THE ULSTER QUESTION SINCE 1945

SECOND EDITION

STUDIES IN CONTEMPORARY HISTORY

Series Editors: T. G. Fraser and J. O. Springhall

THE ARAB–ISRAELI CONFLICT
T. G. Fraser

AMERICA AND THE WORLD SINCE 1945 *T. G. Fraser and
Donette Murray*

THE ULSTER QUESTION SINCE 1945, SECOND EDITION
James Loughlin

GERMANY SINCE 1945
Pól O'Dochartaigh

THE RISE AND FALL OF THE SOVIET EMPIRE,
SECOND EDITION
Raymond Pearson

THE CIVIL RIGHTS MOVEMENT: Struggle and Resistance
William T. Martin Riches

THE UNITED NATIONS AND INTERNATIONAL POLITICS
Stephen Ryan

JAPAN SINCE 1945
Dennis B. Smith

DECOLONIZATION SINCE 1945
John Springhall

**Studies in Contemporary History
Series Standing Order
ISBN 0–333–71706–6 hardcover
ISBN 0–333–69351–5 paperback**
(*outside North America only*)

You can receive future titles in this series as they are published by placing a standing order. Please contract your bookseller or, in the case of difficulty, write to us at the address below with your name and address, the title of the series and the ISBN quoted above.

Customer Services Department, Macmillan Distribution Ltd
Houndmills, Basingstoke, Hampshire RG21 6XS, England

THE ULSTER QUESTION SINCE 1945

SECOND EDITION

JAMES LOUGHLIN

First published 2004 by
PALGRAVE MACMILLAN
Houndmills, Basingstoke, Hampshire RG21 6XS and
175 Fifth Avenue, New York, N.Y. 10010
Companies and representatives throughout the world

PALGRAVE MACMILLAN is the global academic imprint of the Palgrave Macmillan division of St. Martin's Press, LLC and of Palgrave Macmillan Ltd. Macmillan® is a registered trademark in the United States, United Kingdom and other countries. Palgrave is a registered trademark in the European Union and other countries.

ISBN 1–4039–2030–3 hardback
ISBN 0–333–99869–3 paperback

This book is printed on paper suitable for recycling and made from fully managed and sustained forest sources.

A catalogue record for this book is available from the British Library.

A catalog record for this book is available from the Library of Congress.

10 9 8 7 6 5 4 3 2 1
13 12 11 10 09 08 07 06 05 04

Printed in China

For Isabel

CONTENTS

Contents

Contents

Contents

SERIES EDITORS' PREFACE

There are those, politicians among them, who feel that historians should not teach or write about contemporary events and people – many of whom are still living – because of the difficulty of treating such matters with historical perspective, that it is right to draw some distinction between the study of history and the study of current affairs. Proponents of this view seem to be unaware of the concept of contemporary history to which this series is devoted, that the history of the recent past can and should be written with a degree of objectivity. As memories of the Second World War recede, it is surely time to place in perspective the postwar history that has shaped all our lives, whether we were born in the 1940s or the 1970s.

Many countries – Britain, the United States and Germany among them – allow access to their public records under a thirty-year rule, opening up much of the postwar period to archival research. For more recent events, diaries, memoirs, and the investigations of newspapers and television, confirm the view of the famous historian Sir Lewis Namier that all secrets are in print provided you know where to look for them. Contemporary historians also have the opportunity, denied to historians of earlier periods, of interviewing participants in the events they are analysing. The problem facing the contemporary historian is, if anything, the embarrassment of riches.

In any case, the nature and extent of world changes since the late 1980s have clearly signalled the need for concise discussion of major themes in post-1945 history. For many of us the difficult thing to grasp is how dramatically the world has changed over recent years: the end of the Cold War and of Soviet hegemony over eastern Europe; the collapse of the Soviet Union and Russian communism; the unification of Germany; the peace of integration in the European Union; the disintegration of Yugoslavia; political and economic turbulence in South East Asia; communist China's reconciliation with consumer capitalism; the faltering economic progress of Japan. Writing in a structured and cogent way about these seismic changes is what makes contemporary history so challenging and we hope that the end result will convey some of this excitement and interest to our readers.

The general objective of this series is to offer concise and up-to-date treatments of postwar themes considered of historical and political significance and to stimulate critical thought about the theoretical assumptions and conceptual apparatus underlying interpretations of the topics under discussion. The series should bring some of the central themes and problems confronting students and teachers of recent history, politics and international affairs, into sharper focus than the textbook writer alone could provide. The blend required to write contemporary history which is both readable and easily understood but also accurate and scholarly is not easy to achieve, but we hope that this series will prove worthwhile for both students and teachers interested in world affairs since 1945.

University of Ulster at Coleraine   T.G. FRASER
                                                        J.O. SPRINGHALL

NOTE ON TERMINOLOGY

This work often refers to Northern Ireland in the period 1922–72 as a 'statelet'. This term is sometimes used in a pejorative sense. I have employed it simply because it seems most appropriate to an entity which, while having many of the attributes of statehood, lacked constitutional independence.

LIST OF ABBREVIATIONS

AIA	Anglo-Irish Agreement
CDU	Campaign for Democracy in Ulster
CPNI	Communist Party of Northern Ireland
CSJ	Campaign for Social Justice
DPPBs	District Policing Partnership Boards
DUP	Democratic Unionist Party
FARC	Revolutionary Armed Forces of Columbia
FOI	Friends of Ireland
HCL	Homeless Citizens League
IGC	Inter-Governmental Council
INLA	Irish National Liberation Army
INV	Irish National Volunteers
IRA	Irish Republican Army
LVF	Loyalist Volunteer Force
NICRA	Northern Ireland Civil Rights Association
NILP	Northern Ireland Labour Party
NIO	Northern Ireland Office
NIWC	Northern Ireland Women's Coalition
OIRA	Official Irish Republican Army
PD	Peoples Democracy
PIRA	Provisional Irish Republican Army
PSF	Provisional Sinn Fein
PSNI	Police Service of Northern Ireland
PUP	Progressive Unionist Party
RUC	Royal Ulster Constabulary
SAS	Special Air Services
SDLP	Social Democratic and Labour Party

List of Abbreviations

UDA	Ulster Defence Association
UDR	Ulster Defence Regiment
UKUP	United Kingdom Unionist Party
UPNI	Unionist Party of Northern Ireland
USC	Ulster Special Constabulary (B Specials)
UUC	Ulster Unionist Council
UUP	Ulster Unionist Party
UUUC	United Ulster Unionist Council
UVF	Ulster Volunteer Force
UWC	Ulster Workers Council

Map of Northern Ireland

INTRODUCTION

Despite the vast output of academic work on Ulster since 1969 there is much disagreement about the nature of, and solution to, the problem. Recent assessments of the literature (Whyte, 1991; O'Leary and McGarry, 1995) have identified a range of approaches that attempt to explain it: external explanations emanating from the unionist and nationalist traditions that focus on the responsibility of Dublin and London respectively; varieties of Marxist approaches along similar lines; and more academically sourced internal-conflict theories focusing primarily on relations between the unionist and nationalist communities within Northern Ireland. All of these forms of explanation account, to varying degrees, for the problem, but without being entirely satisfactory; and, considered collectively, have cast doubt 'whether any single solution can be applied to Northern Ireland as a whole' (Whyte, 1991: x).

Whyte's conclusion was based on developments before the signing of the Agreement of Good Friday 1998, the most comprehensive attempt, to date, at a solution of the Ulster question. Nevertheless, the euphoria that surrounded the signing of the Agreement has since given way to a deep disillusionment about its effects among a large section of the unionist community, disillusionment intensified by the evident satisfaction it has afforded nationalists and republicans, and which poses an increasing threat to its endurance. That an

1

agreement premised on the embodiment, and demonstration, of fairness of treatment to all sides has had such diver-
gent effects, however, cannot be explained fully by an
assessment of developments since 1998 alone. These effects
have deep historical origins, as indeed most explanations of
the Ulster question, which rely heavily on interpretations of
the region's modern and contemporary history, indicate.

Plantation, Myth and History

History can be said to inform the Ulster question in a two-
fold way: it not only provides the raw material for analysis, but
more importantly, the material out of which the influential
myths of modern unionism and nationalism have been created. No period of Ulster's history has been more fertile in
terms of mythic interpretation than the seventeenth century,
when, in its struggle with Catholic Europe the emergent
nation of Protestant Britain sought to secure its western flank
through the anglicisation of Ireland; a process which in
Ulster involved the confiscation of the estates of the Ulster
chiefs, Hugh O'Neill and Rory O'Donnell, the removal of the
native inhabitants and their replacement with Protestant settlers from England and Scotland. Displacement of the native
inhabitants, however, was never complete and when the
opportunity presented itself in 1641 – a function of the crisis
between King Charles I and the Westminster parliament – the
native Irish, motivated to varying degrees by fear and expectation, rose against the settlers. The ensuing conflict quickly
took on the form of a religious war, fought with propaganda,
no less than the sword, and only ending in the late 1640s
when Cromwell arrived to crush the Catholic forces (Rafferty,
1994). The 1641 Rising was to have a profound effect on the
Ulster Protestant community, acting to consolidate its internal integration and to shape its identity and historical memory.
From this period can be dated the unionist understanding of
their role in Ireland, as a community whose function was to

civilise the country and secure it for the British state. It was also a community that had existed on friendly terms with the native Irish, only to see that friendship betrayed in 1641 when the Ulster Catholics rose and perpetrated frightful atrocities against Protestants. Thereafter, Ulster Protestants saw themselves as living in a state of perpetual threat. The credibility of this view was enhanced by subsequent historical episodes in which the sequence of threat/persecution/deliverance, which characterised the 1641 experience, was repeated. The most important of these was undoubtedly the Irish dimension to the 'Glorious Revolution' of 1688–90. The accession of the Catholic James II to the British throne in 1685 heralded an ill-fated attempt to restore Catholicism, which resulted in his replacement in 1688 by William of Orange and his wife, Mary, James's Protestant daughter. In an attempt to reclaim his throne James raised a Catholic army in Ireland and called a parliament in Dublin which set about restoring their lands to Catholics dispossessed by his predecessors.

The effect in Ulster of James's campaign was to produce a united Protestant resistance; resistance symbolised in the siege of Derry in 1689, when the Protestant garrison, in conditions of near starvation, withstood the efforts of James's army to compel submission. This was rewarded the following year with William of Orange's victory at the battle of the Boyne. The experience of Ulster Protestants in this period resembled that of the early 1640s; however the Williamite period was much more profound in its historical consequences. These years were to provide a foundation myth for subsequent generations of Ulster Protestants; a myth embodied in the cry 'No surrender' that stressed the lesson of Protestant unity and eternal vigilance against the Catholic threat to their rights and privileges, which could only be secured if Catholics were kept in subjection. Moreover, the outlook of Ulster Protestants found a validation both in the Williamite Settlement, which established a constitutional and Protestant monarchy subject to the supremacy of parliament, and in the penal laws that were subsequently enacted against Irish Catholics, designed to ensure that they lacked the material and intellectual resources to mount a serious challenge to Protestant supremacy. The formation of the Orange Order in 1795, named in honour of William of Orange, would ensure that the lessons of 1688–90 were not forgotten.

There was, of course, more to the history of Ulster Protestantism than the conflict with Catholicism. Historians point to the class and religious conflicts between Presbyterians and Anglicans, and the leading role taken by Ulster Presbyterians in the struggle waged by the United Irishmen for national independence in the late eighteenth century. However, what was most important to the Protestant community, and would become increasingly so from the beginning of the nineteenth century, was the service that history could render to their political interests.

Nationalist Resurgence

The turning points of Ulster Protestant history may have been marked by great defeats for Irish Catholics, but despite Cromwellian massacres, dispossession and the effects of the penal laws, by the end of the eighteenth century, Catholic nationalism had revived. It made an important contribution to the insurrection of the United Irishmen in 1798 and would, despite the passing of the Act of Union in 1800, continue to develop. Daniel O'Connell laid the groundwork for modern constitutional nationalism through a mass mobilisation of priests and people which effected Catholic Emancipation in 1829. While a similar mass mobilisation in the 1840s failed to secure the repeal of the Union, the strength of Irish nationalism had nevertheless been registered. It would receive an important long-term endorsement following the Great Famine of the 1840s, for which tragedy, in nationalist legend, England would be held largely responsible. Nationalism exhibited a more militant manifestation in the unsuccessful rebellion of the republican Fenian movement in 1867. It was sufficiently threatening to move Gladstone to disestablish the Anglican Church in Ireland in 1869.

Disestablishment is probably best seen as the latest aspect of a development that was already, with nationalist pressure, well under way by this time; namely Westminster's shift from maximum support for the interests of Protestant loyalism in Ireland towards a position of equidistance between Irish factions. These developments were naturally unsettling to Ulster Protestants. Nationalist mobilisation had brought substantial gains and, convinced that Roman Catholicism was a vast religio-political system bent on the extirpation of their civil and religious liberties, Protestants uneasily contrasted the monolithic character of the Roman Church with their own denominational divisions. Fear of Catholic nationalism worked to intensify extremist attitudes. In the Presbyterian community the liberal spirit that had inspired the United Irishmen in Ulster in the 1790s had become submerged by the 1830s in a sectarian reaction led by the popular demagogue, Revd Henry Cooke. There would still be Presbyterian support for disestablishment in 1869 and also common interests with Catholics on the question of land reform. Yet, on the essential issue of national identity the fundamental division in the mid-1870s, when the Irish home rule movement had developed, was between a Protestant and British community in north-east Ulster and Irish Catholic nationalism. Increasingly, it was a community whose identity was inward-looking, narrowly focused around anti-Catholicism and informed by a historical myth of persecution and atrocity which militated strongly against the development of a sustained community of interests with Irish Catholics. Further, the idea that their interests were now under threat from British indifference as well as Catholic designs was strengthened by the growth of popular democracy. Driven by mainland British imperatives and with little regard for the local balance of power between Irish factions, Westminster

policies were to exert an important influence on the shaping
of the Ulster question as a specifically political issue.

Gladstonian Home Rule and Ulster

While the genesis of the Ulster question can be traced back
to the plantation, it was events in the relatively short period
of 1880–86 that shaped it as the political problem we know
today. Under the leadership of Charles Stewart Parnell from
1880–90 constitutional nationalism was moulded into a
highly effective political movement, combining independent action at Westminster with mass organisation in Ireland.
Capitalising on the Irish land war of 1879–82 and backed by
Irish-American funding, Parnell achieved a position of
unchallenged dominance in nationalist Ireland by 1881.
North-east Ulster remained largely impervious to his influence but external political developments were to create a
crisis that would force Ulster Protestants to respond to the
Parnellite movement.

In particular, the franchise reforms of 1884–85, which
trebled the Irish electorate and re-drew constituencies, transformed nationalist influence in the North. Whereas nationalists held only three seats in Ulster before the 1885 general
election, after it they held a majority (17–16). Moreover,
within the United Kingdom as a whole the result left the
Parnellites, with 86 seats, holding the balance of power
though only able, effectively, to keep the Liberal Party in
office. The price of Parnellite support was home rule, an
Irish parliament. Accordingly, the Liberal leader, William
Gladstone, personally sympathetic to this proposal but motivated also by fear of dislocation in Ireland and Westminster,
and political ambition, moved quickly to construct a home
rule plan for Ireland.

Gladstone's conversion to home rule was rapid and the plan
he formulated was to have a profound influence on the development of the Ulster question. Its effect was to split the Liberal

Party in Britain, while in Ulster the considerable Gladstonian following that existed among Presbyterians virtually disappeared overnight. Accordingly, Ulster Liberalism, which grew significantly in the early 1880s through an uneasy alliance of Presbyterians and Catholics and which, however tentatively, offered a non-sectarian path of political development for the north, collapsed (Walker, 1989). Already suspicious of Westminster, Ulster Protestants saw Gladstonian home rule as a betrayal, entailing the destruction of the Act of Union; the loss of their British nationality and imperial identity; and economic ruin for Ireland generally and Ulster in particular. Moreover, Gladstone's 'betrayal' gave an enormous boost to the growth of the Orange Order, already in revival since the early 1880s. In effect, over the short period from the autumn of 1885 to the spring of 1886 the recognisable features of the Ulster question as a modern political issue emerged. Ulster Presbyterian Liberalism and Anglican Toryism united in an Ulster unionist movement, the unity of which was underpinned by Orangeism. This ensured that anti-Catholicism and the historical myth of papal domination and priestly inspired persecution of Protestants would continue to exert a profound influence on the unionists' understanding of their position in Ireland. In parliament, the province's unionist MPs would form a distinct regional grouping within the wider unionist movement and consolidate an alliance with the Conservative Party that would eventually ensure their exclusion from nationalist rule. Accordingly, it is important to note that from its beginnings as a specifically political issue, the Ulster problem consisted not only of inter-ethnic divisions in Ireland but had a crucial and wider British dimension.

The blueprint for Irish home rule that Gladstone constructed – an Irish parliament for purely internal affairs, within the existing constitutional framework of the United Kingdom and with Westminster retaining control of what are usually considered the most important aspects of independent statehood, defence, coinage, taxation and foreign relations – would, surprisingly, remain the ground-plan not only for the succeeding schemes of 1893 and 1912, but also for the form of autonomy conceded to Northern Ireland in 1921. The most important immediate aspect of Gladstone's scheme of 1886, as it affected the development of the Ulster issue, was the failure to provide any arrangements to meet the specific concerns of northern Protestants. This was also a weakness of subsequent home rule bills and contributed enormously to the failure of home rule as a solution to the Irish question in general.

A number of factors account for the omission, but probably the most important was the nature of the Irish nationalist myth, one which defined the national territory as the whole island of Ireland and its entire people as Irish nationals. It was a myth no less profound in its shaping of nationalist thinking on the Ulster question then and in the future than that of Ulster Protestants for unionism. Accordingly, Protestant rejection of Irish nationalism was regarded as emanating from a form of 'false consciousness', something that would disappear once home rule was implemented. In this view nationalists were supported by Gladstone and his successors. It should also be noted that in 1886 nationalists could make a reasonable case against the exclusion of Ulster from the remit of the home rule scheme. They pointed out, for example, that no specifically Protestant homeland existed in the North, the inter-mixing of the Catholic and Protestant communities, to varying degrees, being characteristic of the region as a whole. Moreover, with their recent electoral successes in mind, nationalists were confident that the problem in the North would be resolved by increasing their parliamentary representation there. Another important factor was the perceived importance of north-east Ulster's industrial prosperity to the viability of home rule. Gladstone's scheme and its successors envisaged an Irish exchequer capable of meeting, as a first charge, its financial commitments to imperial expenditure, but with no great surplus. Accordingly, nationalists, noting that great industrial expansion had taken place in northeast Ulster in the nineteenth century and had brought increasing regional prosperity, saw the region's retention under home rule as essential to the economic viability of Irish autonomy. Nor, it should be added, were Ulster unionists, convinced at this time that home rule *in general* could be defeated, inclined to co-operate in any scheme for the separate treatment of the province.

The split in the Liberal Party, occasioned by Gladstone's conversion to home rule, ensured the defeat of the plan of 1886 in the House of Commons, while his second plan of 1893 was defeated in the Lords. The failures of the Gladstonian period were of fateful significance for the prospects of a non-partitionist settlement of the Irish question. However strong the rhetoric of Ulster unionist opposition to home rule in this period, it lacked the leadership, materiel and organisation to prevent militarily the imposition of home rule in the North. Thus, unionists might have been drawn to accept some form of settlement that provided safeguards for their interests (Loughlin, 1986). From 1893 to 1912, however, constitutional and political changes occurred that greatly diminished the prospects for compromise.

The two general elections of 1910 had been fought on the issue of the House of Lords' refusal to enact Lloyd Georges's controversial budget of 1909, which entailed considerable tax increases on owners of landed property. While the government won both elections it was dependent on nationalist support to retain office and the price of that support was the introduction of a home rule bill. More importantly, the Parliament Act of 1911, introduced to restrict the Lords' ability to resist the passing of Commons' legislation to a two-year suspensory veto, now enabled a home rule bill to be eventually enacted. It would also ensure that a crisis on Irish home rule would have ample time to develop.

In 1905, the Ulster Unionist Council was formed as a permanent body to represent all shades of unionism in the province. It would play a central role in organising the Ulster Volunteer Force (UVF) to oppose the implementation of the third home rule bill on Ulster in the period 1912–14.

Equally important, the leadership offered to Ulster unionism in this period by James Craig and Sir Edward Carson was
considerably more effective than that given by the colourful,
but rather buffoonish, Colonel Edward Saunderson in the
Gladstonian period. Moreover, Ulster unionist MPs were
now more closely tied to constituency opinion and thus
more inclined to allow local extremism to dictate their political stance. Likewise, Tory support for Ulster unionist resolve
to oppose by force the implementation of home rule on
Ulster was more firmly committed under the leadership
of Bonar Law, a leader with strong family connections in
the North.

The opposition to Ulster unionism had also changed
significantly since Gladstone's time. Liberal Prime Minister,
Herbert Asquith, was devoid of the moral enthusiasm that
fired Gladstone's commitment to the solution of the Irish
question. Indecisive and inclined to wait on events, Asquith
allowed unionist opposition to mobilise in Ulster without
taking any effective measures to neutralise it. Nothing better
illustrates the government's mishandling of the Ulster question than the 'Curragh Mutiny' of March 1914, when army
officers were allowed, quite unnecessarily, to demonstrate
their resolve not to be used to put down an Ulster rebellion.
This blunder was capitalised upon a month later when the
UVF succeeded in landing 35,000 rifles and 5,000,000
rounds of ammunition at Larne and other locations in the
North. In fact, by this time the seriousness of the crisis had
already forced a reconsideration of the Ulster question that
would influence its future development. In particular, an
attempt was made to define a unionist territory in north-east
Ulster that might have some legitimate claim to exclusion
from nationalist rule when, in June 1912, a Liberal MP,
T. Agar-Robartes, proposed an amendment to the home rule
bill which defined the four counties of Antrim, Armagh,
Down and Londonderry as an area to be excluded from the
home rule parliament's jurisdiction.

This initiative brought into the open an issue which union- ists realised would have to be tackled. While the hope existed of defeating home rule for any part of Ireland it need not be addressed, but as it became increasingly clear that self- government for nationalist Ireland would have to be conceded, a wide-ranging debate on autonomy developed. It focused around three main proposals: (i) 'home rule all round', which envisaged regional parliaments for all the major national groups of the United Kingdom, including Ulster, subordinate to the imperial parliament at Westminster; (ii) 'home rule within home rule', entailing special powers for Ulster under a Dublin parliament; (iii) exclusion of Ulster from the jurisdiction of a Dublin parliament. Of these proposals, only the third would merit serious consideration as a solution to the Ulster issue; the first being complex and lacking support in Britain and the second being resolutely rejected by Ulster unionists. As exclusion became closely examined the question of the specific area to be excluded had to be addressed. Agar-Robartes's amendment opened the issue but was unacceptable to unionists. They had organ- ised on a nine-county basis and saw the four-county area as being too small. Yet, close examination had also shown that a unionist majority in Ulster as a whole was narrow. According to the 1911 census, Ulster had a Catholic popula- tion of 690,816 (43.7 per cent) and a non-Catholic population of 890,886 (56.3 per cent). Catholic growth and the vagaries of the electoral system might leave the unionist majority in an Ulster parliament vulnerable. Political reality dictated that a smaller area would have to be considered, and while Agar-Robartes's four-county option was unacceptable as it stood, with the addition of the two western counties of Fermanagh and Tyrone it constituted a territory that union- ists felt was the largest that they could effectively control. But Fermanagh and Tyrone had small nationalist majorities and their inclusion in partition proposals would complicate negotiations on the Irish question until 1921 and beyond.

From the end of 1913, both Liberal and Tory leaders began to focus more earnestly on the religious and political realities of Ulster; and Asquith finally succeeded in forcing the nationalist leader, John Redmond, to accept, as a final concession, that Ulster counties might vote themselves out of the jurisdiction of a home rule parliament for a period of six years. Emboldened by their successful defiance of the government, Tories and Ulster unionists rejected the proposal, and despite negotiations between the parties at Buckingham Palace in July 1914, the crisis intensified, especially when the nationalists, having organised their own Irish National Volunteers (INV) in reaction to the formation of the UVF, succeeded in landing a shipment of guns and ammunition at Howth, outside Dublin. Moreover, while plans for rebellion in the North were being finalised parliamentary time was running out. Unless a home rule bill was enacted by the end of the parliamentary session in August, the whole lengthy process would have to be repeated. In the event, a temporary agreement on home rule did emerge, stimulated externally by the deteriorating international situation and Bonar Law's concern that the Irish question should not undermine national unity. Law proposed that, in the circumstances, they postpone their attempts to solve the Irish question, something that Asquith was prepared to accept. A few days later the United Kingdom was engaged in war.

However, despite Tory and Ulster unionist opposition, the home rule bill, together with an amendment stipulating that home rule would not come into operation until after the war and until special legislation had been enacted for Ulster, was placed on the statute book (Buckland, 1973, 1989; Laffan, 1983; Loughlin, 1986; Jackson, 1989).

From War to Partition

The postponement of home rule was based on the premise that, like the short wars of the Victorian era, this war would also be of short duration. Redmond's commitment of the INV to the British war effort encouraged the hope among some British politicians that engagement in a common struggle with the rest of the United Kingdom would strengthen the bonds of British patriotism and diminish the virulence of the Irish quarrel. But the war was not of short duration and by late 1915 the appalling slaughter on the western front was common knowledge, especially in Ulster where the enthusiastic mass enlistment of loyalists in the autumn of 1914 had now reduced to a trickle. Moreover, home rule was now on the statute book, but Redmond was unable to point to any beneficial consequences for Irish nationalists, while his party, having achieved the goal for which it existed, went into decline. Most seriously for Redmond, his commitment of the INV to the war effort in 1914 was not wholeheartedly accepted. A minority of around 11,000 radical nationalists refused the call, and it was from their ranks that the insurgents who effected the 1916 Rising, led by Padraig Pearse in alliance with the Marxian socialist, James Connolly and his tiny Irish Citizen Army, would come.

The Rising, though a military failure, had profound consequences. It provoked the government, through Lloyd George, to attempt a hasty resolution of the Irish question involving the implementation of home rule with exclusion for the six northern counties that Carson had proposed in 1914. The plan, however, initially accepted by both Carson and Redmond, collapsed when it became known that while Redmond had been assured that exclusion would be temporary, Carson was promised it would be permanent. Opposition to it came also from members of the government, unionists in the three Ulster counties not included in the exclusion plan, and from nationalists in the western 'border' regions of the six counties. In fact, the plan provoked an east–west split in northern nationalism, leading to the emergence of the anti-Redmond Irish Nation League which would pave the way for Sinn Fein's successes in the North at the general election of 1918. In sum, the plan resulted in both the weakening of Redmond and his party, and in the prioritising of partition as a central element in any settlement.

The Irish question as a factor in the British national interest was to change significantly as a result of the war, especially after the USA became involved in 1917. With the influential Irish-American lobby in mind, a settlement of the problem in the interests of the war effort became increasingly urgent. And the government was now inclined towards a non-partitionist solution. But the Irish Convention of 1917, set up to effect this, and in which the Ulster unionists were expected to play a conciliatory role, found them recalcitrant, concerned only with safeguarding their own interests. By the end of the war the context of the Ulster problem had changed significantly since 1914. The general election of 1918 marked the demise of the home rule movement, with Sinn Fein, benefiting from a wave of popular support that followed the execution of the leaders of the 1916 Rising, triumphant everywhere apart from north-east Ulster and committed to establishing an independent Irish republic. Northern nationalism had split into two groups; 'border' nationalists rejecting inclusion in any partitioned area, and eastern nationalists, led by Joseph Devlin, reluctantly inclined to consider it, aware that partition, however devised, was unlikely to exclude them. At the same time, Ulster unionists no longer attracted the level of support in Britain that they did in 1914 and would have to fight to maintain exclusion (Laffan, 1983; Phoenix, 1994).

In this they were facilitated by the decision of the Sinn Fein movement to boycott Westminster, which ensured that the northern minority was effectively precluded from any influence in shaping its own fate at a crucial juncture. Indeed, the Sinn Fein leadership, like nationalist leaders before them, had little real understanding of the northern mentality and the complexity of the Ulster question. Their primary concern was not to solve the question but to achieve national independence. Accordingly, in the crucial period from the general election of 1918 to the enacting of the Government of Ireland Act of 1920, the political initiative lay, respectively, in Dublin with a national leadership remote from the realities of Ulster and in Westminster with a Conservative-dominated coalition government, inclined to a non-partitionist settlement and keen to disengage from direct involvement in the government of Ireland, but subject to pressures, not least from the Tory leader, Bonar Law, to honour the pledges given to Ulster unionists in the pre-war period. In this context, Sinn Fein's boycott of Westminster allowed the Ulster unionist MPs a great advantage in making their case (Phoenix, 1994).

This was the background against which a committee, chaired by Walter Long in October 1919, considered the Irish question. The committee's remit covered a range of proposals, including 'home rule within home rule', the option for counties to opt out of the jurisdiction of an Irish parliament, and the simple exclusion of Ulster from the jurisdiction of the home rule parliament with direct rule from Westminster. Problems, however, were found with all of these proposals and in the end a scheme based on the home rule act of 1914 was decided on as best suited to solving Westminster's Irish difficulties. Embodied in the Government of Ireland Act of 1920, this was a scheme whereby Ireland would have two parliaments, one for the six-county area defined in 1914 and one for the remaining 26 Irish counties – to be known, respectively, as Northern Ireland and Southern Ireland. Elections to them were to be conducted by proportional representation, while, as in the home rule schemes, their powers would be strictly limited to internal affairs, with little control over taxation and with all major departments of state retained by Westminster, in which both Northern and Southern Ireland would have rep-resentation. Yet, it is also clear that this constitutional arrangement was intended to be ultimately transitional; for it also included a provision for a Council of Ireland with a view to the establishment of a parliament for the whole of

Ireland. Composed of a president, to be nominated by the crown on the advice of Westminster, and of 40 representatives, 20 each chosen by the two Irish parliaments, the council was intended to deal with areas of common concern, while its powers could be increased by agreement between the two parliaments.

The prospects for the success of this arrangement were never good. In the South, Sinn Fein, having boycotted Westminster, set up its own parliament in Dublin, Dail Eireann. At the same time, a military struggle to expel the British and establish an independent Irish republic was under way and lasted until 1921. Only in the North did the unionists, initially reluctant, set about implementing the Government of Ireland Act. It was soon recognised that the possession of their own parliament, a permanent institution not easily removed, would allow them considerable control over the North's constitutional position (Boyce, 1970; Buckland, 1973; Laffan, 1983).

At the elections to the northern parliament in May 1921, three weeks after the passing of the Government of Ireland Act, unionists, following an extensive gerrymander of constituencies and extensive personation during the campaign, won 40 of the region's 52 seats. In the South, only the two Dublin University representatives attended the new parliament. Ulster unionists had begun the process of consolidating their position long before May 1921. The war of independence allowed for the reconstitution of the UVF in July 1920 and it soon established close links with the British forces. In October 1920, the Ulster Special Constabulary (USC), a part-time Protestant paramilitary force, was established and, effectively, assumed responsibility for law and order. Within a year it had a membership of 16,000. Moreover, an assistant undersecretary for Ulster affairs moved to Belfast, while separate administrative powers and responsibility were also effectively being established in the North. Accordingly, when Sinn Fein leaders reached agreement on a truce with the British authorities three weeks after

16

King George V opened the northern parliament in June 1921 and made a plea for peace, the Ulster unionists were firmly entrenched (Laffan, 1983).

Northern Ireland: The Statelet Secured

In the negotiations that took place between Lloyd George and Sinn Fein representatives following the truce, attempts to persuade Sir James Craig to accept Northern Ireland's inclusion as an autonomous region, holding the powers conferred by the Government of Ireland Act, in an Ireland having dominion status within the Empire, were sternly refused. Ultimately, Lloyd George, the Prime Minister of the Coalition government, was left with the difficult task of arranging a scheme which appeared to offer a united Ireland but which at the same time did not threaten conflict with the Tories and Ulster unionists. This was achieved in the Anglo-Irish Treaty of 1921, imposed on the Irish delegation under duress, and which conferred dominion status on Ireland. It also embodied a clause that set up a boundary commission to determine the border between Northern Ireland and the new Irish Free State should, as was allowed for under the treaty, the Ulster unionists decide to opt out of its operation. This the unionists did at the earliest opportunity, within one month of the treaty's enactment in December 1922 (Boyce, 1970).

Yet, however sensible this arrangement for resolving the Ulster question may have seemed at the time, it was inherently flawed, while the treaty in general would initiate a conflict that allowed the consequences of those flaws to be magnified. The Sinn Fein leadership was riven with personality divisions between Michael Collins and Arthur Griffith on the one side, and Eamon de Valera on the other. These divisions complicated relations between the Irish delegation in London and de Valera, who remained in Dublin. Moreover, the Irish delegation was inexperienced in negotiation, so that when the original offer of a boundary commission that would make territorial decisions based on the wishes of area inhabitants was formalised in print, with the crucial addition, 'so far as these may be compatible with economic and geographic conditions', the change was not apparently noticed. Further, when the treaty was taken back to Dublin for consideration by the Dail, the major concern was the oath of allegiance to the Crown rather than Ulster, which all sides regarded as a subsidiary issue. And it remained a subsidiary issue when the Dail's ratification of the treaty by a very narrow margin was rejected by de Valera and his followers and Southern Ireland descended into civil war. The civil war did not end until May 1923, but it was only one of a number of factors that delayed the formation of the boundary commission, the clause embodying which became operative once the Ulster unionists had opted out of the treaty settlement. A general election in the South; an imperial conference in London followed by a general election and change of government; together with both Craig and the southern Prime Minster, W.T. Cosgrave, falling ill; all combined to ensure that it was April 1924 before the issue was seriously addressed. The three governments met in an attempt to negotiate, between them, a settlement of the boundary issue. It soon emerged, however, that they would be unable to do so and that the commission would have to be formally established. The refusal of the Northern Ireland government to nominate a representative to the commission meant that another delay ensued while the treaty was modified to allow the British government to nominate one on its behalf. Only in November 1924, nearly three years after the treaty had been signed, did the commission meet.

The delay did affect how the commission – composed of J.R. Fisher for Northern Ireland, Eoin McNeill for the Irish Free State and Richard Feetham, a South African judge, as chairman – would set about its work. Political circumstances had changed since 1921: the northern government was firmly in place and arguments about the temporary nature of the existing border were now less persuasive than they once were. Further, the British government in 1921 still contained some Liberal members, while there was considerable sympathy for nationalist Ireland. But by the time the commission had begun to seriously get down to work in early 1925, the short-lived Labour government of 1924 had been replaced by the Conservatives, led by Stanley Baldwin. Freed of the circumstantial pressure to conciliate Irish nationalism that had existed in 1921 and more inclined to remember its wartime activities, the Tory government was unlikely to adopt the Free State interpretation of the commission's task. More sympathetic to Craig, Tories were unfavourable to large territorial transfers. Indeed Craig lost no time in informing Feetham that he would tolerate no significant border changes, while the actual wording of the boundary clause, with its balancing of popular opinion against social and economic considerations, tended to facilitate Craig's view. Accordingly, Feetham came to interpret his role in a minimalist way and concerned himself with minor boundary rectifications. In this he was accommodated by McNeill, who accepted his role fatalistically and without much hope of a successful outcome.

In these circumstances it was hardly a surprise that when the commission drew up an agreed report in October 1925 it recommended only minor changes. Northern Ireland's territory was to be reduced by 3.7 per cent and its population by 1.8 per cent. This trimming would take place mainly along the outer edges of Armagh and Fermanagh, while all the major nationalist areas remained under northern rule. More importantly, not only would Northern Ireland remain intact, some reduction of southern territory was also envisaged, mostly in east Donegal, entailing a loss of 78 square mile of territory and 7500 people. The report, however, was never implemented. An exaggerated account of the commission's findings was leaked in the *Morning Post* of 7 November 1925 and created a scandal. Opinion in the Irish Free State was affronted by the report giving so little while actually taking something away, and the latter was regarded as more significant. There followed three weeks of negotiation between the governments which resulted in an agreement on 3 December 1925 by which the boundary as it stood remained unchanged, while some financial concessions were made by Westminster to the Free State. The Council of Ireland, the prospects for the success of which were never good, was abolished and its powers transferred to the Dublin and Belfast governments (Laffan, 1983; Canning, 1985; Buckland, 1989).

The conclusion to the commission's proceedings registered a substantial success for northern unionists. Their territory and constitutional position had been secured: constitutional change in Southern Ireland in the future would have little effect on Northern Ireland. Even the prorogation of the Stormont parliament in 1972 would still leave the six-county statelet as the primary framework within which a settlement of the Ulster question would be pursued. Yet it was, and would remain, a fundamental weakness of the unionist outlook that the Ulster question was defined primarily in terms of territorial control and constitutional status. The success of Craig in these areas in the period 1920–25 tended to mask the failure of his regime within Northern Ireland, especially his pursuit of policies that alienated the Catholic community.

Ulster Nationalists and Northern Ireland

Already affronted by the failure of the British government to consult them on a constitutional settlement, Ulster nationalist opposition to partition was intensified by the impact of sectarian violence which broke out in the North in July 1920 and which involved the wholesale expulsion of Catholics from their employment. It would appear that all shades of Catholic opinion became convinced that the anti-Catholic violence of the period 1920–22 constituted a pogrom designed to drive the Catholic population out of the new statelet, a belief given credibility by the fact that 58 per cent of those killed in Belfast disturbances in this period were Catholics. The formation of the USC, the 'B Specials', reinforced this view and also enabled the Irish Republican Army (IRA) to establish itself as the protector of the Catholic population.

Some actions of Ulster nationalists also facilitated unionist designs, especially the agreement of Devlinites and Sinn Feiners to a policy of non-recognition of the new regime during the May 1921 Northern Ireland elections; thus enabling the unionists to portray the minority as implacably hostile and not deserving of special treatment. Intending to strengthen the hand of the Dail delegation in its negotiations with Lloyd George, non-recognition was a gesture that only hurt Catholic interests without having any real effect on negotiations in which Ulster was a secondary issue. When the terms of the treaty, as they affected the North, were made known, they only served to further dissension in northern nationalist ranks, encouraging border nationalists in hopes of final deliverance and dissuading them from joint action to secure Catholic interests within the North. For their part, eastern nationalists, led by Devlin, realising that no conceivable border revision was likely to include them in the Irish Free State, placed their hopes on a settlement between the Belfast and Dublin governments that might substitute some semblance of unity for a revised boundary, but would at least include guarantees for the nationalist population in such vital areas as representation, the police force and education. These hopes were to prove misplaced, while the split in the South over the treaty was only to erode further the position of Ulster Catholics.

The policy of the Irish government and especially Michael Collins – the only southern leader for whom partition and the plight of Ulster nationalists were major concerns – was confusing and complicated. His desperation to assist northern nationalists produced an ineffectual and damaging blend of 'non-recognition', diplomacy and coercion. Non-recognition of the northern regime by Catholic teachers and anti-partitionist local authorities increased antagonism between the two nationalist factions in the North, while being impracticable and counter-productive. The Craig government responded to recalcitrant authorities by dissolving them and by abolishing proportional representation for local elections in 1921. Again, two pacts which Collins arranged with Craig in 1922 and which were intended to improve the Catholic position failed to have any significant result, something which provoked a military campaign to make the North unworkable, and which, in turn, only intensified the sectarian backlash against Catholics. Collins's death in August 1922 was a further blow to morale, while the decision of the southern government, after his death, to pursue a 'peace policy' towards the North while at the same time encouraging Catholic non-recognition – with the boundary commission in mind – continued the mood of demoralisation and confusion. The result of the boundary commission scandal in 1925 was a final blow, which shattered the morale of Catholics, leaving them disillusioned, bitter and alienated.

The Inter-War Period

Increasingly, from 1926, the Irish question as viewed especially from London was regarded as being solved. The almost impossible task of meeting the conflicting demands of nationalists desiring independence with Ulster unionist demands that the status quo be maintained, had, however imperfectly, been met. Ireland as a complicating factor in British politics had been removed, while at the same time it was kept within the Empire. In the process the international aspect of the Irish question – especially in its Irish-American aspect – had been neutralised. Nevertheless, this was to solve the Irish question – or the Ulster question as it would in future be chiefly known – only in its 'external' aspects; and it was only achieved at the cost, over time, of intensifying its 'internal' dimensions. Probably the most important factor that facilitated this process was the resolute refusal of British politicians to become involved in Northern Ireland's affairs.

The Government of Ireland Act conferred a Westminster form of government in conditions that guaranteed it would fail to function effectively. It consisted of a Governor of Northern Ireland, representing the monarch, and a bi-cameral parliament – a House of Commons and Senate – with the second chamber composed of the Lord Mayors of Derry and Belfast as ex-officio members, together with 24 members elected from the 52 member House of Commons. This was done to ensure that the unionist dominance in the lower House was reflected in the upper and, unlike the Senate in the Irish Free State, which was elected on a high franchise qualification to ensure that the small Protestant minority was well represented (Harkness, 1983).

The problematic early years of the northern statelet saw the enactment of several measures designed to consolidate unionist control, especially the Special Powers Act of 1922, which effectively abrogated the civil rights of those affected by it. It was kept in force long after the IRA threat to the regime had faded and was made permanent in 1933. Of wider significance was the Local Government Act of 1922, which abolished proportional representation. The latter had been introduced as a measure designed to strengthen minority group representation so as to undermine Sinn Fein at the local elections of 1920 but had enabled nationalists to win control of 25 out of 80 local councils. The bill of 1922 restored the pre-existing franchise and re-shaped electoral areas so as to put the 'natural rulers' in marginal constituencies back in control. So effectively was this objective secured that after the local elections of 1924 nationalists had control of only two councils. Yet nationalists, in generally boycotting the one-man Leech Commission set up to prepare the local government changes, created a situation in which unionist representations became the basis for change, and so, effectively, assisted in the gerrymander (Phoenix, 1994). Local government reorganisation had yet more profound consequences. For despite having been quickly enacted by the Belfast parliament it was refused the royal assent by the Governor of Northern Ireland. The refusal was justified by Westminster officials offended at the changes and who pointed to article 75 of the Government of Ireland Act, which stipulated that despite the powers given to the Northern Ireland parliament, ultimate sovereignty over the region's affairs remained with Westminster. Westminster, however, backed down when Craig threatened to resign and leave it with the responsibility for governing the region. In so doing a fateful precedent was set, whereby Westminster abrogated any attempt to oversee the internal affairs of Northern Ireland, thus allowing the regime to pursue policies that would eventually result in the civil disorder of 1969. Control of local government gave control of the patronage within its gift and the issue of discrimination in council jobs and housing would be at the centre of the civil rights campaign of the 1960s. More immediately, in 1929 there was no protest from Westminster when the northern government set about abolishing proportional representation for elections to the Belfast parliament.

Discrimination would affect the Catholic minority in other areas, especially education. The refusal of the Catholic hierarchy to nominate representatives to the Lynn Committee, appointed in September 1921 to examine the educational system, again left decisions in an important area affecting Catholic interests in the hands of Protestants; and while the Protestant representatives claimed to keep Catholic interests in mind, it was their own concerns that naturally shaped the committee's recommendations (Birrell and Murie, 1980; Buckland, 1989).

By the end of the 1920s, Northern Ireland had demonstrated, substantially, that it had what Craigavon (ennobled in 1927) would boast of in the early 1930s, a 'Protestant parliament and a Protestant people'. A policy of border politics was pursued throughout this period, fed by the verbal anti-partitionism of southern leaders, and designed to accentuate the differences between the two communities in the statelet. Even when obviously secure in its powers there was little political opening offered to Catholics, as Joseph Devlin found repeatedly when he attempted to develop a politics of social reform. The brief unity of Catholic and Protestant workers that was effected at the height of the great depression in 1932 was easily destroyed when the regime played the sectarian card. Moreover, the divisions that emerged within northern nationalism in the years leading up to partition, between constitutional nationalism and militant republicanism, were to persist, offering a demoralised community uninspired leadership.

By the late 1930s, the stability of Northern Ireland was established on the basis of unionist domination, with the minority community – equipped with its own social infrastructure of churches, schools, hospitals, sporting activities, newspapers, businesses and its own sectarian organisation in the Ancient Order of Hibernians – alienated and existing as a kind of 'state within a state' (Phoenix, 1994).

Unionist treatment of the Catholic community cannot be justified, but it can be understood. The historical myth of unionism, effectively socialised within the Protestant community by the Orange Order, was exclusivist, defining Catholics as the eternal enemy. From 1921 especially, the Ulster Protestant perception of their place in Ireland was shaped substantially by a unionist press which reported the affairs of the newly independent southern state in a way which distorted reality and pandered to Protestant anxieties. The early 1930s, which had seen Eamon de Valera come to power with anti-partitionist rhetoric and a policy of breaking Ireland's imperial links, kept unionists on their guard and intensified their unwillingness to conciliate Catholics (Kennedy, 1988). And while their removal from office electorally was highly unlikely, the fact that unionists could lose individual seats – 25 over the life of the regime with a further 13 marginal

(Mulholland, 2002) – sustained their constitutional anxieties and served to validate discriminatory practices. Further, while Westminster did not interfere in Northern Ireland's affairs the relations of the Belfast government to the imperial parliament were rather more involved than they sometimes have seemed and worked to facilitate unionist practices.

Given the close margin separating victory and defeat at general elections in the 1920s, the North's 13 MPs, usually unionists, were a significant addition to Tory strength. Throughout the 1930s there was steady stream of leading party figures as guest speakers at the annual conferences of the Ulster Unionist Council, there to applaud the close relationship between the two parties and their common British identity. Such contacts helped enormously to persuade unionists that the manner in which their form of Britishness was expressed was not inconsistent with that of the mainland.

This belief would induce a deep sense of betrayal in the future when British condemnation of Stormont practices gathered force. In the immediate term, IRA activity, however ineffectual in ending partition, succeeded at least in demonstrating that Northern Ireland could never be regarded as an uncomplicated and integrated region of the United Kingdom, while British assurances about its constitutional position could appear duplicitous as Westminster politicians attempted to conciliate de Valera in the late 1930s. Despite London's assurances eternal vigilance was needed to secure Ulster's interests (Canning, 1985; Loughlin, 1995), even in the highly favourable conditions provided by the Second World War.

King's Men

The war of 1939–45 was fought in Europe to eliminate the menace of Nazism, but for Ulster unionists it was also fought to deliver the North from the menace of Irish nationalism.

In this unionists were, for at least twenty years, highly successful. British expectations in the late 1930s that Irish ports which had been retained for imperial defence under the Anglo-Irish Treaty of 1921, and which had only been handed back in 1938, would be made available again in the event of war, were to be disappointed. Under de Valera's leadership the Irish Free State, or Eire as it was titled under the constitution of 1937, remained neutral and refused all blandishments to become involved on the Allied side, even a rather ambiguous offer of a united Ireland from Sir Winston Churchill. Southern neutrality only served to highlight Northern Ireland's loyalty and certainly during the early years of the war Northern Ireland played a vital role in the battles of the north Atlantic. It also contributed significantly to the production of war materials and was an area for the stationing of American troops in the preparations for the invasion of Europe in 1944. Just as they had in the Great War, Ulster unionists were able in this one to create bonds of indebtedness in Britain that would serve them well in the post-war period. And yet, their narrow and fearful mentality would often prevent them from accurately assessing the reality of their political position. A people for whom the past had such a central role in shaping their political under-standing were unlikely to forget the lessons of the period since 1912. Northern Ireland's constitutional position within the United Kingdom may have been secured, but as the *Belfast News Letter* had acknowledged on the day that King George V opened the northern parliament in June 1921, Ulster unionists, in the intensity of their patriotism, exhib-ited more the characteristics of a 'frontier' community rather than those of the British heartland (Loughlin, 1995). And the future would demonstrate the persistence of those characteristics – especially an adherence to rigid ideas of patriotism, many of them anachronistic and morally indefensible – as the unionist position came under attack (Clayton, 1995).

1

ULSTER: A RECONSTITUTED QUESTION

The Post-War Position

Probably the most significant consequence of Northern Ireland's wartime contribution was the fact that it now had the support of both major political parties, the new Labour government – traditionally sympathetic to Irish nationalism – no less than the outgoing Tory-dominated administration. Accordingly, as the London–Stormont relationship strengthened, reinforced as the cold war took off by the belief that Northern Ireland was essential to western national defence, the position of Irish nationalists on the Ulster question weakened. The security now enjoyed by unionists was to rule out any serious consideration of the constitutional question until after the outbreak of civil conflict in 1969.

The clearest indication of the new state of affairs came in 1949 when Eire abruptly departed from the Commonwealth and became a republic. Westminster's response was the Ireland Act of 1949, designed to regulate Anglo-Irish relations and which declared, as part of that process, that in no event would any part of Northern Ireland cease to have membership of the United Kingdom without the consent of the parliament of Northern Ireland. There were other reassuring developments. Attlee's government enacted a number of measures which transformed the North's finances and guaranteed parity of services and taxation with the rest of the United Kingdom (Buckland, 1989), while on the rare occasion when it was possible to raise at Westminster the issue of Stormont misgovernment and discrimination against Catholics – in 1951 during a debate on the working of the Government of Ireland Act – nationalist hopes were disappointed when the Home Secretary, Chuter Ede, expressed a pro-unionist viewpoint (Loughlin, 1995). Within Northern Ireland Eire's departure from the Commonwealth allowed the regime to call a general election on the border issue, a development which forced the Northern Ireland Labour Party (NILP), the only party not primarily concerned with border politics, to declare itself in support of partition, thereby losing much Catholic support (Buckland, 1989). Brian Faulkner did not exaggerate when he described the Ireland Act of 1949 as having afforded Ulster unionists over twenty years of constitutional security (Faulkner, 1978). Moreover, it added greatly to their sense of security that an anti-partition campaign organised by parties in the South in this period failed so abysmally to enlist popular support either in Britain or, more importantly, in the USA.

Ironically, the only threat to Northern Ireland's constitutional position in the immediate post-war years came from within the ranks of Ulster unionism. A number of unionists, impressed by the North's economic progress under the artificial conditions of wartime; concerned about the emergence within the Labour Party of a 'Friends of Ireland' group; by the government's 'socialist' policies and the increased taxation needed to pay for them, demanded dominion status for the North. It was a short-lived campaign, being killed off by a greater appreciation of Northern Ireland's real economic condition in the context of post-war austerity and its implications, both for an independent Ulster in general, and class unity

29

within the unionist family in particular; by the unlikelihood
of Westminster agreeing to independence; and by the resurgence of nationalist activity within Northern Ireland
(Buckland, 1989; Patterson, 2002). But while the constitutional position was to remain unchanged in this period, the
Ulster question would be transformed in other ways.

Change and its Effects

The post-war social and economic environment of Northern
Ireland was shaped both by expectations derived from wartime prosperity which stimulated government attempts to
attract foreign capital (Darby, 1983), and by the effects of
the radical policies pursued by the Attlee government. With
the weakness of the dominion status option exposed, the
Stormont authorities settled down to establishing a working
relationship with Westminster.

In fact, the policy pursued by the Brooke administration
was a balancing act in which, on the one hand, it demonstrated its conservatism by supporting Tory opposition to
proposed Labour legislation, and on the other, accepting,
once enacted, the implementation of that legislation in
Northern Ireland. The major nationalisation measures, such
as affected heavy industry and coal, had little impact on the
North where there was no heavy industry or coal to nation-
alise, while transport, gas and electricity were already in public ownership. However, the National Insurance Act of 1946,
the Education Act of 1947 and the National Health Act of
1948 were measures which had an enormous impact in the
North. The acts of 1946 and 1948 provided a comprehensive
scheme of social insurance with benefits and contributions
at the same level as applied in Britain. The Education Act
was of equal, if not greater, importance. It provided univer-
sal secondary education, including free transport, milk,
meals, medical services, books and materials, increased free

scholarships and more school buildings – thus preparing able students from whatever background to take advantage of university education (O'Leary, 1979; Birrell and Murie, 1980).

In the political sphere, the enacting of the Elections and Franchise Act of 1947 was important in a negative sense. While the Westminster government had assimilated the parliamentary and local government franchises, abolishing plural voting in both, the Stormont measure maintained the pre-war local government election structure, based on rated occupation, and actually increased the number of business votes, a local government elector could claim, to six. Perceived as a major injustice designed to strengthen unionist hegemony in local government in a blatantly sectarian manner, it would provide one of the most emotive and symbolic civil rights grievances in the 1960s (O'Leary, 1979; Arthur, 1994). In sum, it was the legislation enacted in the 1940s that provide the seedbed for the crisis that developed in the 1960s. The effects of that legislation were gradual and cumulative, but were already evident in the 1950s.

In education, for example, the total number of pupils in secondary schools doubled between 1947 and 1952, while Catholic schools in particular, and from a lower starting point, made disproportionately good progress. Also, by 1955 significant progress was made in house-building and the provision of water and sewerage, while health and welfare services had expanded beyond all recognition (Harkness, 1983). Moreover, with the addition of national assistance, family allowances – especially beneficial to large Catholic families – and non-contributory pensions, Northern Ireland, within a decade, had passed 'from the status of an exceptionally backward area to full membership of the welfare state' (Buckland, 1989: 89).

By the same token these post-war changes created a marked division between the standard of living in Northern Ireland and that obtaining in the Irish Republic. By so doing they served to reinforce partition. Thus, although it had less than half the population of the Republic,

> Northern Ireland had in 1964 95,000 children in second-
> ary education compared with 85,000 in the South; while
> expenditure on higher education was almost three times
> higher. ... welfare payments were almost 50 per cent higher
> in the North, while the difference between the health
> services was so great that little comparison was possible
> (Ibid.: 103).

This vastly improved state of affairs was facilitated by a
Westminster policy of allowing Stormont to spend well beyond
its means, a policy predicated substantially on the need to
pacify a perceptibly rebellious Catholic minority. (Mulholland,
2000). It undoubtedly influenced the attitudes of Catholics to
the northern statelet, reflected in a growing tendency to focus
more on their position as citizens of Northern Ireland rather
than their subjective identity as Irish nationals. Perhaps the
clearest pointer to this development was the failure of northern Catholics to support the IRA's military campaign of
1956–62 – the resultant fatalities of which were 12, six IRA and
six RUC personnel, and equivalent to a typical 10-day toll
for 1972, the worst year of the post-1969 troubles (Moloney,
2002) – something that was more central to its collapse than
the actions of the Royal Ulster Constabulary (RUC) and B
Specials. The new realities facing the Catholic community
were addressed at a social studies conference at Garron Tower
in north Antrim in 1958 when a leading Catholic, G.B. Newe,
called for greater Catholic participation in northern affairs, a
suggestion favourably received by Captain Terence O'Neill,
the future Prime Minister. In this context the failure of the
Anti-Partition League at the Stormont elections of 1958 is
worth noting, as is the fact that the NILP won four seats, while
at the Westminster general election held the following year
Sinn Fein saw its vote plummet from the 24 per cent it received
in 1955 to 11 per cent, with the unionists winning every seat.
But perhaps most significant at this time were the calls made

by some leading members of the Unionist Party that Catholics should be permitted to join it.

In fact, even Lord Brookeborough (ennobled in 1952 on Elizabeth II's accession to office) had adopted a more conciliatory approach to the Catholic minority in the late 1940s and early 1950s, hoping that the North's socio-economic improvement under the welfare state would diminish the attraction of Irish unity. Fundamentalist Protestant and Orange reaction, however, soon forced a reversal to type (Patterson, 2002). That prime ministerial and vehement Orange opposition killed the membership proposal – continuing IRA activity added force to their opposition – was less significant than the fact that it was made (O'Leary, 1979; Darby, 1983; Mulholland, 2000). Yet, for all the signals that seemed to point to political tolerance and the easing of ancient divisions, fundamental problems remained. Indeed they were in some respects deepened by the policies pursued from 1945.

Economic Decline and its Consequences

One of the most serious problems was that the social advances of the period were not accompanied by significant economic regeneration. Concerned in 1945 that the prosperity of the war years would end, the Stormont government introduced measures to attract new industries. But this policy was soon reversed in favour of one supportive of the predominantly family-owned, local businesses that were closely connected with unionism. This remained the thrust of government economic policy until the end of Brooke's premiership in 1963. The problem, however, was that Northern Ireland's traditional industries – textiles, shipbuilding and agriculture – proved incapable of delivering sustained economic progress. Competition from lower-cost foreign producers together with the effects of modernisation resulted in large-scale employment reduction in all three areas.

The decline in staple industries was reflected in a high level of unemployment throughout the 1950s. While various government initiatives did attract new enterprises they failed to compensate adequately for the decline in traditional industries, with the result that throughout the decade unemployment never fell below 5 per cent of the workforce and averaged around 7.5 per cent – four times the United Kingdom national average – and was also occurring in the context of a better performance by other regional blackspots (Bew *et al.*, 2002). A number of factors complicated the revival of the old industries, ranging from climate, lack of fuel and remoteness from British markets, to lack of initiative and innovation in a business sector and market that was too small to attract investment. These went together with Westminster taxation policies which took little heed of Ulster's interests and the fact that in Northern Ireland ministers and civil servants sometimes stood too close to supplicants (Harkness, 1983).

The unemployment problem had worrying political consequences for unionism, illustrated by the success of the NILP in gaining four seats at the Stormont elections of 1958. As Prime Minister, Brookeborough carried most of the responsibility. Accordingly, when the Hall Committee – a Westminster–Stormont initiative to investigate the unemployment problem and how it might be solved – delivered its report in October 1962 against the background of threatened massive job losses at the Shorts aircraft factory, its rejection of Brookeborough's economic policy in favour of attracting new industries fatally damaged his leadership (Bew *et al.*, 2002). Brookeborough's influence at Westminster had depended on his elite contacts, but the passing of the pre-war generation left these a diminishing commodity. Also, the collapse of the IRA campaign reduced Westminster's fears of a Catholic uprising at the same time as global military strategy made Northern Ireland less central to British national defence. All combined to make Brookeborough expendable. Within six months he had resigned and was replaced by Captain Terence O'Neill, a politician more attuned to a new era of professional government (Mulholland, 2000).

O'Neill and Reform

Judged by his rhetoric the O'Neill era (1963–69) was a period when a reforming Prime Minister, repelled by the sectarianism endemic in Ulster politics, found his efforts to modernise the region's politics along the lines of the liberal democratic traditions characteristic of mainland Britain thwarted both by unionist extremism and the unreasonable demands and confrontational politics of the civil rights movement (O'Neill, 1973). The reality was rather different.

In fact, O'Neill's politics, while couched in the rhetoric of political modernisation and the need to abandon sectarianism, were directed chiefly towards the traditional unionist objective of consolidating the hegemony of the party, and especially to thwarting the recent advances among the Protestant working class of the NILP. As much as he wanted to integrate Northern Ireland with Britain, O'Neill wanted to avoid the replication of its class-based politics. He also saw much to admire in Sean Lemass's reformist economic programme in the Irish Republic, a programme promising economic modernisation and enhanced national cohesion, though, unlike Lemass, O'Neill would fail to adequately prepare his ground, and take due note that the national unity evident in the South was singularly absent in ethnically divided Northern Ireland (Mulholland, 2000). Accordingly, the project of undermining the NILP to the advantage of the Unionist Party would objectively serve sectarian ends.

The means settled on to effect this purpose were initiatives to reduce high unemployment, especially the creation of high growth areas, new towns, infrastructural investment and large-scale public works in housing, motorways, a new airport and improved port facilities. O'Neill's strategy worked. The Stormont elections of 1965 showed a 7 per cent swing to the Unionist Party with the NILP losing two of its four seats.

These gains, however, were not made without cost. Massive job-creation schemes may have stemmed the Protestant working class defection to the NILP, but only at the expense of disrupting traditional unionist power structures at local level (Bew *et al.*, 2002). The Matthew Plan of 1963 – which originated with the civil service rather than O'Neill, whose skill lay in recognising its political utility and appropriating it (Mulholland, 2000) – had recommended a new ministry of planning and development which, formalised as the Ministry of Development, took over powers on planning, transport, roads, local government and housing. The local government reaction to loss of control, especially that of unionist-controlled councils west of the Bann river, was hostile and would contribute to charges of O'Neill's supposedly 'dictatorial' style of government. O'Neill attempted, with partial success, to defuse that criticism by locating such high-profile projects as a new university and a new city in mainly Protestant east Ulster, in the Coleraine and Lurgan-Portadown areas, respectively. Despite misgivings in the Unionist Party no serious opposition materialised so long – as the result of the 1965 Stormont elections demonstrated – O'Neill's policies were seen as successful. In fact, O'Neill felt it necessary to demonstrate his commitment to traditionalist unionist ideology and, effectively, the practices that went with it. The outstanding weakness of his reform programme was the failure to address Catholic complaints in a substantive way.

It was inevitable that tensions would develop between the promise of O'Neill's modernising rhetoric and his failure to meet the expectations it aroused. His failure in this regard was attacked strongly by liberal unionist opinion in the North, which noted that a policy of attempting to attract Catholic support for the regime through increasing material well-being in general – which was the most that could be said for O'Neill's policies – without tackling the structures of sectarianism, was bound to fail. Not only did the modernising rhetoric highlight, by contrast, O'Neill's failure to address sectarianism, it threw into sharp relief the attacks he made on the Catholic Church when his lack of action was publicised by leading Catholics (Mulholland, 2000; Bew *et al.*, 2002).

Thus even his rhetoric of non-sectarian modernisation was not consistent.

A comprehensive assessment of O'Neill's political failure, however, has to account for a range of interacting factors, personal, circumstantial and ideological. Coming to power due to his neo-ascendancy background, modernising image, military credentials and ambition for power, O'Neill's support-base was a liberal, middle-class constituency that found expression in the *Belfast Telegraph*, rather than a solid constituency within the parliamentary party. Moreover, as a political manager he was less than accomplished. A product of an English upper-class background, he was vain, aloof and disinclined to take his less sophisticated colleagues into his confidence or seek their advice, relying instead on a small coterie of trusted civil servants. However much political necessity might dictate a need to placate them at times, he was contemptuous of local political traditions, whether Protestant or Catholic. Towards the latter, O'Neill appears to have assumed that to appeal to Catholics it was enough that he could claim a historical lineage back to the great O'Neill chiefs of Ulster through the female line (O'Neill, 1973). At best this was an aid to self-delusion. Certainly O'Neill made no attempt to establish an Irish cultural presence in the propaganda of the regime, while his claims to an Irish identity tended to be made in reaction to criticisms of the northern statelet emanating from the Irish Republic, and associated with vehement expressions of Ulster's Britishness. Moreover, clearly intending that the Catholic community should wait until economic prosperity in general improved their lot, he demanded of Catholics immediately their allegiance to the state.

The closer one examines O'Neill's 'modernisation' project the more it becomes apparent that its intended audiences were not only the unionist and nationalist communities in Northern Ireland but, perhaps primarily, the British government and people (Loughlin, 1995). He made assiduous efforts to communicate his modernisation message to the British political elite and press; and more substantially at a popular level through the institution of 'Ulster weeks' in various British cities, designed to promote Ulster industries and tourism, and which deliberately copied the 'Irish weeks' that the southern government had already been promoting for some time (Mulholland, 2000). His vocabulary borrowed freely from 1960s British popular culture with its themes of anti-militarism, the 'generation gap' and the celebration of consumerism. O'Neill re-worked these themes in an Ulster context to cultivate a constituency, especially among the young, that would carry his hopes for the non-sectarian future of the North and effect a cultural homogeneity of Northern Ireland and Britain. By so doing the region's constitutional position could be secured. It was, however, wishful thinking to assume that the superficial media materialism of 1960s Britain could provide a solution for the fundamental community divisions of Northern Ireland (Loughlin, 1995); especially as O'Neill failed to appreciate their depth. Needing to contain the right-wing unionist reaction to his liberal overtures, he would publicly deny the legitimacy of the civil rights case (Mulholland, 2000).

What gave O'Neill's consumerist approach to the Ulster problem credibility was the fact that his administration's efforts to attract outside investment did have significant success. Over the period 1964–69 60 new factories were set up, including a complex of six synthetic factories, the greatest of its kind in the world (O'Leary, 1979). More generally, growth in the regional economy was significantly higher than that for the United Kingdom as a whole in the years up to 1970, while expenditure per head of population in these years doubled, especially in the areas of housing stock, roads, education and training. Twenty-nine thousand new manufacturing jobs were also created, but as these were counterbalanced by the continuing decline in traditional industries the net gain was only 5000 (Mulholland, 2000). Accordingly, against a background of continuing job scarcity, Ian Paisley's accusation that O'Neill was creating jobs for Catholics at the expense of

Protestants continued to resonate with his working class and petty bourgeois constituency.

O'Neill's achievement was cited in Britain as evidence of the value of regional autonomy working both to advance local prosperity and constitutional security (Loughlin, 1995). If increased material well-being was the solution to Ulster's problems all that was needed was time for it to develop. The unintended consequences of O'Neillism, however, would ensure that time was in short supply.

Minority Grievances

The emotive impact of Catholic complaints against the Stormont regime became enhanced as the political temperature rose in the late 1960s, and given that the Catholic case was apparently validated by the oft-quoted statements of previous unionist leaders such as Lords Craigavon and Brookeborough encouraging discrimination and boasting, effectively, that unionists had a Protestant parliament for a Protestant people.

The minority case covered six broad areas, electoral practices, public employment, private employment, public housing, regional policy and policing; and that a strong case against the Stormont regime in several of these areas could be made is beyond question. It was incontestable, for example, that the repressive Special Powers Act was employed only against the Catholic community and that local electoral boundaries had been deliberately manipulated to enhance unionist power. The most notorious example was Derry City, where the substantial Catholic majority in the population failed to translate into a corresponding majority on the city corporation due to blatant manipulation of ward boundaries. On the housing issue, extensive house building programmes that local authorities had engaged in from 1945 offered ample scope for discrimination in public housing allocation. Likewise, in public and private employment, discrimination existed and was seen to account for the fact that Catholics were disproportionately relegated to low-pay sectors such as construction, clothing and footwear. Indeed, the view that this was a system of repression and discrimination *organised* by Stormont was seen to be validated by actions of the supposedly liberal O'Neill government.

Strategies apparently undertaken to retain working-class Protestant support for the regime, and which provoked criticisms from unionist-controlled councils of O'Neill's 'dictatorial' reduction of local government powers, took on a completely different aspect when viewed from the Catholic perspective. The building of the new city of Craigavon in the Lurgan-Portadown area and the siting of a new university in Coleraine rather than Derry, which already had Magee University College on which to build, seemed to be two significant examples of a policy which was directing the great majority of new enterprises attracted to Northern Ireland away from Catholic areas for the purpose of maintaining the existing sectarian power-balance in the region.

The picture, however, was rather more complicated than it appeared. In fact, the problem of discrimination under Stormont rule was chiefly one of local, rather than regional, government, with the great majority of cases relating to the west of the province, especially counties Tyrone and Fermanagh, parts of counties Londonderry and Armagh, and Londonderry County Borough. All the accusations of gerrymandering, virtually all the complaints about housing and regional policy, and a disproportionate number of the complaints about public and private employment came from this area. Having less than a quarter of the population of the statelet, it generated almost three-quarters of the complaints about discrimination. Injustices existed elsewhere. The B Specials were a blatantly Protestant militia; police decisions were sometimes partisan; there were fewer Catholics in the higher echelons of the civil service than were willing and qualified to serve; and some private firms discriminated against Catholics. Nevertheless, in the main, discrimination was a problem of local government in the west of the province. Stormont, of course, was ultimately responsible. The northern government had effected the original gerrymander of electoral boundaries which underpinned many of the subsequent malpractices, which it then did little to stop (Whyte, 1983; Patterson, 2002). However: 'The most serious charge against the Northern Ireland government is not that it was directly responsible for widespread discrimination, but that it allowed discrimination on such a scale over a substantial segment of Northern Ireland' (Whyte, 1983: 31). It is unlikely, though, that had the complexity of the issue been more widely appreciated in the 1960s, the case against Stormont, and the emotions it generated, would have been greatly modified. Sins of omission were scarcely less damnable than sins of commission.

Party Politics and the Catholic Community

The transformation in Ulster Catholic politics that occurred in the 1960s has to be seen against the background of a variety of changes, social, economic, cultural and political. The effects of the welfare state in diverting Catholic attention away from the partition issue was reinforced when Eamon de Valera retired and was replaced as Taoiseach of the Irish Republic by Sean Lemass in 1959. Lemass, taking his cue from a more accommodating attitude to Northern Ireland expressed by de Valera towards the end of his period of office, went further than de Valera by acting upon it. Almost immediately he signalled to northern Catholics that they should take a more active part in the public life of the region, especially in pursuing dialogue with Protestants. He gave de facto recognition to Northern Ireland's constitutional position during a speech at the Oxford Union in October 1959. In doing so he echoed G.B. Newe's conclusion at the Garron Tower conference in 1958. Indeed, Lemass's attitude to northern nationalism was dismissive, bordering on contempt, notwithstanding occasional anti-partitionist utterances made for the benefit of the more republican elements in Fianna Fail. In a period when the Irish Republic, under his direction, was entering a period of economic modernisation, and possible partnership with Stormont, northern nationalists and their grievances were an irrelevant irritation, with the result that as the civil rights movement began to stir Dublin appeared to be less concerned about minority grievances than London (Patterson, 2002).

Another important development of this era was the initiation by Pope John XXIII of the second Vatican Council at the turn of the decade, and which marked a dramatic change in Catholic attitudes to the Protestant churches. The hostility of the past was to be replaced with tolerance and conciliation. This development, in turn, was associated with the much greater understanding of the wider world that television made possible. Television would also be an important medium for the provision of political forms and tactics as minority politics became transformed in the 1960s. In its coverage of northern affairs, moreover, local television channels facilitated the belief that a new era had opened by a policy of avoiding controversial political issues.

The development of Catholic politics away from the partition issue towards that of citizenship rights would also be greatly encouraged by the return of Harold Wilson's Labour government in January 1964. Before the election Wilson had declared a willingness to address Catholic grievances, while within the Labour Party itself a group of MPs came together to form the Campaign for Democracy in Ulster (CDU). Its activities – especially attempts to thwart the convention that Northern Ireland affairs could not be discussed at Westminster – would be energised considerably by the adhesion of Gerry Fitt, a Belfast labourist politician who became Republican Labour MP for west Belfast at the general election of 1966 (Arthur, 1994; Rose, 2001). But if individuals such as Fitt played an important role in the process of political change, existing parties and movements generally failed to meet the challenge of the times.

Following the failure of the IRA campaign of 1956–62, the republican movement did mark a radical break with the past when it rejected violence and embraced Roy Johnson's Marxist analysis of the Irish question, popularly known as the 'stages' theory. This theory envisaged workers in the North prosecuting a civil rights campaign to establish social equality for the Catholic community, a development that would remove sectarian barriers between the two communities and lead to a recognition of a proletarian class interest. When this point was reached, a Sinn Fein campaign in the South would transform the reactionary outlook of the working class there into a progressive non-sectarian attitude. Simultaneously, the dynamics of capitalism would forge a strong bourgeoise over the island as a whole, one oppressive to workers of all creeds. Accordingly, the scene would be set for a working-class revolt to overthrow capitalism by whatever means (Bishop and Mallie, 1987; Patterson, 1989).

Johnson's plan was imaginative and clearly recognised that the Ulster problem could only be solved by a reconciliation of divided peoples rather than by territorial unity. Moreover, in focusing on civil rights it was, at one level, attuned to the political developments of the period. Significantly, its emphasis on politics rather than the gun as a means of resolving the national question was attractive to a young Gerry Adams, who would return to it as the futility of the Provisional Irish Republican Army (PIRA) campaign for this purpose became evident in the late 1970s (Moloney, 2002). The theory, however, suffered from significant weaknesses.

Promotionally, the basic mistake was made of forcing new ideas on a traditionalist movement at too early a stage, and the resultant opposition dealt with by means of open confrontation, thereby making a split likely – mistakes Adams would note and take care to avoid in the future (Moloney, 2002). But most seriously, the plan vastly underestimated the problem of religious sectarianism as a divisive factor in Ulster society, while its evolutionary perspective would leave republicans woefully ill-equipped to respond to the rapidly deteriorating political environment of Northern Ireland in the late 1960s. Nevertheless the republican movement, however imperfectly, did at least respond imaginatively to a new situation, something that could hardly be said for the constitutional Nationalist Party led by Eddie McAteer.

By the 1960s it was increasingly anachronistic. It had never been a political party in the normal sense of the term, lacking a formal organisation, structure and policies. Only in November 1964 would a party policy document be issued and only in 1965 an annual conference initiated. As a party it consisted mainly of a loose alliance of local leaders operating at the parliamentary level, while its close association with the Catholic community entailed substantial clerical involvement in party affairs. Geographically, the party's electoral base was entirely rural.

That it was woefully ill-equipped for the politics of civil rights was demonstrated in a televised debate on discrimination in February 1964 between the party's representative, James O'Reilly, MP for Mourne, and Brian Faulkner. Despite the fact that this issue had been a long-established element of the anti-partitionist case, Faulkner, defending the weakest case imaginable, easily demolished O'Reilly. Moreover, even though the Nationalist Party's major focus was partition, even here it failed to establish a distinctive position of its own. At the urging of the blatantly unsympathetic Sean Lemass it took up the position of official opposition at Stormont in 1965 and was soon identifying with the institution, agreeing to the provision of extra funds for the B Specials and uncritically applauding O'Neill's gestural conciliationism. The party's stance at Stormont pointed up its failure to effectively address the new political agenda increasingly important to the Catholic community: that it was completely sidelined by the civil rights movement is not surprising (McAllister, 1983; Lynn, 1997; Bew *et al.*, 2002). In fact, the only political party that might have been able to embrace the politics of civil rights was the NILP.

In the early 1960s, the NILP developed a distinct set of non-sectarian policies, such as reform of the electoral law and electoral boundaries, housing allocation and an end to discrimination. It was, however, primarily a party which saw its natural arena of operation as Stormont and was unsuitable as a vehicle for the creation of an extra-parliamentary mass movement. Indeed, its leaders were ideologically incapable of pursuing such a course of action. Despite its non-sectarian programme the party's membership was not free from sectarian prejudices. The NILP failed to increase its parliamentary seats at the general election of 1962 and sought to remedy this by a sustained pitch for Catholic support, a policy that produced significant results, but which discomfited Protestant members many of whom were sympathetic to Paisleyism. Their outlook was reflected in a scandal in November 1964, when three of the party's six councillors on Belfast Corporation voted to support a Protestant Unionist motion on keeping children's playgrounds closed on Sundays, an action in direct contradiction to the party's manifesto. This issue caused Catholic disillusionment and a controversy between right and left in the party that almost caused a split. In fact the NILP had already responded in a contradictory way to the re-emergence of sectarian conflict on Belfast's streets. This was occasioned by a hard-line Protestant reaction, led by Revd Ian Paisley, to the display of an Irish Tricolour in Sinn Fein offices in Divis Street during the general election of 1964. It resulted in three days of rioting. These disturbances, Gerry Adams has claimed, aroused his interest in politics, and seems to have been a major factor in his decision to enlist in the IRA (Purdie, 1990; Adams, 1996; Mulholland, 2000; Moloney, 2002).

The NILP, as we have seen, was also the main focus of attack in O'Neill's campaign to re-establish Unionist Party hegemony over the Protestant working class. As part of that campaign O'Neill quite successfully tainted it by association with the 'anti-partitionist' Labour government in Britain. The result was that by 1966 the NILP was largely a spent force in Ulster politics. With its decline, virtually, the last parliamentary restraint on the development of street politics was removed (Purdie, 1990).

The Civil Rights Campaign

The novelty of the civil rights movement in Northern Ireland has perhaps suggested a sharper break with the political mentality of the past than was, in fact, the case. Certainly the verdict of the Cameron Commission, set up in January 1969 to investigate the violence surrounding the civil rights march of 5 October 1968 in Derry City, emphasised its novelty by focusing on the vanguard role for the Catholic community performed by a new Catholic middle class that had been created by post-war welfare and educational reforms (Anon., 1972). Subsequent analyses of developments in Catholic politics in the 1960s, however, painted a more complex picture, one which illustrated the magnitude of the political upheaval which took place in the minority community.

In fact, one of the first civil rights organisations in 1964, the Campaign for Social Justice (CSJ), was founded in Dungannon by a doctor's wife, Patricia McCluskey, *in response* to a mass protest organised by a local organisation, the Homeless Citizens League (HCL), against anti-Catholic discrimination in housing allocations by Dungannon Council. As a whole, the civil rights movement was the product of the coming together of several such pressure groups. The tactics employed by the HCL and CSJ – direct action in the form of petitions and pickets – also established the political forms of the future. Unlike previous Catholic complaints which were localised and easily contained, the HCL took its protests and well-rehearsed arguments over the head of Dungannon Council to Stormont and was able to gain some significant successes. By so doing it also served to expose the weaknesses of the local nationalist leadership. The issues the HCL were concerned with were, of course, not localised in Dungannon but prevalent to varying degrees across Northern Ireland. Accordingly, the organisation gave a lead to other areas. Moreover, the HCL emerged at a time when the Black civil rights movement in the USA was attracting world-wide attention and comparisons between injustices in the USA and the

North were already being made. Certainly the CSJ, which superseded the HCL, had a title which was influenced by developments in America.

Although, as an organisation, the CSJ was more concerned with publicity and soliciting the support of British parties than mass protest, in so doing, it copied the HCL tactic of going beyond the local authority to the national level. Further, it was fortunate enough in that when it did so the CDU existed within the British governing party as a receptive audience for its grievances. Indeed, the attention of the Labour Party was likely to focus on Northern Ireland for quite a different reason. Its majority at the general election of 1964 was only four, and as Harold Wilson noted, it was a majority that could be easily overturned by the Ulster unionist MPs supporting the Tory Party on an issue such as English housing, which they could vote on in Westminster though Westminster could not discuss Northern Ireland affairs. Persuaded largely by Gerry Fitt, the CDU had committed itself by 1968 to abolishing this convention.

Another important body within the civil rights movement was the Northern Ireland Civil Rights Association (NICRA), an organisation formed on 1 February 1967 and which was to be increasingly seen as the dominant force within the movement. It was a view given colour by the organisation's formal structure, composed of a ruling executive body of 13, a regional council of 240 delegates, together with local civil rights committees providing the groundwork. In reality, however, prior to October 1968, the executive body *was* the association, and the executive consisted of individual activists, largely based in Belfast, and consisted of members of the CSJ, the NILP, the Communist Party of Northern Ireland (CPNI), republicans of the Belfast Wolfe Tone Society, the Republican Clubs, and private individuals. Only in the aftermath of the 5 October march in Derry would it become a truly regional mass organisation (Purdie, 1990).

Constitutional nationalism would also make its contribution to the civil rights movement. In 1964, the National

Democratic Party (NDP) was formed. It was the product of a generation of young Catholic graduates who had attempted unsuccessfully to convert the Nationalist Party, both to the view that Catholics should be more actively engaged in the political system, and that Irish unity could only come about with unionist consent (Arthur, 1994).

The variety of groupings that came together to make up the civil rights movement points to a heterogeneous consciousness, prompting the question of how far the embracing of a new political agenda entailed the abandonment of old ideologies. The best insight we have into the political consciousness of the Catholic community generally in the period before the outbreak of civil strife in 1969, is provided in a study undertaken by Richard Rose (Rose, 1971). It shows that only 15 per cent of Catholics questioned regarded themselves as 'British', and of these only around half accepted Northern Ireland's constitutional position as part of the United Kingdom. Rose's conclusions suggest that a Catholic sense of grievance rather than an active embracing of British citizenship, which the slogan 'British rights for British citizens' indicated, was the most important driving force behind the civil rights struggle.

The most significant source of disaffection within the Catholic community has been located in the deteriorating social and economic position of the Catholic working class. Whereas everywhere else and also in the Protestant community the unskilled sector of the working class was diminishing as a proportion of the workforce, in the Catholic community it was actually increasing. Around a quarter belonged to this category, and as such, constituted a sector of the population excluded from political life and substantially from social rewards. Its mentality had not been 'modernised', but instead embodied traditional opposition to unionism and was to find ready access for the expression of its grievances in the new forms of political activity such as street marches and sit-downs that the civil rights movement provided. Thus, while the Catholic middle class may have been growing in this period and throwing up political leaders concerned to mark out new paths in minority politics, this was only one factor in a more complex situation (Bew *et al.*, 2002). Tellingly, one member of People's Democracy (PD), a student-based group which emerged in the wake of the Derry march of 5 October 1968, noted: 'Everyone applauds loudly when one says in a speech that we are not sectarian, but really that is because they see this as a new way of getting at the Protestants' (quoted Purdie, 1990: 247). Certainly the civil rights movement, though ostensibly non-sectarian, focused heavily, and perhaps inevitably, on the grievances of the Catholic population, much of which had also been embodied in a long-established nationalist case against partition.

From Agitation to Conflict

By early 1968, politics in Northern Ireland were moving into a highly unstable stage. Despite a 'law and order' rhetoric popular unionism all too easily accommodated and exploited mob violence, as the Divis Street riots of 1964 demonstrated. At the same time, traditional parties had never established deep roots within a Catholic community which now motivated by a combination of discontent, O'Neill's expectation-raising rhetoric, and a political environment being reshaped by new political forms, was becoming a volatile political constituency whose demands Stormont was finding difficult to accommodate.

The point at which politics began to shift from parliament to the streets came in May 1967. The NILP, which had regularly offered parliamentary support for the civil rights demands of extra-parliamentary groups, proposed a resolution demanding a reform of the local government franchise. Unlike the rest of the United Kingdom where the practice had been eliminated in 1947, the franchise allowed businessmen (usually unionist) to hold a number of votes, thereby consolidating unionist control of local government in many areas. The resolution, however, was promptly defeated. As the civil rights movement got under way in 1968, 'One man, one vote' became the central demand, one that was out of proportion to the real, practical significance of the issue (Arthur, 1994).

Despite the mythology that would later surround the NICRA, it was, in fact, very reluctant to engage in public protests and played no major role in the most important demonstrations. The first civil rights march of 2500 people from Coalisland to Dungannon on 24 August 1968, for example, was the inspiration of Austin Currie, a young Nationalist MP at Stormont, while the organisation's presence during the crucial Derry march of 5 October 1968 was almost non-existent. That march was initiated by a local group, mainly from the Derry Housing Action Committee. A massive follow-up march on 16 November was organised by another local body, the Derry Citizens Action Committee. In fact, in the main, street protests were largely the province of local organisations, with only indirect links to the NICRA.

The October march in Derry was the crucial event that initiated the political crisis of 1968–69. It was attended by RUC mismanagement and brutality inflicted on non-violent marchers. Witnessed by the world's media together with three British Labour MPs, a major political controversy ensued. Thereafter, the NICRA mushroomed into a movement with branches and associated bodies throughout areas of Northern Ireland with substantial Catholic populations, together with supporting organisations in the Irish Republic, Britain, Australia and New Zealand. By this time also the NICRA had acquired a specific set of objectives:

1. One man, one vote in local elections.
2. Removal of gerrymandered electoral boundaries.
3. Laws against discrimination in local government and machinery to deal with complaints.
4. Allocation of public housing on a points system.
5. Repeal of the Special Powers Act.
6. Disbanding of the B Specials.

The development of this new and greatly expanded movement, especially the emergence of the student-based PD – a group that would exert a political influence out of proportion to its numbers – transformed politics in Northern Ireland. But as it did so it produced sectarian tensions, instability and violence. This was due in large part to the nature of the movement. The primacy of local autonomy; a programme that unionists perceived as directed at overthrowing the government; direct action methods that flouted traditional sectarian territorial boundaries; all combined to present insuperable problems for the leadership in terms of controlling events (Anon., 1972; Purdie, 1990). Thus, when it called for a temporary truce on street demonstrations in December 1968 – a call made in response to O'Neill's 'Crossroads' speech of 9 December, in which he appealed for restraint to prevent a collapse into civil chaos – the call was heeded only for a few weeks. In January 1969, 14 marches were held, the busiest month for the movement.

The most important of these was the watershed march of 4 January from Belfast to Derry and organised by PD. This 'Long March' not only broke the truce on marches, but in deliberately taking a route which brought the marchers through loyalist areas was organised in such a way that inter-community tensions would be heightened. What had made the truce acceptable to mainstream civil rights opinion was that it came in the wake of a promised five-point reform programme announced by O'Neill on 22 November 1968. The programme included a points system for the allocation of public housing; abolition of the company vote in local government elections; a review of the Special Powers Act; the appointment of an Ombudsman; and the establishment of a development commission to replace the corrupt Derry City corporation (Anon., 1972; Cochrane, 1997).

Seeking change of a more far-reaching kind, this programme was rejected by PD as too little, too late, while O'Neill's emotional appeal for restraint was dismissed with contempt. In fact, PD, a distinctive grouping that was rapidly developing in a left-ward direction, succeeded not in radicalising the civil rights movement but in dragging it, via the Burntollet experience – a savage loyalist attack on the marchers involving members of the B Specials at Burntollet Bridge outside Derry – into the sectarian political realities of Northern Ireland (Arthur, 1974).

The Belfast–Derry march was followed a week later by a civil rights demonstration in Newry, where the tensions raised the previous week found expression in a riot, during which seven police vans were destroyed, 18 people – 10 of them policemen – were injured, and 24, mostly PD members, were arrested. Probably the most serious consequence of the Belfast–Derry march, however, was its effect on the Protestant people, which tended to view the Burntollet attack as a just retribution for a series of arrogant invasions of its territory. More specifically, the march allowed the return to the streets of the Protestant religio-political agitator, Revd Ian Paisley, intent on mobilising his lower middle-class and working-class followers for confrontation with the civil rights movement.

Paisley and the Resurgence of Loyalist Extremism

There was nothing novel in Ian Paisley adopting the role of public defender of traditional unionism. With family roots in the plantation, he was merely the latest in a historical line of religious demagogues going back to the Revd Henry Cooke and Revd Hugh Hanna in the nineteenth century; clerics whose deployment of impressive oratorical abilities in the cause of anti-Catholicism ensured them a large following. As Northern Ireland's political crisis deepened in the 1960s, a development to which he made a substantial contribution, Paisley emerged as the most authentic standard-bearer of the unionist right-wing.

He first emerged as a controversial figure in the 1950s with attacks on the mainstream Presbyterian Church for its per-ceived departure from biblical Protestantism, in defence of which he established his own Free Presbyterian Church. This occasionally led to brushes with the law, as in 1956, when he was associated with the Maura Lyons case, a controversy involving the removal by evangelical Protestants of a 15-year-old Catholic girl whom they claimed to have 'saved' from the control of her parents. Paisley was especially alert to treachery in high places, with even the ultra-right-wing Brookeborough occasionally coming under the lash for slackness in defence of the unionist faith.

With the emergence of ecumenism following Vatican II in the early 1960s and the conciliationist response to it from Ireland's mainstream Protestant denominations, Paisley redoubled his efforts (Moloney and Pollak, 1986). Certainly the report of the 'committee on national and international problems' within the Presbyterian Church in 1966, which condemned discrimination in the workplace, in housing allocation and in the drawing of electoral boundaries (Rafferty, 1994), could only have seemed from the Paisleyite perspective a deeply ominous consequence of ecumenism.

While Paisley could, at this time, still be dismissed as a marginal extremist, his potential for political progress was more solidly based than O'Neill's. The strain of anti-Catholicism that runs deeply throughout the Protestant community is the single most important ideological factor binding the community together (Rose, 1971; Pollak ed., 1993; McKay, 2000). In the 1960s, a desire by Protestants for better relations with Roman Catholics went together with support for more government attention to the views of strong loyalists; discrimination against Catholics in jobs and housing; stronger measures to defend the border and no change in the existing relations between the two communities. These views were deeply embedded in the right-wing unionist outlook which Paisley had, by then, come to personify. By contrast, for a number of reasons, O'Neill's position was weak.

He had attained the premiership by appointment, due it seems, to his perceived ascendancy background, an advantage over his rivals from a business background, J.L.O. Andrews and Brian Faulkner, whose success as Minister of Commerce would make him indispensable to O'Neill at the same time as his frustrated ambition and resentment served to complicate the O'Neillite project. Politically astute, Faulkner was a complex personality, combining strong personal ambition with equally strong right-wing impulses – evidenced in a record of promoting Orange marches through Catholic areas, with attendant violence – together with a recognition of the need for reform. Indeed, it was, apparently, Faulkner's threat to outdo O'Neill on the reformist front by pursuing his own high-level North–South dialogue, despite having dismissed Lemass's overtures for practical co-operation as a form of devious anti-partitionism, that moved the latter to initiate his controversial meetings with the Irish Taoiseach in 1965, and which demonstrated his poor party-management skills (Mulholland, 2000; Patterson, 2002).

The visit of Lemass to Stormont in 1965 was taken on his own initiative and sprung on his colleagues as Lemass was about to arrive. The visit was easily portrayed by Paisley as evidence of political treachery. It was always easier for Paisley to make political capital by defending beliefs deeply embedded in the unionist community than it was for O'Neill through promoting change, with the uncertainties it entailed and in the face of an ever-more demanding minority community.

Paisley, indeed, proved adept at creating situations which heightened grass-roots unionist antagonism to O'Neillite ideas. He protested, for instance, against the expression of condolences on the death of Pope John XXIII by O'Neill and the Lord Mayor of Belfast. Even events unassociated with O'Neill – for example, the display of an Irish Tricolour in a Sinn Fein office window in west Belfast in 1964 and the celebrations of the fiftieth anniversary of the 1916 Rising in 1966 – could be exploited to the same effect. Again, it was an especially adept move to bring Sir Edward Carson's son to Belfast in 1966 to condemn O'Neill, with the sanction of the great hero of Ulster unionism that the son's presence implied. It is also worth noting that the damage accruing to

Paisley as a result of the heckling of Lord Erskine, the Governor of Northern Ireland, and his wife at the Presbyterian General Assembly in 1966, was short term.

Demonstrations and protests, however, were only a part of Paisley's campaign against O'Neill. His *Protestant Telegraph* pursued unremitting vilification not only of O'Neill, but the Irish Republic and the Catholic Church, while a flirtation with loyalist paramilitarism was maintained through the Ulster Constitutional Defence Committee and its vanguard, the Ulster Protestant Volunteers; though this organisation, established in 1966, officially rejected illegal activities.

The year 1966 is noteworthy for the murder of a Catholic barman and the wounding of two others in Malvern Street, Belfast, by a small loyalist group calling itself the UVF, but it is of some significance that these shootings, perpetrated by Augustus 'Gusty' Spence and two followers, took place against the background of a low-level campaign of petrol bomb attacks against Catholic schools, homes and public houses, which was symptomatic of extreme loyalist feeling, at least in the Belfast area. When the NICRA emerged the following year it was easily portrayed as a republican front organisation, a belief neatly conveyed in the slogan, 'CRA = IRA' (Farrell, 1976; Bruce, 1986).

This charge is unsustainable, but given the near paranoid mindset of extreme loyalism, enough grains of truth could be found to validate it. In the South, for example, Nelson's pillar in O'Connell Street, Dublin, had been blown up in 1965, while 1966 was to see an IRA splinter group stage a number of bank robberies. But most seriously, on 7 May police in the Republic found an IRA document of policy suggestions which, in the section on Northern Ireland, outlined a plan for the takeover of Catholic areas of Belfast; the intervention of the republic in the North; and the infiltration of labour and civil rights organisations, trade unions, the British army and the RUC (Hezlet, 1973). The plan was an extreme republican wish-list with no possibility of implementation. Nevertheless, when published in the *Belfast News Letter*, on 21 May 1966, it caused considerable unionist apprehension. These proposed activities must have been a significant element of MI5 intelligence reports to the effect that the IRA planned to use the forthcoming commemoration of the fiftieth anniversary of the 1916 Rising in the North as an occasion to create a violent agitation, and which caused a quiet dispatch of troop reinforcements to Northern Ireland (Rose, 2001).

In its membership and modes of operation the civil rights movement gave some colour to loyalist claims. In fact, republicans of the Wolfe Tone Societies had largely been responsible for creating the NICRA, but as the organisation came to take shape republicanism was only one among a number of elements that made it up, and was certainly not in a position to dictate membership or direct its operations. Likewise, unionist accusations of communist influence in the organisation had an element of truth, but greatly exaggerated the influence of people such as Betty Sinclair, the chairperson of the NICRA in 1968, who, though a member of the CPNI, became involved in the organisation from personal, not party, motivation. Inclined to moderation, her influence was marginal.

It was the mistake of right-wing unionists, especially those in government positions like William Craig – whom O'Neill had made the mistake of moving from the Ministry of Development to Home Affairs and was thus responsible for dealing with civil rights marches – to note republican and communist involvement in the civil rights movement, fail to assess their real influence, and to conclude that what was afoot was a thinly disguised threat to the constitution of Northern Ireland. It was this understanding that shaped Craig's approach to the 5 October march in Derry.

It was also the case, however, that the model and tactics that the civil rights movement employed were imperfectly suited to Northern Ireland. The Black civil rights movement in the USA was a model adopted superficially from television coverage without due consideration of its suitability in the very different Ulster environment. Street marches, sit-downs, passive resistance and songs such as 'We shall overcome' had a very different implication in Armagh than in Alabama. In a society fundamentally divided on questions of national identity and state legitimacy, to march in an area was to demonstrate control, or, as was invariably the Paisleyite view of civil rights marches in loyalist areas, territorial invasion. It was true, of course, that for many involved in the civil rights struggle, especially those Protestants who became involved, the claim of 'British rights for British citizens' defined the extent of their ambitions. Nevertheless, it was inevitable, given the main support-base of the movement, that the campaign would also provide occasions for the expression of more traditional political and sectarian viewpoints. In this context, the argument that the movement's leadership should have realised the political dangers involved in over-identification with the Catholic sector of the population and made a greater attempt to address the concerns of Protestants, has some validity.

Certainly it could be argued that, unlike the USA where the federal government and courts responded to the demands of the civil rights movement, their Ulster equivalent had no option but to take to the streets. Once street protest became the usual form of political activity, however, the initiative lay with local groups and in the process the organisational weakness of the movement was exposed. One of the most serious weaknesses was the lack of an authoritative leader that could perform the role that Dr Martin Luther King did for the Black movement in the USA. The absence of such a figure in Northern Ireland left the leadership of the civil rights movement having to respond to the uncontrolled initiatives of individual groups, as the example of the PD's Belfast–Derry march so clearly demonstrated. Consequently, as a movement it was a very difficult one to effectively negotiate with (Purdie, 1990).

Ironically, it was only on the extreme loyalist side that such a leader, in the person of Ian Paisley, was emerging, and by the time the civil rights campaign got seriously under way from October 1968 he was effectively placed to lead the loyalist reaction. In this he was assisted considerably by the fact that the leadership of the Orange Order, an organisation that in the past was the strongest defender of traditional unionism, had by this time grown so close to the government that it was inhibited from explicitly criticising O'Neill (Cochrane, 1997). Paisley's mobilisation skills were effectively displayed on 30 November 1968 when a planned civil rights demonstration through Armagh led to a mass convergence on the town by thousands of loyalists armed with clubs, thereby inducing an RUC capitulation and the prevention of the march. It was a most impressive demonstration of the growth of Paisley's political power, and as his power grew that of O'Neill diminished.

In fact, O'Neill's leadership was under threat from 1966 when a number of attempts were made to replace him with Brian Faulkner. But his position greatly weakened from December 1968. On 11 December and in opposition to the reform package he had announced in late November, William Craig, the Minister of Home Affairs, voiced his dissent and was sacked. On 15 January 1969, following the resumption of street demonstrations, O'Neill appointed the Cameron Commission to investigate the causes of the disturbances that occurred following the Derry march of the previous October, a development used as a pretext for resignation by Brian Faulkner. Faulkner was followed the next day by another hardliner, William Morgan, while on 3 February, 12 unionist backbenchers met in a Portadown hotel – the 'Portadown Parliament' – and called for O'Neill's resignation. With a majority of backbench opinion now against him O'Neill called an election for 24 February (Farrell, 1976).

This election was unlike any other that had occurred under the Stormont regime, for it involved conflicts both between unionists and an assorted opposition, and perhaps most importantly, conflicts between the liberal and right-wing sections of the Unionist Party, between those support-ing and those opposing O'Neill. This was a defining moment for the party, when it had to choose between two distinct paths of development, but the election would fail to clearly resolve the issue. For his part, O'Neill had hoped to attract the support of both the Protestant and Catholic middle classes. But his appeal to Catholics suffered from the same triumph of appearance over substance that had characterised his conciliationist project in general, for although some Catholics were willing to stand as O'Neillite candidates, none were asked.

As an attempt to restore his leadership, the election was a failure. In 23 constituencies where pro- and anti-O'Neillite candidates stood, the former got 141,914 votes and 11 seats, and their opponents 130,019 votes and 12 seats. O'Neill himself just scraped home with an overall majority in Bannside against Ian Paisley. On the opposition side the upheaval that had been developing in minority politics now produced its results. In Derry, the Nationalist Party leader, Eddie McAteer, was decisively ousted by John Hume, one of the new civil rights leaders, while other Nationalist Party incumbents were defeated in Mid-Londonderry and in South Armagh. In South Down, the PD candidate just failed to oust his nationalist opponent. In sum, far from resolving O'Neill's difficulties, the election served to mobilise both loyalist extremism and Catholic militancy (Farrell, 1976; Arthur, 1994; Mulholland, 2000).

Seriously weakened, O'Neill carried on, but over the next two months confrontation on the streets accelerated, with protests taking place against the implementation of a Public Order Bill aimed chiefly against the forms of protest employed by the civil rights movement, accompanied by occasional police brutality. The most serious incident occurred on 19 April, two days after the Catholics of Mid-Ulster had united to elect Bernadette Devlin to Westminster in a by-election. In the heat of a riot, a group of RUC men in pursuit of local youths followed their route of escape through the home of Samuel Devenny in the Bogside area of Derry; and having failed to apprehend the youths vented their frustration on the uninvolved householder, beating him unconscious in front of his family. Devenny died three months later as a result of his injuries.

The tension on the streets increased substantially in April when a number of explosive attacks against public utilities occurred. Immediately attributed to the IRA, they were, in fact, the work of the UVF and intended to force O'Neill's resignation. This was to come before the month was out. Following several days of rioting on the Falls Road in Catholic west Belfast, O'Neill, on 22 April, at last conceded 'One man, one vote'. It was a concession, however, only reluctantly endorsed by the Unionist Party (28–22) and also provoked the resignation of his cousin, Major James Chichester-Clark. Under pressure from continuing civil disturbances and facing a meeting of the Standing Committee of the Unionist Party which he was unlikely to survive, O'Neill resigned on the 28 April (Farrell, 1976; Arthur, 1994). But while O'Neill's demise is largely explicable in terms of his personal failings and political developments within Northern Ireland, it cannot be adequately accounted for without some consideration of the contribution made to those developments by the Labour government of Harold Wilson.

Labour and Northern Ireland

If the Stormont regime bridled at Westminster's interference in Northern Ireland's affairs in the 1960s this was only understandable given the uncritical support previous administrations had given it since the end of the Second World War. At a time when Britain was about to initiate a massive programme of decolonisation, the strongly pro-unionist Home Secretary, Herbert Morrison – grandfather of the future Secretary of State for Northern Ireland, Peter Mandelson – ensured that its sympathies did not extend to Irish nationalist aspirations. By the mid-1960s, however, the memory of Northern Ireland's wartime loyalty to Britain was fading and the political capital derived from it constantly diminishing. Indeed Harold Wilson was unlikely to place too high a value on that loyalty in any event. As a young wartime civil servant and joint secretary of the Cabinet's Manpower Requirement Committee, he was appalled at Northern Ireland's failure to contribute adequately to the struggle against fascism (Rose, 2001).

O'Neill recognised that times had changed and the consequent need to consolidate the North's constitutional position on a more substantial basis. Given the existence of a significant constituency among Labour MPs sympathetic to Catholic grievances, however, and Harold Wilson's personal sympathy for Irish nationalism – expressed during the election campaign of 1964 in a stated readiness to deal with Catholic grievances in Northern Ireland – it was unlikely that Westminster would be content to simply go along with O'Neill's hopes of eliminating Catholic alienation through a general and gradual rise in economic well-being, especially after Gerry Fitt's election to Westminster in 1966 (Arthur, 1994; Loughlin, 1995; Rose, 2001).

Accordingly, when Wilson and his Home Secretary, Roy Jenkins, met O'Neill in August 1966 the connection between the high financial subvention Northern Ireland received from Westminster and the need for an effective reform package was pointedly made. Yet, events from 1967 onwards were to demonstrate the lack of substance behind O'Neill's reformist rhetoric. Increasingly it was seen that reform would only come if pressed by Westminster and the controversy produced by the events in Derry in October 1968 provided the occasion for action. O'Neill's reform package of November 1968 was, in fact, dictated by the Wilson government. But while reforms could be pressed on O'Neill there was a substantial cost involved in terms of his authority, for in so doing his position in the unionist community and his relationship with the Catholic community was bound to suffer. If he was seen to be only a puppet of the Wilson government it made more sense to address Westminster directly. Wilson's concern to urge reform on O'Neill was, of course, motivated by the realisation that if he did not, Westminster might well have to intervene directly, a prospect nobody wanted to contemplate (Rose, 2001). Yet, in being seen to force reform on O'Neill that prospect was brought closer.

As O'Neill's authority waned in early 1969 the Wilson government turned its attention more closely to the North with the creation of a Northern Ireland Cabinet Committee, which included leading Labour figures such as Denis Healy, Roy Jenkins, Jim Callaghan, Richard Crossman and Lord Gardiner, the government's senior legal adviser. The formation of the committee was a recognition of the deterioration of the political situation in the North, but no serious measures for dealing with it – for example, preparations for mass disorder – were made (Callaghan, 1973; Boyce, 1988). Thus, Northern Ireland drifted increasingly towards civil conflict after the fall of O'Neill, with ever more insistent Catholic demands for reform and an intensifying loyalist reaction. Nor was O'Neill's successor as Prime Minister, his cousin, Major James Chichester-Clark, any more effective than he had been at reversing the drift of political power away from Stormont to the streets. Indeed, as Catholic expectations quickened, Stormont, a parliamentary institution modelled on Westminster and geared to the *gradual* implementation of legislation, was increasingly unsuitable for this purpose (Wilson, 1989).

British intervention in Northern Ireland became inevitable following the eruption of violence sparked off by the Apprentice Boys march in Derry on 12 August 1969, permission for which we now know was given, not by the Stormont Minister for Home Affairs, Robert Porter, but by the Home Secretary in London, Jim Callaghan, and against the advice of Cabinet colleagues and informed opinion in the North (Rose, 2001). And it came only after two days of massive civil disorder, not only in Derry, but shortly afterwards in Belfast, the latter being the more destructive for being fuelled by antagonistic ethnic myths in which an RUC–Loyalist alliance attempted a pogrom against Bogside Catholics, on the one hand, and the forces of law and order struggled to contain an IRA-inspired rebellion, on the other (Patterson, 2002). It was, however, the Catholic community that suffered most; 1500 Catholic families, five times that of Protestants, were forced to move between July and September 1969 (Moloney, 2002); and the terms of the intervention – in aid of the civil power – testified to the reluctance with which it was undertaken (Callaghan, 1973).

The record of the Wilson government on Northern Ireland was unimpressive. Acknowledging on coming to office that injustices in the region needed to be addressed, and expressing intent to do so, Wilson failed to act effectively. A combination of factors were to blame; historically based fears about being dragged into the 'Irish bog' – not least a Protestant backlash against London interference – expressed in undue adherence to the convention of Westminster's non-interference in Northern Ireland's affairs; a delusionary reliance on the 'liberal' O'Neill to deliver reforms, in spite of evidence to the contrary; and, from the mid-1960s, Wilson's preoccupation with non-Irish issues, especially threats to his position as his government was buffeted by economic crises, internal Cabinet conflict over trade union reform and Rhodesia. In the context of domestic and wider Common-wealth issues Ulster seemed relatively unimportant and was pushed to the margins, meriting only erratic and occasional consideration until events dictated closer engagement, and even then the nature of that engagement would serve to deepen rather than alleviate the Ulster problem (Rose, 2001; Patterson, 2002).

2

BRITISH INTERVENTION

Crisis Management

With British engagement in August 1969 a new and critical phase of the Ulster question opened up. The policies Westminster pursued from then until the prorogation of Stormont in April 1972 would have fateful consequences.

Having been forced to intervene directly in the North's affairs Britain at once became the most important political actor. Intervention was greeted with relief by Catholics as Britain would restrain the Stormont authorities and have a determining role in shaping future policy. In both these areas, however, reality would be rather different from Catholic expectations. Fundamentally the extent of Westminster's engagement in the crisis in this period was determined by the hope of extricating itself at an early date. Rather than accepting that intervention had made a sham of devolution and that its retention was an evasion of the disagreeable fact that London would have to take control, the mistaken policy of working through Stormont was pursued (Wilson, 1989; Rose, 2001). This resulted in ambiguity about governmental responsibility and the creation of a policy vacuum which allowed the strongest, and not necessarily the wisest, counsels to prevail at crucial junctures.

While British intervention brought the region back from the brink of civil war, it nevertheless intensified the developments that had brought the Ulster problem to a crisis point, namely nationalist expectations of fundamental reforms and unionist dismay at the perceived Catholic successes. The former intensified almost immediately. The Home Secretary, Jim Callaghan, having 'triggered' the conflict, now made Northern Ireland a personal priority and in so doing was one of the few British politicians to enhance his political reputation on the Ulster question. He also had strong cross-party support. The publication in September of the Cameron Report on the causes of the disturbances of the previous year made a damning case for reform and Quintin Hogg, the shadow Home Secretary, a man with historic family links with Ulster, made plain the Tory Party's support for reform with a trenchant attack on religious discrimination.

Stormont–Westminster relations were re-established by the Downing Street declaration of 19 August 1969. It declared equality of treatment for all citizens in Northern Ireland 'irrespective of political or religious views'. It said nothing, however, about mechanisms to give effect to this, and except for what was being done in Derry the government of Chichester-Clark, though committed to reform, yet feared its effect on party unity and was reluctant to move. Callaghan's commitment to taking charge of the situation was regarded, therefore, with some relief. His proactive approach to Ulster was evidenced in the appointment, on 21 August, of the Hunt Inquiry to investigate the whole structure of the North's security forces and Sir Leslie Scarman, a High Court judge, to investigate the causes of the violence and civil disturbance that took place in the previous six months.

Callaghan's purpose was to build on the O'Neill reform package of the previous autumn. An inquiry by the new Ombudsman, Sir Edmund Compton, into accusations of abuse by the Stormont regime was under way and the Derry

Commission, which replaced the old corrupt city corporation, was allocating houses on the basis of need. Callaghan hastened the reform process for the region as a whole by establishing three working parties, on housing allocation, job discrimination and community relations, to be composed of members of both the Stormont and Westminster governments. They were due to report by mid-October, when Callaghan planned to return to Belfast. In the meantime, a 'UK representative', Oliver Wright, a diplomat seconded from the Foreign Office, would keep an eye on Stormont (Anon., 1972).

Callaghan's initiative contributed powerfully to the extensive range of reforms that were enacted in the period from August 1969 to June 1971, and which conceded virtually the entire case made by the civil rights movement. British standards of public administration would replace sectarian clientism in local government. Reform of local government would accompany a franchise based on 'one person, one vote' and the creation of an independent commissioner to draw up electoral boundaries. The RUC would be disarmed (though quickly re-armed again as republican violence increased) and an independent Police Authority established to oversee policing. The B Specials would be disbanded and replaced by the Ulster Defence Regiment, a local force under British Army control (though almost inevitably, it would be overwhelmingly Protestant). A Housing Executive would be established to take over the housing allocation powers of local authorities, while a Commissioner of Complaints would investigate accusations of discrimination against them. Further, a significant reform of the public prosecution system would take place with the appointment of a Director of Public Prosecutions, independent of the RUC. Legislation making incitement to religious hatred an offence was framed in July 1970, while a Ministry of Community Relations was also established (O'Leary and McGarry, 1993).

Impressive as this list of reforms was, however, its effectiveness as a solution to the Ulster problem was undermined by developments in the increasingly volatile political sphere. The reforms caused great dismay among unionists at the same time as repressive security measures were leading to a re-emergence of the national question in the Catholic community.

Reform and Reaction

Having seen violence on the streets subside by the end of 1969, the British government became somewhat complacent about its successes: the problem had been 'licked', reforms would transform the North. Troops' numbers were reduced.

Anxious to initiate reform so as to quickly disengage, Westminster politicians failed to consider how their obviously directing hand and the reforms, especially those affecting the RUC and the B Specials, would impact on the relationship between the Chichester-Clark administration and the loyalist population. That relationship was gravely weakening and contributing to an increasingly tense atmosphere in the confrontation zones of working-class Belfast, where sectarian conflict was traditional. The result was a gradual proliferation of inter-community conflict over the next year with the attendant involvement of the security forces (Bew and Patterson, 1985).

The revival of street violence on 10–11 October was rather novel in that it involved loyalists pitted against the RUC and the British Army. It resulted in three deaths, that of Constable Arbuckle, the first policeman killed in the troubles, and two loyalists killed by the army. The most serious effect of loyalist violence, however, was its role in the revival of militant republicanism.

Republicanism and Nationalism Re-form

The Belfast riots of August 1969 had demonstrated the irrelevance of Marxist republicanism to the needs of the Catholic community. Republicans had taken a leading role in forming the Central Citizens Defence Committee on 16 August but this was a community-wide, rather than a republican, movement. Accordingly, and with the purpose of re-asserting both the IRA's traditional roles as defender of the Catholic community and an army of Irish liberation, a group of republicans that included many future leaders of the PIRA such as Joe Cahill and Daihi O'Connell, met on 24 August. Their objectives were to replace the discredited republican leadership both at the local Belfast and national levels, and then to force the British to abolish Stormont and impose direct rule, thereby setting in train a process that, it was believed, would inevitably lead to Irish unity. This group soon achieved a hegemonic position within the IRA in Belfast – though Gerry Adams, apparently, did not bring his, Ballymurphy, unit into the PIRA camp until April 1970, when the political situation had clarified (Moloney, 2002) – but its ability to pursue traditional republican militancy in the immediate term was constrained by the favourable attitude of the Catholic community towards the British Army, and by the reformist agenda of Callaghan, which made it possible to have barricades taken down in the Falls Road area of Belfast and the Bogside in Derry. In this context the most important developments took place within the republican movement.

A secret meeting of the IRA leadership in Dublin in December 1969 adopted proposals in line with the still prevailing Marxist ethos, in particular a National Liberation Front between Sinn Fein, the Irish Communist Party and other left-wing groups, with the purpose, having abandoned the traditional policy of abstentionism, of electing representatives to the Dail, Stormont and Westminster. With the resurgence of traditional republicanism in the North, this policy was bound to cause a split. Opposition to the leadership focused around Sean McStiofain, a republican with an English background who was opposed to all constitutional activity. McStiofain became the Chief of Staff of a group of Belfast traditionalists who formed a Provisional Army Council, the term

'Provisional' being adopted to establish the legitimacy of the new organisation by connecting it with the 'Provisional Government of the Irish Republic' declared by the leaders of the 1916 Rising. The rift in the IRA, represented by the dissident PIRA and the mainstream 'Official' IRA (OIRA), became public and political on 11 January 1970 when the political front of the IRA, Sinn Fein, also split, with Provisional Sinn Fein (PSF) establishing its own premises in Kevin Street, Dublin.

From its inauguration in January 1970 until the Labour government in Britain left office the following June the new organisation marked time and consolidated its position, especially in Belfast and Derry where it saw its primary task as preparing to protect Catholic areas from an inevitable resurgence of loyalist violence. The process of building up to a position where it could launch an all-out assault on the British presence in the North was gradual, but stimulated enormously by a loyalist campaign of intimidation and violence against Catholic districts which accounted for 80 per cent of the 1808 families identified by the Community Relations Commission as having been forced from their homes in the greater Belfast areas between August 1969 and February 1973 (McStiofain, 1975; Coogan, 1995). In the meantime the re-shaping of constitutional nationalism took place.

The civil rights movement had discredited the old Nationalist Party and, in the aftermath of the Callaghan reform package, John Hume recognised the need for the creation of a modernised replacement to ensure the implementation of reform and to respond positively to a political situation in which Catholic Liberals and O'Neillite unionists had come together to form the non-sectarian Alliance Party. It was largely Hume's directing hand that created the Social Democratic and Labour Party (SDLP) in July 1970. He brought together political figures with strong personal followings such as the labourist Gerry Fitt and Paddy Devlin, and the nationalist Austin Currie, representing, respectively, the predominant urban and rural traditions in minority politics. And despite his own superior intellectual claims, Hume, to ensure unity, allowed Fitt, the MP for west Belfast who had done so much to rouse Westminster's attention to injustices in Northern Ireland, to assume the party leadership (White, 1984). The period from August 1969 to summer 1970, however, saw fundamental and enduring changes not only in minority politics but also within the unionist family.

Unionism: A Fracturing Movement

The failure of the Unionist Party to halt the violence of August 1969 provoked vocal opposition to its policies both within and outside its ranks. Two groups emerged, one consisting of the majority of unionists inside the party who retained their membership but opposed the leadership's policies; and another, which demanded stronger security measures, greater constitutional guarantees and which would form a pressure group entitled Ulster Vanguard in 1972. In 1973, it would strike out as a separate party under the name Vanguard Progressive Unionist Party. Outside the party, right-wing evangelical unionism was being marshalled by Revd Ian Paisley. On a platform combining biblical fundamentalism with economic populism, he was elected to Stormont in a by-election in April 1970. After 1969, with Westminster taking increasing responsibility for Northern Ireland and with the reform package greatly weakening Stormont's powers of patronage, Unionist Party unity was progressively eroded and the authority of the post-O'Neill leaders, Major James Chichester-Clark and Brian Faulkner, undermined (McAllister, 1983).

Westminster Changes and Ulster Consequences

The general election of 18 June 1970 saw the Labour government replaced with a Tory administration under Edward

Heath. As Home Secretary with responsibility for Northern Ireland, James Callaghan was replaced by Reginald Maudling. Heath's government pursued the same bi-partisan policy on Northern Ireland as its predecessor; nevertheless, significant changes on the ground in Ulster soon became apparent. These were facilitated by the fact that both politically and militarily the relationship between Westminster and Stormont was ambiguous. Politically, no one was certain about who was actually in charge. Westminster was clearly the dominant partner but insisted on working through the Stormont government. Militarily, a confusing situation existed. The General-Officer-Commanding (GOC) of the British Army in the North assumed overall responsibility for security operations and was directly answerable to the Ministry of Defence in London. At the same time, he had to work 'in the closest co-operation' with the Stormont government and the head of the RUC. Apart from security matters the latter remained under Stormont control. Moreover, both the GOC and the Chief Constable, as members of a joint security committee headed by the Northern Ireland Minister of Home Affairs, came under local political pressure. Further, the pursuit of a coherent security policy was hampered by the fact that each party tended to define the nature of the Ulster problem differently, with the Stormont government blaming the IRA for civil unrest and at least some British military leaders inclined to spread the mantle of blame to include the regime itself (Arthur and Jeffery, 1996).

As no formal structures existed to determine how a Home Secretary should deal with the North, the effectiveness of government policies depended very much on the character of the office holder. Callaghan had taken a vigorous approach to the Ulster issue, prioritising the implementation of the reform programme. Maudling, however, though very intelligent, was lethargic, and more willing to let local politicians take the initiative. And while a change of government did not signal a change of policy on Northern Ireland, the fact that a Tory government was now in office did register subtle changes in the political environment of the North. It was evident in the tendency of the army to deal more aggressively with nationalist troublemakers. In fact, signs of change began to emerge towards the end of the Labour administration.

Street violence in west Belfast had intensified in April, with riots in the Ballymurphy housing estate and the expulsion of Protestants from the nearby New Barnsley estate. At the same time, Westminster failed to adequately appreciate the extent to which the vigorous implementation of reforms, especially police reforms, would alienate the loyalist community at a time when nationalist 'no go' areas, from which the security forces were excluded, were being tolerated. Paisley's election to Westminster in June 1970 was evidence of that alienation, and also indicated that the reform package would not solve the Ulster problem. Callaghan's support in parliament for a statement by General Freeland, the British Army GOC, to the effect that petrol bombers could be shot, signalled that Westminster's patience was running out. But while the loyalist population was alienated by the reform programme, the Stormont regime, conscious of its historically close relationship with the Tories, looked on the Heath administration in a distinctly friendly light (Bew and Patterson, 1985; Kelley, 1990).

The clearest indication of a more aggressive approach to the nationalist community came on 26 June when Bernadette Devlin was imprisoned for her part in the August disturbances of the previous year. Her conviction provoked serious rioting in Derry and was followed, the next day, by the first major engagement of the PIRA. This occurred during riots which followed an Orange march along the perimeter of the Catholic Ardoyne area of west Belfast, and which soon degenerated into a gunfight in which three Protestants were killed. Loyalist retaliation took the form of an onslaught on the small Catholic enclave of Short Strand in overwhelmingly Protestant east Belfast. Here again the PIRA was called in to defend the area. The death toll was three Protestants and one Catholic. But the PIRA had only been called on when repeated appeals to the army for protection had failed to elicit any response, and its failure to respond clearly worked to the PIRA's advantage, whose action re-established militant republicanism's traditional role as defenders of the Catholic community after the failure of 1969. The Ardoyne and Short Strand experiences were significant markers in the progressive alienation of the Catholic working class from the forces of the British state. It was a process that was completed with the army onslaught on the Lower Falls area the following week.

Apparently concerned to assert the army's authority after the recent killings, the Heath government authorised a curfew and a house-to-house search on Friday, 3 July. It provoked an inevitable confrontation between locals and soldiers which led to the search being extended over the whole weekend, with attendant harassment of the community, extensive destruction of homes and property, and five civilian deaths. The search did yield significant results: 52 pistols, 35 rifles, six automatics and 250 rounds of ammunition. But the cost to the army far outweighed the gains. The sight of two unionist politicians being given a tour of the area by the army at the end of the curfew only confirmed the opinion among Catholics that there was now no distinction to be made between the British and the unionists (Kelley, 1990; Adams, 1996). Moreover, it could be argued that the apparent success of the operation persuaded the generals that if internment was to be introduced any Catholic backlash could be contained (McStiofain, 1975).

The Falls curfew and the method of its implementation indicated a caste of mind focused on short-term gain with little consideration of wider implications. As such, it reflected the failure of British politicians to develop a clearly defined analysis of how their involvement in the North might impact on the problem. Increasingly, attempts to find a constitutional solution to the Ulster problem would be complicated by repressive security measures and the consequent strengthening of the republican movement.

The Crisis Escalates

The ability of the Stormont regime to redress the situation in the North in a way that precluded closer Westminster involvement diminished rapidly from July 1970. Heading a party deeply antagonistic to the reform process, the Stormont regime was riven with factional disputes and incapable of both pursuing reform and retaining mass support. Increasingly it was driven to conciliate the party's right-wing, a tendency indicated in the appointment of John Taylor as Minister of Home Affairs to replace the pro-reform Robert Porter a month after the Falls curfew and, as violence on the streets intensified, in persistent demands for repressive measures against Catholic areas from Maudling and the Heath government (Bew and Patterson, 1985).

At the same time the reform process was slowed down. Reform of the housing system was accompanied by attempts to continue discrimination in allocation. Dungannon Council's efforts to resist change in this area, for instance, were only stopped by a High Court injunction, while SDLP complaints about housing were dismissed by Brian Faulkner, the Minister for Development, as a 'plot' against the local authorities (Coogan, 1995). Violence did diminish in the autumn of 1970, but only to allow the PIRA to consolidate its weapons supply. It accelerated dramatically from January 1971. The PIRA was the inevitable beneficiary of the Catholic community's increasing alienation from crown forces, whose coercive house searches rose from 17,000 to 75,000 in the period 1971–74. However, acceptance of the PIRA's role as the defender of vulnerable communities did not necessarily mean endorsement of the military campaign to remove the border.

Nevertheless, as the PIRA's position in the Catholic ghettoes strengthened, republican violence intensified. The first British soldier to die in Ireland in 50 years was killed on 6 February, to be followed on 10 March by the particularly brutal murder of three young Scottish soldiers. Such acts, especially the latter, brought intensified loyalist attacks on the Catholic community. But the loyalist reaction only consolidated further the PIRA's base of support. At the same time, the army was induced to consider even more extreme measures. Of these, the most radical was internment. Until Sir James Chichester-Clark resigned on 20 March 1971, having lost the confidence of his party and unionist right-wing opinion, the view prevailed that internment would only exacerbate the republican menace. That view would change under his successor, Brian Faulkner (Farrell, 1976; Kelley, 1990).

Faulkner and Internment

Faulkner's accession to the leadership of the Unionist Party, by a margin of 26 votes to four, reflected the closeness of his own politics to that of mainstream party opinion, especially in its desire to restore the pre-August 1969 status quo. He was also, however, a versatile political operator and recognised the need to balance his own preferences with an acknowledgement of political realities. Thus, the inclusion of the right-wing Harry West in his Cabinet was balanced by the appointment of David Bleakley, a former NILP MP, as Minister for Community Relations. Accordingly, while it was a Cabinet balanced in favour of the right-wing, it had a more reformist image than its predecessor. The initial effect was to satisfy mainstream unionist opinion while denying the opportunity for the simplistic condemnation of a reactionary administration.

The pace of political development, nevertheless, was still being set by the PIRA, whose activities took on a somewhat novel dimension with a bombing campaign directed against business and commercial premises across the North. This was officially justified by the argument that the mounting economic cost, which would be borne by the British exchequer, would force Westminster to accede to the PIRA's primary demand for the abolition of Stormont. However, the recent past had demonstrated that hasty, repressive action, by the security forces worked to republican advantage, and this was clearly a central motivation (Moloney, 2002). In this context, it should be noted that the campaign included individual atrocities, apparently unsanctioned by the PIRA leadership, but which were perpetrated by its personnel. These inflamed unionist opinion and accordingly moved Faulkner to greatly extend the parameters within which the security forces could use firearms, citing persons merely acting 'suspiciously' as being legitimate targets.

The search for a political way forward also continued. Faulkner was astute enough to recognise in the constitutional nationalists at Stormont men of ability, frustrated with their lack of position; still, ideologically, of a civil rights, reformist cast of mind, and thus amenable to an offer of parliamentary reform. Accordingly, on 22 June 1971 he proposed to add three new powerful committees to the Public Accounts Committee, to consider government policy on social services, industrial development and environment matters. But most significantly, he proposed that the Opposition should provide salaried chairmen for two of them.

Faulkner gauged Opposition opinion well enough. Both Paddy Devlin and John Hume greeted the plan enthusiastically and in this respect reflected middle-class nationalist opinion. There was every chance that these reforms would have been taken up had not two of Hume's constituents, Seamus Cusack and Desmond Beattie, both innocent of any involvement in paramilitary activity, been shot by the army in a riot situation on 7 July; shootings legitimised by Faulkner's recent statement on justifiable targets.

Nationalist opinion was outraged by the killings, and Hume gave expression to that anger with a demand for an independent inquiry and, when this was rejected, by leading an SDLP boycott of Stormont. Such action was needed if Hume was to retain his credibility as a political leader. In the Bogside, no less than in west Belfast, the intensifying level of violence was sharpening the growing alienation between the people and the security forces. Moreover, his constituents had already made known to Hume that they were less enamoured of Faulkner's committee proposals than he was. Thus, in a deteriorating political context he needed to demonstrate that he was not a creature of Stormont, especially as the PIRA continued to prove effective at exploiting incidents such as the Cusack and Beattie killings for their own advantage. For his part, Faulkner, witnessing the collapse of his committee initiative and under pressure from both his right-wing and the increasing street violence – there were 91 explosions in July – gave serious consideration to internment (Anon., 1972; Farrell, 1976; White, 1984; Kelley, 1990).

Personally Faulkner needed little persuasion about this option. He had implemented it during the IRA's 1956–62 campaign. It was a central factor in the defeat of the IRA then, he believed, and would be equally effective again. And there was now a much better chance of getting Westminster support. With the killing of British soldiers in Northern Ireland Tory backbench opinion wanted strong security measures (Bew and Patterson, 1985). Moreover, Heath had no specific policy for the North while Maudling seems to have held the view that though the prospect of direct rule was distasteful, it was going to have to come and in the meantime gave the impression that any form of political activity was useless, the only effective approach in this context being a military one. The impression was somewhat misleading. In the Cabinet Maudling pressed unsuccessfully for a radical re-partition of Northern Ireland with the purpose of creating a 'truncated' Ulster that would leave a numerically more dominant Protestant community feeling secure, reduce the security problem presented by the existing border, and 'be a splendid public relations exercise in the eyes of the world' (Cabinet papers, 1971, in *Guardian*, 13 April 2002).

Faulkner, who wanted internment as part of a much wider operation involving the sealing of the border and raids into the Irish Republic to arrest suspected IRA men, felt in a strong position. He informed the British Cabinet that unless internment was implemented he would have to resign, leaving them with the prospect of a Paisley premiership or direct rule. At a crucial meeting with the British Cabinet, Faulkner convinced Heath of the case for internment (Coogan, 1995), a decision taken against the advice of the GOC, General Harry Tuzo and the Defence Secretary, Lord Carrington (*Guardian*, 13 April 2002).

It was a botched operation from the beginning. A practice-run for internment on 23 July, consisting of dawn raids throughout the North, alerted the PIRA to what was coming, so that when it was actually implemented on 9 August 1971 the organisation's leadership largely managed to evade it. In fact, the internment lists were hopelessly out of date, having been framed with the old IRA, rather than the PIRA, in mind, with the result that in many cases entirely innocent people were lifted. Of 342 people arrested without charge during the first 24 hours of internment – 'Operation Demetrious' – fewer than 100 were actually PIRA or OIRA members, and within 48 hours, 116 of the original 342 detainees had to be released. Furthermore, unlike the 1950s the Irish Republic was neither involved nor sympathetic. Indeed popular opinion in the South would force the Fianna Fail Government of Jack Lynch into a more anti-partitionist stance, while British opinion was only likely to accept internment in the very short term and only if it produced results.

This it was not likely to do. Nationalist opinion was outraged. Internment was applied only against the Catholic community, despite the fact that loyalist violence was ongoing. Faulkner refused to take any action against loyalists – not even re-routing the controversial Apprentice Boys march in Derry on 12 August – to improve the situation. More seriously, loyalist 'rifle clubs' were allowed to proliferate. Emulating a device employed by Orangemen in 1913, whereby a Justice of the Peace could grant gun licenses, the unionist community proceeded to legally arm itself. By November 1971 there were 110,000 licensed weapons in Northern Ireland, the great majority in loyalist hands.

Internment: The Consequences

The failure of internment to quell paramilitary violence and civil disorder is reflected statistically. In the four months to 9 August eight people had been killed in the North, four of them civilians. In the four months following that date the death toll included 30 British soldiers, 73 civilians and 11 members of the RUC and Ulster Defence Regiment (UDR). In August alone 35 people were killed, 100 bombs went off and some 200 houses in Belfast were burned down. Nevertheless, despite its failure it would be persisted with for four years, during which a total of 2158 internment orders would be made, while the anger the policy provoked in the Catholic community would intensify as well-founded allegations of brutality against internees came to light (Kelley, 1990; Coogan, 1995). Together with a policy of cratering border roads that alienated rural nationalist communities, internment served to enlarge the PIRA 'into a six-county-wide army and transformed it into a force that could now seriously challenge British rule in Northern Ireland' (Moloney, 2002: 103).

To understand the sheer scale of the disorder that attended the implementation of internment, it is necessary to see it in the context of a series of abuses of the law by state forces in the recent past. The case in April 1971, for instance, when a mentally retarded Catholic was jailed for a year for shouting abuse at Orangemen, was one of many in which the law was applied much more harshly against one side of the community than the other (Anon., 1972). The verdict of a respected academic study into law and order in Northern Ireland at this time was damning. The law, it declared, was used blatantly as a buttress of the existing order:

> The Unionist government reacted repressively when its authority was called into question, and sought to suppress any criticism or complaint raised against it. The Westminster government reacted similarly to allegations

over misconduct by the security forces.... Both showed utter contempt for the rule of law (Hadden and Hillyard, 1973: 67).

One of the most enduring consequences of internment for the development of the Ulster problem was its role in stimulating Irish-American involvement. Internment and the treatment of internees were ideal issues for exploitation by PIRA support groups in the USA, especially Northern Aid, or Noraid as it would be more commonly known. Even newspapers which had supported internment, such as the establishment organ, *New York Times*, turned against it. In sum, internment made Ulster a major issue for Irish-Americans and the politicians who depended on their support (Wilson, 1995).

Historically, Irish-American engagement in the Irish question has been a symptom of acute crisis, and what was true for the Fenian era in the 1860s, Parnellism in the 1880s and the War of Independence from 1919–21, was true once again with the Ulster problem. Irish-American financial and political support would be vitally important to the PIRA's ability to sustain its military campaign over the next 20 years. As the campaign intensified it was important to develop a clear statement of the objective to be gained. Rather belatedly PSF did this in June 1971 when it produced the document, *Eire Nua* (New Ireland), which envisaged a liberated Ireland having a federal constitution consisting of four provincial assemblies. The federal solution was PSF's way of addressing unionist fears of Irish unity, as they would have the predominant influence in the Ulster assembly. In September 1971, the PIRA set out a five-point plan for the cessation of hostilities: an end to British violence; abolition of Stormont; free elections to a new Ulster assembly, Dail Uladh; release of political prisoners; and compensation for the victims of British violence. Britain was given four days to accept the plan, rejection would be followed by the intensification of the military campaign (Smith, 1995).

There was, of course, no hope of the PIRA's ultimatum being accepted. Nevertheless, it tells us much about the buoyant frame of mind the organisation was in at this time. Internment had not only failed in its purpose, but had greatly radicalised the political environment of Northern Ireland. The limited reformism which had until recently been the limit of the SDLP's political ambitions was discarded as the party embarked on a rent-and-rates strike intended to force an end to internment, while even those reluctant revolutionaries, the OIRA, were forced into more extensive military activity against the British presence in Ulster (Kelley, 1990).

Prorogation

The failure of internment made direct rule almost inevitable. The alienation of the Catholic community was expressed in the SDLP's refusal to negotiate with the British government until internment was ended, so no political accommodation was possible. Even the British Labour Party moved away from bi-partisanship on Ulster, recognising the transformation of the question from one which could be resolved on a civil rights agenda to a nationality issue; one which the Labour leader, Harold Wilson, now argued could only be settled by Irish unity.

On the ground, the region became virtually ungovernable. On the loyalist side, the consequences of internment led to the creation of the Ulster Defence Association (UDA), signalling a murder campaign against the Catholic population. In the political sphere extreme unionism found another avenue of expression with the creation of Revd Ian Paisley's Democratic Unionist Party (DUP). Meanwhile, the SDLP's rent-and-rates strike gathered pace and the NICRA revived, now largely under the control of the political wing of the OIRA, the Republican Clubs. October 1971 was to see the formation of the Northern Resistance Movement, consisting of

81

PD and other radical groups friendly to the PIRA, and demanding the complete overthrow of Stormont. In the face of security force harassment, these groups organised a campaign of anti-internment rallies across the North, flouting a decree by Faulkner of 9 August banning all marches for a year.

It was at one of the largest of these, in Derry on 30 January 1972 – Bloody Sunday – that soldiers of the 1st Parachute Regiment opened fire on the marchers, killing 13 unarmed civilians and mortally wounding another. Attempts by the army to displace blame on to the victims was wholly unsuccessful. Too many witnesses, not least from the British media, had observed the killings. A government inquiry under Lord Widgery was overly sympathetic to the soldiers' defence of their actions and lacked credibility. Successive British governments refused either to apologise for the killings or to instigate a new inquiry into their cause, while evidence demonstrating army culpability continued to build up. Only with the election of the Blair government in 1997 was an independent investigation initiated – the Saville Inquiry – whose proceedings are ongoing.

The killings had traumatic consequences. Both John Hume and the Dublin government were moved to declare that only Irish unity would solve the Ulster difficulty, while the OIRA planted a bomb at the Paratroopers' headquarters in Aldershot which killed seven people, all civilians with no connection to Northern Ireland. In Dublin, the British Embassy was burned to the ground (Coogan, 1995). It was, however, in the USA that the consequences of the killings were most serious. Extensively reported by all the major television channels and newspapers, the sight of a priest, Fr Edward Daly, attempting to get medical aid to one of the victims while being harassed by British soldiers, provoked outrage. Most importantly, the killings created a permanent base of Irish-American support for the PIRA (Wilson, 1995).

In the aftermath of Bloody Sunday the PIRA campaign took on greater ferocity, with bomb attacks on the Abercorn

Restaurant and Donegall Street, Belfast, in March that caused appalling deaths and injury to civilians. The PIRA knew that it lacked the military might to forcibly expel the British from Ulster. Rather it hoped to coerce withdrawal by making the human and economic cost of staying too much to bear. In this respect it was much heartened by opinion polls in Britain, such as that which appeared in the *Daily Mail* in September 1971 showing that 60 per cent of the British public favoured withdrawal. At the same time, PIRA violence provoked loyalist retaliation against the Catholic community in general. February 1972 saw the emergence of the neo-fascist Vanguard movement led by the former Stormont cabinet minister, William Craig. Adopting the führeristic leadership style common to such movements in the 1930s, complete with motorcycle outriders, Craig called for the 'liquidation' of Ulster's enemies.

The situation in Northern Ireland simply could not be left to deteriorate. An attempt to find a way out of the impasse created by internment emerged in January 1972 when Heath met Faulkner and Jack Lynch. Heath was initially inclined to increase Catholic representation at Stormont, but was progressively impelled to more radical measures by violent threats from Vanguard and the loyalist groups. With disorder continuing on the streets Faulkner was summoned to London for a series of meetings, and finally, on 21 March, he was informed that internment was to be phased out and that control of the entire law-and-order apparatus of Northern Ireland – police, prosecution, judges, courts and prisons – was to be transferred to Whitehall. Faulkner and his Cabinet found this proposal unacceptable and threatened resignation. But the time was past when this kind of threat could work. On 24 March, Heath rose in the House of Commons to announce the prorogation of Stormont, ostensibly for one year. The emotional shock to unionism was severe, but despite a mass protest meeting of 100,000 at Stormont and a Vanguard-led loyalist workers' strike lasting two days, the situation had to be accepted. A threat to declare a unilateral declaration of independence for Northern Ireland by William Craig came to nothing (Farrell, 1976; Coogan, 1995).

For the PIRA the fall of Stormont was a great achievement, a result of their military struggle and which they believed would soon be followed by British withdrawal, a view reflected in the slogan, 'One more year'. It cannot be denied that PIRA's campaign of violence was an important factor in producing the crisis that brought down Stormont. It was followed, however, not by the onward rush to Irish unity, but the consolidation of the Ulster problem. In this context, militant republicanism, with the power of surprise, would be capable of mounting lethal attacks on crown forces yet without the ability to inflict a decisive defeat. This also applied to the security forces. The PIRA would be contained but not eliminated. But while tied to the North essentially by the constitutional guarantee given to unionists, Britain would fail to develop an effective strategy for dealing with Ulster beyond a crisis management that left it constantly responding to events. For their part, unionists, harking after the return of the old Stormont system, would play their part in perpetuating the problem by rejecting any settlement that offered substantial concessions to the Catholic population.

The Irish Republic, despite its constitutional claim to the territory of Northern Ireland, established a position at the beginning of the troubles in 1969 that would remain substantially unchanged. This entailed a defence of nationalist interests in the North, a repudiation of violence, the promotion of reforms and an 'Irish dimension' in any political settlement. Irish unity could only come by the consent of a majority of the people of Northern Ireland. As they watched the northern security forces grapple with republican and loyalist violence this was a position all southern governments were basically content with (Buckland, 1989; Girvin, 1994).

3

NEW INITIATIVES AND OLD PROBLEMS

A New Order

Direct rule was premised on an optimistic scenario. Stormont would be prorogued for one year, during which time Westminster would assume control of the government of Northern Ireland while discussions between all parties to the Ulster problem were pursued to resolve it. From April 1972 onwards attempts were made to establish common ground between them.

Constitutionally direct rule was unproblematic. The Acts of 1920 and 1949 enshrined Westminster's sovereignty over the North, but there was no attempt to assimilate the government and administration of the region to that of Britain. Under the Northern Ireland (Emergency Provisions) Act of 1973 the region was accorded a system of legislation through Orders in Council. Under this system bills for implementation in Northern Ireland are introduced in the House of Commons by the Secretary of State for Northern Ireland. Once introduced they cannot be amended and, when passed by the Commons, become law. Moreover, Orders have tended to be introduced late at night to a depleted House and with little time allowed for detailed consideration. The fact that many proposed Orders are circulated to interested parties in Northern Ireland before legislation is proceeded with is a poor substitute for democratic accountability, especially since, until very recently, no Northern Ireland Select Committee existed in the House of Commons to consider legislation for the area.

Executive administrative power in the North was to be exercised in all important areas – agriculture, education, economic development, the environment, health and social services, law, order and security – by, or on behalf, of the Secretary of State. This concentration of power was reinforced at local level. A review body on local government of June 1970, the recommendations of which were embodied in the Macrory Report (named after its chairman, Patrick Macrory), established a reformed system of local government. Framed very much against the background of the discrimination controversy in the 1960s, it recommended that 26 district councils be established but with powers restricted to subsidiary services in non-controversial areas, such as refuse collection, leisure centres, crematoria and graveyards. Non-elected, nominated Boards – Education and Library Boards, the Housing Executive, Health and Social Services Boards and the Police Authority – were established to exercise the more important powers at local level. Moreover, the essential framework of unionist administration in the North, the Northern Ireland civil service, was subordinated to a new ministry, the Northern Ireland Office (NIO), which would become the pinnacle and co-ordinator of the whole administrative machine (Bew and Patterson, 1985; Hadfield, 1993; Cunningham, 2001).

Power arrangements such as these were created to ensure fair administration and also to create an environment in which a political settlement could be arrived at in the near future. In the latter respect, British perspectives on the problem were informed largely by their own political experience.

Opinion polls in Britain since 1971 may have identified the Ulster problem as essentially Irish and 'un-British', but Westminster politicians sought to deal with it on the basis of British political assumptions; namely, a belief in negotiation, that all problems have accessible solutions once the concerns of the 'centre' – supposedly consisting of the great, politically moderate, majority of the population – were identified and addressed. This outlook informed the British approach to the making of the Sunningdale agreement of 1974 (Loughlin, 1995).

Government hopes of a political settlement along the lines of reformed devolution were premised partly on the observable fragmentation, and consequent weakening, of the unionist movement that had occurred during the last months of Stormont, and on the belief that constitutional nationalism, represented chiefly by the SDLP, was amenable to an agreement that gave it a guaranteed position in a new administration. The major task was to develop a unionist grouping that found this idea acceptable.

As a solution devolution appeared the most realistic given the dearth of practicable alternatives. The constitutional guarantee to unionists prevented withdrawal from Northern Ireland; unionists would not accept a united Ireland; and no major British party was prepared to accept the complete integration of Northern Ireland with the rest of the United Kingdom. Moreover, the increasing acceptance by Westminster that the Irish Republic had to be involved in any solution made this option even more unthinkable, while the fact that the only major Ulster politician pressing this option after the prorogation of Stormont was Revd Ian Paisley did not increase its attractiveness.

There was again the security situation to consider. A significant factor in persuading Heath that the Stormont regime had to go was a change in the army's assessment of the PIRA campaign, to the effect that it could not be contained while law and order powers remained in Stormont's hands. Thus, PIRA violence could not be ignored, nor was it possible to negotiate it out of existence if integration was pursued. Optimistically, there were indications from the PIRA at this time that it was considering negotiations as well as violence to achieve its ends. Accordingly, when, following pressure from the Catholic community and the SDLP, the PIRA called a ceasefire in June 1972 the Secretary of State for Northern Ireland, William Whitelaw, initiated talks (Bishop and Mallie, 1987; Cunningham, 2001).

PIRA Violence and British Responses

From the PIRA perspective their military campaign had secured a place at the negotiating table with the British. It had, republicans believed, brought down Stormont. But while an important factor in Stormont's removal, it was less the crucial element than a highly aggravating one. Stormont fell ultimately because of its own failings and because there was a stronger case for removing it than for keeping it. PIRA violence 'widened the cracks and highlighted the flaws by constantly heaping up the burdens it had to carry' (Bishop and Mallie, 1987: 170). The question now was, with Stormont gone, how far could the PIRA advance towards its ultimate objective of a British withdrawal? In fact, Stormont's fall 'opened up a fault line within nationalism that would never really close. Moderate nationalist opinion now sought a polit-ical deal and reform, while the [P]IRA fought on for revolu-tion and the elusive republic' (Moloney, 2002: 112).

Certainly from mid-1972 the organisation's activities inten-sified, with increasing use of the recently invented car bomb, while in June the security forces suffered more deaths and injuries than in any previous month of the campaign. Nevertheless, there was a nagging fear about how well the campaign could be sustained. The sympathy that PIRA gained from the implementation of internment was wearing off, largely due to the atrocities resulting from the bomb-ing campaign, while British Army intelligence was becoming more effective. Militant republicanism came under increased pressure after the OIRA called a permanent ceasefire on 29 May 1972 and with the prospect of being marginalised by a constitutional settlement that enhanced the standing of the SDLP in the Catholic community (Bishop and Mallie, 1987). The question was whether the PIRA leadership, among whose negotiators were the future republican leaders, Gerry Adams – whose ability was apparent even then (Moloney, 2002) – and Martin McGuiness, had the skill to further their cause. That they had not, soon became apparent.

Fundamentally the PIRA's position was unchanged from that of traditional republicanism since the 1920s. 'Negotiation' was defined merely in terms of arranging the facilities for British withdrawal:

> As demonstrated by the controversy over the 1921 Treaty, the concept of negotiation was, in many respects, alien to the republican tradition. ... 'negotiation' was almost demand, threat and coercion – in other words, a complete British surrender (Smith, 1995: 106).

This was a wildly optimistic expectation. In fact, Whitelaw's chief concern in holding talks with the PIRA leadership was not to concede a British surrender but to define its position. Further, to have refused to talk would have given the PIRA a propaganda coup, while the impossibilism of their position would also be useful to cite to the SDLP if stronger security measures were found necessary.

The talks did clarify just how difficult finding a solution would be. Holding to the absolutist position of a British withdrawal the PIRA yet lacked the military might to compel it. The British negotiators, for their part, made plain that however devastating the PIRA campaign was in the North it made little impact in Britain. But it was an argument militant republicans preferred to ignore. Two days after the talks ended the military campaign resumed. In part this was due to loyalist action in preventing the re-housing of evicted

Catholic families in a religiously mixed area of Belfast and the refusal of the army to effect the re-housing. But it was unlikely to endure in any event. The only lesson the PIRA took from its meeting with the British was the need to inten-sify its campaign. In part this was due to inconsistencies in the British position. The latter had acceded to one of the PIRA's fundamental conditions for the holding of talks; namely the concession of political status. Thus, while it was made clear to the Provisionals that their campaign could not succeed, at the same time the British effectively recognised that the republican struggle was legitimate (Bishop and Mallie, 1987; Smith, 1995). But more crucially, the Belfast members of the delegation were convinced that the British merely wanted to draw the ceasefire out to make the PIRA more exposed and vulnerable to arrest, while the recent acquisition of 200 powerful armalite rifles from the USA, together with the development of the car bomb – which both allowed the PIRA to increase substantially the amount of explosive at each location while reducing the vulnerability of its personnel – appeared to offer the prospects of a more effective military campaign (Moloney, 2002).

The resumed campaign entailed an orgy of violence involving PIRA attacks and loyalist retaliation, which saw 33 people killed in a week. The most serious single atrocity – the product of bungling rather than intent – occurred on 'Bloody Friday', 21 July 1972, when 22 no-warning bombs were exploded in Belfast in 75 minutes, killing nine and injuring 130 (White, 1984; Moloney, 2002). These atrocities allowed the security forces to peacefully occupy the 'no-go' areas of the Bogside in Derry and west Belfast. The loss of these areas had a debilitating effect on the Provisionals in terms of propaganda, men and support, with the result that the level of republican paramilitary activity dropped signifi-cantly over the next few years. Increasingly, their strategy for removing the British presence in the North was seen to be unrealistic (Coogan, 1995; Smith, 1995). But while the repub-lican campaign had been dealt a serious blow, this did not occur before its effects had exacerbated the Ulster problem significantly.

Loyalist Paramilitary Resurgence

The development of the UDA into the largest loyalist paramilitary force in the aftermath of internment entailed a rather ambivalent stance on the part of the security forces. Both had a similar attitude to the institutions of the British state and the latter, fully occupied with the nationalist reaction to internment, were anxious not to fight a war on two fronts. This was a situation more likely to produce amicable rather than antagonistic relations. Accordingly, despite clear evidence of loyalist responsibility for the second most serious atrocity of the troubles to date – the explosion at McGurk's Bar in Belfast on 14 December 1971 which killed 15 people – the security forces insisted on regarding it as a PIRA 'own goal'. From 8 February 1972 and over the next 18 months over 200 Catholics would be killed by loyalist murder squads. Loyalist killings tended to be more openly sectarian than those of the PIRA, the sectarian nature of which was often masked by a rhetoric of national liberation (McKittrick, 1989).

Collusion between the security forces and loyalist paramilitaries assumed an especially ominous aspect as indications emerged that the latter were being used to perpetrate acts that the crown forces did not wish to be publicly associated with, and that dual membership of the UDA and the UDR was common. From this period onwards, as the security presence in working-class Catholic ghettoes became increasingly oppressive, with widespread intimidation of the population, republicans took the view that no real distinction between the crown forces and loyalist paramilitaries could be made (Farrell, 1976). This perception was consolidated by a virtually complete failure to make British soldiers charged with murder amenable under the law and by the introduction of no-jury courts.

These had been introduced in 1973 on the recommendation of the Diplock Commission, established to inquire into legal aspects of the government's response to paramilitary violence. They allowed for suspects to be arrested without warrant and detained for up to 72 hours; for trials of all terrorist-related offences to be held by a senior judge sitting without a jury; and for convictions on the basis of statements made by defendants provided these had not been obtained forcibly (Arthur and Jeffery, 1996). In this context, the presentation of the conflict in the British media as one in which a terrorist organisation (PIRA) was imposing its will on the community was one that accorded ill with the reality of life in Catholic ghettoes. At the same time, British security policies were providing excellent propaganda for republican support groups in the USA, especially Noraid. From Bloody Sunday to 29 July 1972 this organisation sent $312,700 to Ireland (Wilson, 1995). Nevertheless, an effective counter-attack by crown forces to PIRA's activities threw the political advantage back to the SDLP.

Towards Political Accommodation

In July 1972, John Hume took the initiative with a policy document entitled 'Towards a New Ireland', which proposed joint authority of Britain and the Irish Republic over Northern Ireland, and a declaration by the British government that it would work for Irish unity (Coogan, 1995). The document effectively outlined a gradualist approach towards the same objective aimed at by PIRA through armed struggle.

For their part, Whitelaw and the NIO were also attempting to make political progress, first with a conference at Darlington, county Durham, in late September, designed to chart a political way forward in the North, and afterwards with the discussion paper, 'The Future of Northern Ireland'. This document combined guarantees for unionists on the North's constitutional position, so long as a majority of the population supported it, with a proposal that the minority be given a share in executive power. But most significantly, it proposed that any political settlement should embody an 'Irish dimension', recognising institutionally Northern Ireland's relationship with the Irish Republic. Given its source this was a radical document and testified to the growing influence of the SDLP at this time and more especially Hume.

Hume had spelt out his party's refusal to attend the Darlington conference, partly because of the continued existence of internment, but also because the conference had not allowed for Irish representation. For Hume the Irish dimension was an essential element of the Ulster question. A purely internal settlement based on Northern Ireland, an unstable entity, could not be final. The unionist proposals, presented by Brian Faulkner, consisted of the committee proposals of the previous year and were now considered by many as irrelevant to current political realities.

This was confirmed by the government White Paper of 20 March 1973 which, following a poll on the existence of the border earlier in the month intended to reassure unionists, laid out the government's proposals for a political settlement. These included an 80-seat Assembly elected by proportional representation for a fixed four-year term headed by an Executive that would include representatives of both communities. There was also a vaguely expressed willingness to consider the establishment of institutional arrangements for consultation and co-operation between Northern Ireland and the Irish Republic. This was clearly a set of proposals designed chiefly with the SDLP's concerns in mind and the party gave them a cautious welcome. It reflected their position as the voice of majority opinion within the Catholic community, something that would be confirmed in elections to the new local councils in the North. The poll, held on 30 May 1973, delivered 83 of 103 anti-partitionist seats to the party and signalled a similar result in elections to the new Assembly in June, when the SDLP took 19 of the 78 seats.

The consolidating of nationalist support behind the SDLP, however, was not matched on the unionist side. The Faulknerite unionists, pledged to co-operate with the government's proposals for the North, won only 23 seats against 18 for a right-wing unionist coalition, and nine for unionists 'unpledged' to the proposals (White, 1984). For the SDLP, committed to reunification and seeing the government's proposals in that light, these developments were not uncongenial. If, as they thought at this time, the only real obstacle to Irish unity was the British presence, unionist divisions were a sign of weakness and inability to resist the reunification process (Bew and Patterson, 1985).

The Sunningdale Experiment

The government proposals outlined a settlement that prioritised an internal administration with the Irish dimension a subsidiary aspect, dealing with issues of mutual concern to North and South. This balance, however, would change significantly in the process of negotiation over the following months, entailing profound political consequences as the Irish dimension became objectified in a proposed Council of Ireland. Originally both London and Dublin governments were agreed that a weak Council be established. But the necessity of conciliating the SDLP entailed acceptance of their preference for a stronger institution, one that might become the engine for Irish unity. This was also deemed necessary as a heavy security presence in Catholic areas and the continued existence of internment was putting pressure on the SDLP to deliver substantial concessions. And since the government was not prepared to consider significant concessions on security the Irish dimension became the focus of attention.

Accordingly, while the Council of Ireland was initially envisaged as having some executive functions and a 'consultative' role, it was finally agreed that it would have 'executive and harmonising functions'. The gains made by the SDLP on the Council of Ireland, however, would prove fatal to the future of the whole experiment, called the Sunningdale Agreement after the civil service staff college in Berkshire where the final negotiations took place in early December 1973. Of all aspects of the agreement it was the one that most angered unionists. The non-unionist belief that the result of the border poll, with its expected large majority for the Union, would reassure unionists, ignored the deep insecurities embedded in the unionist mentality, especially regarding Westminster's intentions towards the North (Bew and Patterson, 1985).

As an initiative Sunningdale leant heavily towards addressing the Ulster problem as defined from a nationalist perspective. But even without the Council of Ireland it could only be read as a weakening of the unionist position. The 50-year existence of the Stormont parliament had set a standard, or index, of United Kingdom membership. Any replacement not of equal status and which diminished the political and administrative control of the unionist majority over the region was likely to be seen as a threat to the Union. That the political structures to be established under the Sunningdale Agreement were of a lower status than those of the old Stormont parliament could not be denied.

In fact, Stormont's prorogation itself entailed a diminishing of the constitutional guarantee embodied in the Ireland Act of 1949. This Act had secured the North's place within the United Kingdom unless the Stormont parliament decided otherwise. Stormont's demise made that guarantee redundant and its replacement, embodied in the Northern Ireland Constitution Act of 1973, stipulated that constitutional security depended on a majority for the Union being registered in a poll on the border question. Again, the Constitution Act dispensed with such designatory forms as 'Parliament', 'Prime Minister', 'Cabinet', 'Acts' and replaced them with 'Assembly', 'Chief Executive', 'Executive' and 'Measures', while the powers to be exercised by the new institution were also of a lesser order.

The Act not only abolished the position of Governor of Northern Ireland but gave the Secretary of State a central role in the formation of the Executive. The Assembly, elected by proportional representation, was given wide legislative powers over a range of internal matters, such as education and the environment, though any measure embodying discrimination either on grounds of religious or political belief would be void. Further, the Act established a Standing Advisory Commission on Human Rights to advise the Secretary of State on the effectiveness of the law in preventing discrimination, while power to enact laws that might prove divisive would also be withheld from the Assembly.

The second element of the reform package was embodied in the Sunningdale Agreement of December 1973, made between the London and Dublin governments and the Northern Ireland Executive-Designate. It provided for a Council of Ireland, consisting of a Council of Ministers (seven representatives from North and South) with executive and harmonising functions, and a Consultative Assembly (30 representatives from North and South) with advising and review functions (Hadfield, 1993). In sum, from the unionist, and especially the extreme loyalist, perspective, the reform package, shaped to conciliate nationalists, was clearly a threat to the Union. For the Faulknerite unionists, whose participation in the power-sharing initiative was premised on the belief that it was necessary if Northern Ireland was to survive, and for whom the supreme prize was Dublin's co-operation in combating terrorism and acceptance of the constitutional status quo, the enhanced role accorded to the Council of Ireland came as a surprise. Nevertheless, given that both governments were against re-negotiation and that unionists would have a majority of one in the power-sharing Executive, with Faulkner as Chief Executive, their belief was that they would be able to mould it to their own liking.

Both nationalists and unionists needed to have enough from the negotiations to sell the Sunningdale Agreement to their own communities. For Hume the objective was to undermine the PIRA by demonstrating to the nationalist community that constitutionalism offered substantial gains on the long road to Irish unity. Power sharing and the Council of Ireland were offered as proof of this. Certainly, set against the old Stormont system, the Sunningdale package could only be read as a major gain for the nationalist community. Hume hoped that it would be put to the Irish people, North and South, for ratification in referendums to be held on the same day. His intention was to invalidate the republican argument that the last election on the national question to have validity was that of 1918, when the great majority of the Irish people, outside the north-east, voted for independence, and which provided the legitimation for their campaign of violence. Faulkner, however, was in a much weaker position than Hume and, recognising the deep misgivings in the unionist community about the reform package, was not persuaded that this was the best way to sell it.

The Faulknerite unionists had hoped to get a formal recognition of Northern Ireland's constitutional position and an extradition agreement from Dublin, but neither was forthcoming. Clause five of the Agreement did recognise that there could be no change in the constitution of Northern Ireland until the majority desired it, but whatever effect this might have had on unionist opinion was undermined when a Fianna Fail politician, Kevin Boland, challenged the Irish government's recognition of Northern Ireland in the courts as contravening articles 2 and 3 of the Irish constitution, which claimed jurisdiction over the whole island. The court did eventually find for the defendants in a judgement which declared that the sovereignty claim had no legal standing. But defence submissions had included the argument that the government did not agree that any part of Ireland belonged to the United Kingdom and the damage was done. Faulkner was to lose a vote of confidence at a meeting of the Ulster Unionist Council (UUC) in January 1974. On resigning as party leader he lost control of the party machine and cut himself off from the bulk of his followers. He hoped, nevertheless, that he could show by results that the Sunningdale experiment could work. This strategy was undermined when Edward Heath, grappling with the effects of a miner's strike in Britain, and despite warnings about the consequences for the reform programme in the North, decided to put the issue before the nation in a general election in February 1974.

The election was guaranteed to clarify the weaknesses of the pro-Executive parties – which, in addition to the SDLP and the Faulknerite unionists (soon to be formed into a political party under the name, Unionist Party of Northern Ireland (UPNI)), included the small cross-community Alliance Party headed by Oliver Napier – and maximise the strengths of their opponents. The former had to fight on three separate and conflicting platforms, the latter, united in a loyalist alliance under the title, United Ulster Unionist Council (UUUC) campaigned on the slogan, 'Dublin is just a Sunningdale away'. Accordingly, with the Executive denied the opportunity to prove its worth, the opposition case was easy to make and was to result in the UUUC winning 11 of the 12 Northern Ireland seats at Westminster.

Against this background, and with the PIRA campaign as a further aggravating factor, prospects for the Sunningdale experiment were bleak. An attempt by Faulkner to postpone the implementation of the Council of Ireland, on the grounds that Dublin had failed to recognise the constitutional position of Northern Ireland or to deliver on extradition, was forestalled by the Ulster Workers Council (UWC) strike which brought the Executive down (Faulkner, 1978; White, 1984).

The UWC Strike

The UWC originated in a grouping set up in the wake of a loyalist strike that took place in March 1973 to protest against the internment of loyalists. It devoted itself to the quiet recruitment of Protestant workers in key industries.

The strategy of Hugh Petrie and his co-planners in the Short and Harland aircraft factory in Belfast was to effect a withdrawal of labour by these workers, especially those in the power industries, which would bring about maximum disruption to economic life. The grouping would be separate from the UDA and UVF but would work with the leaders of both to enlist paramilitary support, thus ensuring the intimidation that would be essential to the strike's success. With the formation of the Executive and the proposals for a Council of Ireland, the grouping, with the addition of Harry Murray and Bob Pagels, who would lead the strike, adopted the title UWC. It also founded a co-ordinating committee headed by Glen Barr, a Derry trade unionist with UDA and Vanguard connections. The committee included UDA and UVF members and co-opted the leading unionists Ian Paisley, Bill Craig and Harry West, while throughout the North shop stewards were recruited and plans made for electricity cuts.

UUUC politicians were unhappy about backing a strike that lacked public support and the UWC was not even invited to a conference at Portrush in late April at which plans for opposing the Executive were drawn up. The count-down to action took the form of a threat that if a motion condemning power sharing and the Council of Ireland was rejected by the Assembly, the UWC and the Protestant paramilitary groups would call a general strike on 14 May. This they duly did, putting a stranglehold on the social and economic life of the North for two weeks, during which time popular Protestant support increased and unionist leaders came on board. And while the strike was confined to the North, loyalist rejection of Dublin's interference in northern affairs was registered brutally when, on 17 May, no-warning bombs went off in Monaghan town and Dublin killing 35 people. Merlyn Rees, the new Labour Secretary of State for Northern Ireland, and Harold Wilson, the Prime Minister, refused to talk to the strikers. After two weeks Faulkner resigned and the Executive collapsed (Fisk, 1975; Nelson, 1984; Rees, 1985).

Thus ended the most radical attempt to solve the Ulster problem until the signing of the Agreement of Easter 1998.

The failure of the Sunningdale experiment had grave political consequences for the North, demonstrating to the PIRA and its supporters that constitutional nationalism had failed, thereby ushering in a further 20 years of violence. Probably the most important reason for its collapse lay in the failure of its supporters to appreciate the fear within the unionist community that it engendered, and how fear could be employed as a unifying factor among those groups opposed to it. It was a fear that was significantly enhanced by the differing interpretations of the role of the Council of Ireland given by the SDLP and the Faulknerite unionists (Bew and Patterson, 1985).

The role of the British government during the crisis especially that of Merlyn Rees, was also questionable. It came as a surprise to the leaders of the UWC how easily they were able to impose their will on the streets of Northern Ireland without interference from the security forces. In fact, collaboration between soldiers, the RUC and loyalist paramilitaries manning the barricades was common. Certainly there was no attempt to dismantle the barricades. Moreover, the crisis was deepened by the failure of Rees and Wilson both to call on the army to restore law and order or to talk to the strikers, at the same time as Wilson's contemptuous description of them as 'spongers' on the Westminster government who wished to set up a sectarian state, stiffened their resolve. At its height all classes of the Protestant community had come on board (Fisk, 1975; Coogan, 1995).

The Sunningdale experiment embodied the elements any future settlement of the problem would have to include – power, or responsibility, sharing within the present constitutional framework, together with institutional links between North and South to acknowledge the national identity of nationalists and to deal with common areas of concern between North and South. But for such a scheme to succeed would require a greater degree of commitment to the problem's resolution than was shown by either the Tory administration of Edward Heath or the Labour government of Harold Wilson in 1974.

In justification of his inaction during the UWC strike Merlyn Rees would later claim that he was faced with the naked force of Protestant nationalism, something which could not be dealt with simply by security measures (Rees, 1985). This is an argument, however, more indicative of the thinking in British government circles after the strike than during it. Certainly in its wake there were clear indications of British exasperation with the North and of a desire to distance Westminster from it, something the recognition of a separate nationality could be used as an excuse for. In formalising the fall of the Executive the debate in the House of Commons found agreement between Labour and Tory Parties that full integration of Northern Ireland with the rest of the United Kingdom was undesirable, as it would 'overburden' Westminster. Such a policy, Rees argued, would run counter to the nascent 'Ulster nationalism' that the UWC strike represented. This was a line of argument unionists found very disquieting. Ulster nationalism had never struck deep roots in the Protestant community and UDA attempts to develop it in the late 1970s and early 1980s would be singularly unsuccessful (Nelson, 1984; Loughlin, 1995; Cunningham, 2001). The most significant effect of Westminster's exasperation, however, was the belief that a solution to the Ulster problem had to originate with, and be agreed between, the political parties in the North rather than be determined by London and Dublin.

The Ulster Convention

Despite the existence of Stormont rule for 50 years there was less than a completely unified unionist commitment to its restoration in 1974. Immediately after its prorogation in 1972 the Revd Ian Paisley had argued for complete integration with Britain. His enthusiasm waned when it became clear there was no British enthusiasm for this option and when the success of the UWC strike encouraged the idea that the old Stormont could be restored. The 'official' Ulster Unionist Party (UUP, a name adopted by the mainstream unionist party to distinguish it from Faulkner's UPNI), also demonstrated a less than unambiguous commitment to its restoration. By 1975, some of its leading members were arguing for devolved government with varying degrees of enthusiasm, while others were attracted by the integrationist arguments of Enoch Powell, now a UUP MP, having been elected for South Down at the general election of October 1974. The Alliance Party remained committed to devolved government on the power-sharing model, a position it shared with the SDLP and the Irish government, though the latter were firmly committed to recognition of the 'Irish dimension' in any settlement (Maguire, 1992). Thus, while support for the restoration of devolved government existed to varying degrees across the party spectrum in Northern Ireland, the differing meanings attached to it did not augur well for the success of any attempt to effect it.

Encouragement to do so came with the publication of the government White Paper, 'The Northern Ireland Constitution', on 4 July 1974. The paper proposed the establishment of a Constitutional Convention, purely consultative in character, with a remit to consider 'what provision for the government of Northern Ireland is likely to command the most widespread support throughout the community there'. At the same time, rather vague parameters were outlined to shape the nature of a settlement. It would have to be based on 'partnership', and allow for an Irish dimension, defined in terms of mutual interests and co-operation. It would also have to be acceptable to Westminster, while a statement with distinct 'withdrawal' connotations was included, to the effect that British willingness to commit financial aid to Northern Ireland would 'be affected by the progress of events there'. Thus, the Convention proposals were framed in the context of Sunningdale's failure, hoping to maximise support for partnership in government, while abandoning the institutional cross-border structures that loyalists had taken most exception to.

The Convention proposals could be assured of majority support at Westminster and measures were duly taken to give effect to them. Elections to a 78-member assembly, on the Single Transferable Vote system and based on the 12 Westminster constituencies, took place on 1 May 1975. The result largely mirrored the political divisions of the 1974 general elections, with the UUUC winning 54.8 per cent of the votes and 47 seats. The pro-power-sharing parties took 42.6 per cent and 31 seats. These realities determined that the Convention would not reach agreement on a political settlement. The UUUC view prevailed in a draft report submitted to the Secretary of State on 7 November 1975. It virtually recommended the restoration of the old Stormont system, allowing only for opposition representation on parliamentary committees. It was a report that the SDLP naturally opposed. The only unexpected development was a proposal by William Craig for 'voluntary' power sharing with the SDLP, a proposal opposed by other UUUC leaders and which destroyed his political career.

The Convention Report was debated in the Commons on 12 January 1976. Its failure to meet the government's terms of political acceptability was reflected in Rees' decision to re-convene the Convention in a rather desperate attempt to achieve some limited form of agreement between the parties. It was, however, a futile exercise and the Convention was formally dissolved on 5 May 1976. The only small satisfaction that the government could take from the exercise was that it had been framed in such a way that if it failed, the responsibility for failure would lie clearly with the parties in Northern Ireland, and not with Westminster (Rees, 1985; Cunningham, 2001). But a constitutional initiative was not the only way in which the British government sought to distance itself from Ulster. It was also evident in how Westminster dealt with security problems.

Ulsterisation

It was perhaps a personal misfortune for Merlyn Rees to have taken up his post on the eve of a major constitutional crisis. Certainly his role during the UWC strike did not enhance his reputation either for political effectiveness or fairness. Indeed, in the North there has been a widespread belief that the low priority given to Northern Ireland at Westminster has generally resulted in politicians of low calibre holding the post of Secretary of State. For unionists at least, however, that perception would be modified in the case of Rees's successor, Roy Mason.

Despite the fact that Labour historically has been more disposed to Irish unity than the Tories, the cornerstone of British policy in the North during the 1970s, regardless of which party was in office, remained the Northern Ireland Constitution Act of 1973, which stipulated that there could be no change in the constitutional status of Northern Ireland without the consent of a majority of its people, *freely* given, not induced (O'Malley, 1983). Nevertheless, given the failure to reach a political settlement the impression was abroad that Westminster would like to withdraw from Northern Ireland, an impression given colour by a decision to place the RUC and UDR in the forefront of the struggle against paramilitary violence, with British soldiers performing a back-up role, and inevitably suffering fewer casualties. Under Roy Mason British policy in Northern Ireland would focus primarily on security, together with social and economic issues.

Mason did hold a succession of talks with the North's political parties, but not in the expectation that progress could be made. In fact, after the failure of the Convention the political alliance of right-wing unionist parties began to unravel. The UUP refused to back the United Unionist Action Council – a body led by Revd Ian Paisley and Ernest Baird, Craig's successor as leader of Vanguard – when it attempted another loyalist strike, from 3 to 13 May 1977. And when it refused to run its candidates for the local elections of 1977 on a UUUC ticket, that organisation folded. At Westminster also, the bi-partisan approach of both major parties on the Ulster problem came apart when Airey Neave, the Tory Shadow Spokesman on Northern Ireland, refused to support Mason's plan for a consultative assembly. Neave declared his party's abandonment of power sharing in favour of enhanced local government, a policy in line with the increasing preference of UUP leader, James Molyneaux and his mentor, Enoch Powell, for closer integration with Britain.

Labour's response was equivocal. While it was ideologically close to the SDLP on the Ulster problem, the government was effectively without a majority in the Commons. In a deal to gain unionist support it pandered to the party's integrationist tendencies by agreeing to increase the number of Northern Ireland seats at Westminster from 12 to 17. This was the only significant political initiative Labour would attempt before leaving office in March 1979 following defeat in a vote of confidence occasioned by Gerry Fitt's withdrawal of support over British security policy in Northern Ireland (Cunningham, 2001).

The relationship between the security forces and the Catholic community had deteriorated badly since Bloody Sunday. State policy had concentrated on a massive coercive presence in Catholic areas while loyalist areas were treated more sensitively. The legislation under which security policy was pursued was the Northern Ireland (Emergency Provisions) Act, 1973, which established the no-jury Diplock courts. Taken together with the phasing out of internment without trial; the recommendation of the Gardiner Inquiry in January 1975 that special-category status be abolished; and the primacy being given to the police and UDR in the struggle with the PIRA, the Ulster problem, in its most difficult aspect, was being re-defined as a law and order problem, to be dealt with through the courts and former political offenders re-defined as ordinary criminals (O'Malley, 1983; Bishop and Mallie, 1987).

The acceptability of these arrangements in Britain was facilitated by the extension of the PIRA's campaign. A bombing outrage in Birmingham, in November 1974, left 19 dead and 182 injured, but instead of producing war-weariness and a willingness to consider withdrawal from Northern Ireland, it merely hardened attitudes. The result was the hurriedly enacted Prevention of Terrorism Act, 1974, which reinforced the Ulsterisation policy by, among other things, allowing persons from Northern Ireland suspected of terrorist activities being excluded from Britain (Rees, 1985; Cunningham, 2001). Having little success in pursuing a political settlement Mason placed greater emphasis on security measures. His 'offensive' against the PIRA involved greater use of the Special Air Services (SAS) in nationalist areas and increased undercover operations by the RUC and regular army. At the same time, greater emphasis on the use of locally recruited personnel saw their proportion of the security forces increase, from 45 per cent in 1970 to 51 per cent in 1977 and to 67 per cent in 1989 (O'Duffy, 1996).

For a time, it appeared that the criminalisation policy was working, as levels of PIRA activity were reduced and convictions increased. The weakness of the policy, however, gradually became apparent. The free rein given to the police in extracting confessions soon became controversial as the police abused the powers accorded them. For example, in one year, 1977–78, over 2800 people were arrested but only 35 per cent were charged with any offence (O'Malley, 1983). But more controversial were the abuses employed in obtaining confessions, evidence of which caused Amnesty International to call for a public inquiry in 1978. Consequently, the Bennett Inquiry upheld the charges and recommended major reforms. The political consequences of adverse publicity were evident in the action of the USA State Department in banning the sale of weapons to the RUC. But another, more serious, consequence, served to undermine the criminalisation policy, when, in an effort to restore political status, PIRA prisoners at the Maze prison entered on a policy of non-compliance with prison regulations which would have profound political consequences. Of more immediate importance, the increasing effectiveness of the security forces forced the PIRA to reorganise (O'Malley, 1983; O'Duffy, 1996).

Security Initiatives and PIRA Reactions

By the time Labour had come to power in 1974, the PIRA had established itself as the most successful republican paramilitary grouping. The OIRA had ceased activities in 1972. But the gap this left in militant Marxist republicanism was filled in December 1974 by the formation of the Irish Republican Socialist Party and, soon afterwards, by the emergence of a paramilitary wing, the tiny, but extremist, Irish National Liberation Army (INLA). The birth of this organisation was attended by a lethal feud with the OIRA (Arthur, 1994). Yet, while the OIRA had functioned as an antagonistic and oppositional force to the Provisionals, the INLA largely operated in its shadow with its policies and actions often subject to PIRA influence. Moreover, within the working-class Catholic community the status of the PIRA remained high and was not significantly diminished by the loyalist retaliation that its activities often called forth. By the mid-1970s, however, the increasing effectiveness of crown forces, combined with a more determined security campaign in the Irish Republic, resulted in a serious weakening of the organisation's ability. Thus, members of the security forces killed by the PIRA fell in number from 103 in 1972 to 14 in 1975 (Bishop and Mallie, 1987; Smith, 1995).

It was against the background of diminishing effectiveness that the organisation, under pressure from within the Catholic community and peace rallies in the North, and having sounded out the Wilson government, called an indefinite ceasefire in December 1974. The basis of the ceasefire was an arrangement whereby, in return for halting its attacks on the security forces – combined with suggestions that the

British wanted to effect their disengagement from the North – 'incident centres' would be set up in nationalist areas of the North, establishing contacts between PSF and NIO officials to ensure that no incidents occurred which could undermine it. In effect, the centres operated as PSF political offices and PIRA police stations, and were thereby used to raise the republican profile and re-build mass support in a context where British withdrawal was widely rumoured.

For the British the truce was advantageous for a number of reasons. It facilitated the criminalisation and Ulsterisation policies if the fighting in the North had actually stopped, and the PIRA might be persuaded to stop its campaign altogether. Again, the cessation could help to undermine the Troops Out campaign, then in progress in Britain, and improve the environment in which the Convention initiative proceeded. But most importantly, it allowed the security forces to embark on an extensive intelligence-gathering operation that would bring the PIRA close to defeat.

The truce was not without its difficulties for both sides. For the PIRA there was the task of maintaining discipline and preventing disaffection within its ranks. Likewise, in the British Army, commanders felt cheated of victory just when they believed the PIRA was on the run. There was again the difficulties created by the alienation of the SDLP, affronted by the concessions given to a terrorist organisation, and also by the antagonism of the loyalist community, enraged at British 'capitulation' to the PIRA. Accordingly, there was no diminishing of the loyalist murder campaign against the Catholic community during the truce; and it was greatly to the advantage of the UDA that, despite clear evidence of its involvement in sectarian murders, unlike the PIRA, it was not an illegal organisation. Its members thus qualified for membership of the UDR, a regiment that would acquire a reputation for involvement in sectarian crimes as the 1970s unfolded. Clearly the likelihood that the truce would become the basis for a permanent cessation of violence was not good, the more so as the PIRA became involved in a murderous feud with the OIRA in October 1975, prompted by a PIRA belief that the OIRA was working with the British to its detriment. Accordingly, Merlyn Rees, evidently feeling that the security forces had got as much out of the truce as they were likely to, formally ended it on 12 November by breaking off the links between the incident centres and NIO officials (Kelley, 1990; Smith, 1995; Moloney, 2002). The ending of the truce demonstrated that the republican hopes of a British withdrawal were misplaced. It was a realisation that forced a re-assessment in their ranks about strategy; a re-assessment driven by bitter recriminations about responsibility for the truce and with the northern republicans, in which an imprisoned Gerry Adams had a leading voice, exploiting the issue to establish a separate Northern Command of the PIRA (comprising the six counties together with Louth, Cavan, Monaghan, Leitrim and Donegal) largely autonomous of its Army Council, and with a Southern Command providing logistical support for the struggle in the North. This was a significant development, one that facilitated both a more coherent and co-ordinated campaign across the six counties, and a marked shift of power within the republican movement that would greatly assist Gerry Adams's future dominance of it (Moloney, 2002).

The struggle was now defined as a 'long war'. In this context, the old system of battalions and companies was largely replaced by a network of cells, or Active Service Units, operating independently of each other and receiving instructions from an anonymous hierarchy. Re-organisation significantly limited the scope for infiltration and consequent arrests: 'In 1978, there were 465 fewer charges for paramilitary offences than in the previous year' (Smith, 1995: 145). Moreover, the PIRA was slimmed down to a core of around 3000 activists.

Re-organisation, however, merely assisted the PIRA to function more effectively with less manpower and public support, and could be read as a sign of weakness. It is noteworthy that Irish-American financial support had diminished significantly by this time. The $600,000 per year sent from the USA in the early years of the struggle had, by 1978, fallen to $160,000 (Bishop and Mallie, 1987; Smith, 1995). In fact, the main pre-occupation of the northern leaders was how to develop their campaign in such a way that the republican movement could become a real political force, not wholly dependent on the violent activities of the PIRA; a movement capable of compet-ing effectively with the SDLP. Gerry Adams, moreover, recog-nised that if the struggle was limited only to armed conflict a truce meant that it effectively ceased, leaving the movement demoralised and confused. Accordingly, he argued, increas-ing political activity and support would strengthen republi-canism, indeed would enable the PIRA to intensify and sustain military struggle. By 1978, the republican leadership, in which Adams's voice was increasingly influential, had been per-suaded to expand its political role, focusing on the social and economic grievances of working-class Catholics (Smith, 1995; Moloney, 2002).

The first significant sign of the new thinking was a re-consideration of the Eire Nua policy of the early 1970s, a policy designed by the southern leadership of the move-ment with southern realities in mind. The Ulster assembly it envisaged would have left northern Catholics still subject to unionist domination. Re-thinking the republican pro-gramme was an essential element of Adams's campaign to wrest control of the republican movement from the south-ern-based leadership of Daihi O'Connell and Ruairi O'Bradaigh, and would be pursued through the promotion of a more Marxist socialist alternative, together with women's issues, policies adopted not least because of their offensive-ness to traditionalist sensibilities while also serving to broaden PSF's political appeal (Moloney, 2002).

This, however, was a slow business; and meanwhile the bombing campaign continued, both in England and Northern Ireland. Atrocities such as the La Mon Restaurant bombing in Belfast in February 1978, which left 12 innocent people dead, was symptomatic of its traumatic effect on the local commu-nity. A radical departure in republican activities did come, not from the PIRA on the ground, or PSF, but from republican prisoners (Bishop and Mallie, 1987; O'Duffy, 1996).

The Blanket Protest

A concomitant of the criminalisation process, which affected prisoners convicted after March 1976, was new single-cell prison accommodation in accordance with that provided for ordinary prisoners. Special category status had allowed the IRA command structure to function effectively within the prisons and it was inevitable that the new regime would provoke strenuous resistance.

From the start prisoners refused to co-operate with a system which refused them the right to wear their own clothes and compelled them to do prison work. By the end of the decade over 200 men and women in Northern Ireland's jails, clothed only in blankets and facing a coercive regime and spartan diet, were involved in the protest. This had extended from a refusal to accept prison clothes and conditions to a blanket and 'dirty' protest, whereby prisoners, rebelling against beatings administered on the way to and from showers and lavatories, remained in their cells and fouled them. Accordingly, relations between warders and prisoners worsened, exacerbated by a PIRA murder campaign against warders, which claimed 18 lives between 1976 and 1980.

Outside support for the protest, however, was generally lukewarm, despite attempts by the Roman Catholic Archbishop of Armagh, Tomas O'Fiaich, to intercede with Roy Mason. The authorities would only begin to take notice when the media in the USA was alerted and when the prisoners' case was taken to the European Court of Human Rights. In the meantime, the prisoners, noting the British refusal to budge, abandoned the view that special category status could be easily restored, and accepted that a greater crisis would have to be provoked before the issue would be resolved. With the accession to power of Margaret Thatcher and the Conservative Party in May 1979 the course was set for just such a crisis (Bishop and Mallie, 1987).

Thatcher and the Hunger Strikes

A resolute politician of firm right-wing ideas, Thatcher was even more determined than had been Roy Mason to face down the prisoners. On the Ulster issue a firm unionist, her resolve on the prison issue was stiffened by the killing of warders, but especially by the INLA killing, during the general election campaign, of Airey Neave, a personal friend and Shadow Secretary of State for Northern Ireland. Neave's killing was followed, later in the year, by that of Lord Mountbatten, last Viceroy of India and the Queen's cousin; and, on the same day, by that of 18 paratroopers at Warrenpoint, county Down. Her position on the prison issue, which intensified from the blanket protest to a hunger strike in late 1980, was supported by the Labour Party, apart from a few radicals.

The first wave of strikes had collapsed by Christmas 1980, but a more effective and sustained wave began in March 1981, led by the PIRA commander in the Maze prison, Bobby Sands. Sands was to gain a great propaganda coup by having himself elected MP for the Westminster constituency of Fermanagh-South Tyrone at a by-election shortly after the hunger strikes began. In June 1981, Sands's colleagues on the hunger strike, Kieran Doherty and Paddy Agnew, were elected to the Dail, while after his death on hunger strike, his election agent, Owen Carron, succeeded him as MP for the constituency. (Bew and Patterson, 1985). In fact, in Sands, Thatcher was faced with someone of like character, a person of limited ideas stubbornly held. The result was that despite attempts by a variety of intermediaries, especially the respected priest, Father Denis Faul, and John Hume, to initiate a settlement, 10 hunger strikers had died by August 1981 with no significant political results. The strike was only brought to an end when the prisoners' relatives took the decision to authorise outside medical attention as soon as they lost consciousness, and when a compromise was arranged with the Prisons Minister, Lord Gowrie, and Jim Prior, the Secretary of State for Northern Ireland. It was agreed that the prisoners should receive a 50 per cent restoration of lost remission of sentences and the right to wear their own clothes at all times, while significant progress would also be made on the prisoners' other grievances (White, 1984; Clarke, 1987; Bew and Gillespie, 1993).

The hunger strikes were an important episode for the republican movement, one that demonstrated that their success was not inevitable and that they should only be embarked on as a last resort, and on the basis of an informed assessment of the opposition's strengths and weakness. But while the cost in human lives was high, politically, much was gained. The strikes had cast the prisoners in the role of victims within an influential Catholic-nationalist frame of reference. The sympathy gained – local, national and international – would be effectively exploited at a time when the republican movement was preparing to engage more actively in orthodox politics and would significantly hasten that process. The marches and demonstrations they initiated and the experience of fighting elections attracted a media coverage that created 'the illusion of a mass movement – the precursor of mass political action' (O'Malley, 1983: 272–4). Moreover, within the republican movement itself – whose leadership had advised against them – the hunger strikes had quite profound effects. The popular campaign in support of them was largely directed from the North, casting the Adams faction as the prisoners' representatives and also as the architects of political success when they won elections. At the same time, the deaths of hunger strikers made the federalism of the Eire Nua policy seem a sop to those responsible for them. On both counts Adams gained a great advantage in his struggle with O'Connell and O'Bradaigh.

Accordingly, at the PSF Ard Fheis of 1981 the movement voted to abandon Eire Nua in favour of a 'democratic socialist republic', though only in 1982 would a two-thirds majority be gained to make the change effective. Of more practical significance, however, was a change of policy in favour of contesting local elections and taking whatever seats were won, with abstentionism remaining for Stormont and Westminster elections. As a result the movement became radicalised. Comparisons were made with other 'liberation' struggles in the international arena, while PSF cut out its own constituency among the Catholic underprivileged, whose interests the largely middle-class SDLP had failed to adequately address. The new agenda ran in tandem with the PIRA's armed struggle and was neatly encapsulated in the phrase 'taking power with a ballot box in one hand and a rifle in the other'. It was a policy that reflected the increasing dominance of the northern republicans – and quite remarkable in that they had successfully opposed electoralism at the 1980 Ard Fheis – a process that would be completed with the formal ousting of O'Bradaigh and O'Connell from all leadership posts in 1982 (Moloney, 2002).

The results of the new political course were seen at the local elections of May 1983 when PSF took 35 per cent of the nationalist vote. It was a product of a vigorous campaign and effective voter registration, and suggested that PSF had the potential to overtake the SDLP as the predominant representative of the Catholic community; a prospect both Dublin and London treated with deep foreboding (Clarke, 1987). In fact, what happened was the mobilisation of a limited constituency unattracted by the policies of the SDLP, and which, at the time, had little scope for expansion. Moreover, while the republican movement's political changes were accompanied by a continued firm commitment to armed struggle, time would show that these strategies were not complementary, that a decision between them would have to be made. Nevertheless, the success of the new political direction was striking enough at the time to force the British and Irish governments to react.

Despite her strident opposition to the hunger strikers Thatcher was yet a radical politician, more inclined to action than inaction when dealing with political problems. Northern Ireland was no exception. Indeed, at an early stage of her premiership she had considered, like Maudling before her, the possibility of diminishing the republican threat to Northern Ireland by ceding some of the most militant areas of south Armagh to the Irish Republic (Thatcher, 1993). This option was not pursued, but movement of some kind was necessary. A confidential British Army report had concluded that the PIRA could not be defeated, so a military resolution of the Ulster problem was not possible (O'Malley, 1983). Further, the controversy over the hunger strikes had internationalised the problem, especially in the USA, and to the advantage of republicans: 'The death of ten prisoners rejuvenated the republican network and won levels of Irish-American support far in excess of that achieved by Bloody Sunday' (Wilson, 1995: 169). The Thatcher administration was incensed at how criticism of her refusal to compromise led easily into anti-British consideration of the problem in general and how it should be resolved, while the British counter-offensive failed abysmally. At the same time, the long standing bi-partisan approach to the Ulster problem by the two major parties at Westminster had also broken down, with the Labour Party declaring itself in favour of a united Ireland achieved by consent. But it was from Hume and the SDLP that the initiative for change would come.

New Directions in Nationalist Politics

Despite pressures which had forced the SDLP to decide against contesting the Fermanagh-South Tyrone during the hunger strikes, Hume had been asserting his party's differences with PSF since the mid-1970s, arguing that unity could only be achieved through a carefully worked out strategy, involving not only the Northern Ireland parties but the London and Dublin governments. A simple British withdrawal from the North was not enough. Hume's thinking on a political settlement had been determined by Roy Mason's insensitivity to Catholic opinion, especially his insistence that Northern Ireland be included in the Queen's Silver Jubilee itinerary in August 1977. The royal visit enhanced community polarisation and, set against the failure of the Convention, cast doubt over the pursuit of community reconciliation. In this context, Hume moved away from any attempt at an internal solution to consider wider perspectives.

Thus, at a seminar at Queen's University in May 1978 he first outlined his ideas about federalism. Urging unionists to rely not on uncertain political developments at Westminster for their security but their own strength of numbers, he suggested a solution in which a self-governing Northern Ireland would function within a federal arrangement and with a constitutional bill of rights to provide civil and religious equality in both parts of Ireland. However, a unionist movement which saw the Labour government about to concede increased representation for Northern Ireland at Westminster – and with the leader of the UUP, James Molyneaux, increasingly wedded to integration – was not interested.

In January 1979, Hume embarked on a campaign to promote his ideas in the USA. Having already established contacts with Senator Edward Kennedy and other leading Irish-Americans, he soon gained their support. At the Westminster general election of May 1979, the SDLP manifesto called for talks between all parties to the Ulster problem and for an end to the 'one-sided' British guarantee to the unionists which, it was argued, encouraged their refusal to negotiate.

Neither Labour nor Tory Parties responded to the Hume initiative, while the SDLP leader, Gerry Fitt, always more labourist than nationalist, remained the party's sole representative at Westminster. Nevertheless, the primacy of Hume as the most authoritative representative of nationalist opinion in the North was demonstrated at the first elections for the European Parliament in June 1979. Fought in Northern Ireland under proportional representation and with the region forming one constituency, Hume gained 140,622 first preference votes. Moreover, unlike the UUP and DUP candidates, John Taylor and Ian Paisley, Hume was strongly pro-European, describing the European community as a 'healing force' for the North's troubles. In the future, the European dimension would be a central dimension of Hume's conception of the Ulster problem. Taking his seat at Strasburg, Hume aligned himself with the powerful Social Democrat bloc of representatives and began to create a whole new circle of influential friends.

From this point his approach to the Ulster difficulty shows evidence of a subtlety not evident in nationalist approaches before. He argued for the abandonment of 'unconditional' guarantees for anyone in favour of guarantees for all; to be gained, not through a predetermined solution – there was none – but through a 'process' that would integrate Ireland's traditions and lead to a solution (White, 1984; Murray, 1998). At the same time the mobilisation of international opinion proceeded. In this respect, Hume, in a 1979 article for the influential American journal, *Foreign Affairs*, sought to engage the interests of the US political elite in Northern Ireland by arguing that political instability there provided fertile ground for Marxists working against Western interests (Bew and Patterson, 1985).

Growing American interest in Ulster would create problems for Margaret Thatcher, who had established an unusually close, and apparently influential, working relationship with President Ronald Reagan, elected in 1980. It is widely accepted that a talks initiative announced by Humphrey Atkins, the Northern Ireland Secretary of State, before the election was intended to prevent Ulster becoming a burning issue during the presidential campaign. As an initiative, however, it came to nothing, a victim of UUP boycotting and DUP intransigence. Yet its failure did allow Hume to obtain a hearing with Atkins at Hillsborough for his own ideas.

In this respect the increasing influence of the European context on his thinking was apparent. Hume proposed an

Anglo-Irish Council in which North and South would be represented as parts of a larger community of the British Isles, and drew parallels with other inter-governmental bodies such as Benelux and the Nordic Council. Under an Anglo-Irish Council certain rights, such as citizenship, could be retained for unionists, to protect the perceived Britishness of the North while a form of majority rule would be acceptable to nationalists in a federal Ireland framework. This was a radical approach to the issue of identity which lies at the heart of the Ulster problem. Federalism, of course, would have been almost impossible to sell to the unionists, but from the very first meetings between the Irish Taoiseach, Charles Haughey, and Margaret Thatcher, the 'unique relationship' between the two nations was recognised and Hume could see evidence of the plan he outlined at Hillsborough (White, 1984; Murray, 1998). Specific policy initiatives for Northern Ireland, however, continued to fail.

The collapse of the Atkins' proposals was followed by that of his successor, Jim Prior, whose plan for a consultative assembly with 'rolling devolution' – incremental powers conferred when cross-community support was demonstrated – collapsed due to the SDLP's refusal to participate and Thatcher's refusal to back the initiative (O'Leary and McGarry, 1993). Accordingly, the only hope for progress was seen increasingly to lie in the Haughey–Thatcher relationship which, due partly to personal attraction, co-operation in the security area and Haughey's acceptance that Irish unity could only come about by consent, was surprisingly close. A successful first meeting between the two leaders, in London on 21 May 1980, was followed by an Anglo-Irish summit in Dublin on 8 December. Here a decision was made to devote their next meeting in London to a 'special consideration of the totality of relationships within these islands' (Arthur and Jeffery, 1996: 15–16). It was a decision, however, with more import for the long, rather than the short, term. The close relationship between Thatcher and Haughey only lasted until the outbreak of the Falklands War of 1982, when

Haughey refused to support European sanctions against Argentina. The breakdown in the relationship was heartening to unionists who saw in Thatcher's vigorous pursuit of the Falkland's conflict evidence of her resolve to defend Northern Ireland's constitutional position. But it was a situation that they proved incapable of capitalising on.

Unionist Immobility

Unlike Hume – whose instinct, once an opening for political progress was perceived, was to build on it – the UUP and DUP were imbued with a rigid ideology shaped to serve the limited task of stubbornly defending the constitutional status quo. Convinced by Enoch Powell, among others, that the unionist position was secure they were content to simply place their faith in Margaret Thatcher. It was, ironically, only from the ranks of extreme loyalism that new political thinking came.

Glen Barr, a member of the UDA leadership and a prime mover of the loyalist strike of 1974, proposed the creation of an independent, non-sectarian Ulster outside the constitutional framework of both the United Kingdom and the Irish Republic. This proposal, however, failed to find significant support from a unionist community ideologically indisposed towards radical ideas, reluctant to *politically* embrace paramilitary loyalism, and, perhaps most importantly, lacking the self-identity of alienated ethnic nationalism that most often supplies the basis for separate state formation (Nelson, 1984). Misled by Thatcher's obsession with issues of sovereignty unionists failed to adequately take account of her radical impulses, and that on Northern Ireland, if reassured about sovereignty, she could be persuaded to embrace far-reaching proposals. By 1982, convinced that the consent principle safeguarded the North's constitutional position, and, like the Dublin government, alarmed at PSF's strong showing at the elections held for James Prior's Northern

119

Ireland Assembly, Thatcher was prepared for radical action (Bew *et al.*, 2002).

From Forum to Agreement

The groundwork for an initiative on Northern Ireland had been laid when relations between Dublin and London were formalised in the creation of the Anglo-Irish Inter-governmental Council in November 1981, inaugurated by Thatcher and Garret FitzGerald during the latter's brief Fine Gael–Labour Coalition government of 1980–81. Political movement on Northern Ireland stalled during the Falklands War but, on returning to office after the conflict, and unassociated with Haughey's refusal to support the British position during it, FitzGerald was well placed to encourage movement.

In fact, FitzGerald's ambitions were grand indeed, involving nothing less than a 'constitutional crusade' intended to liberalise southern society to remove those aspects of it that northern Protestants found most objectionable, especially the political influence exercised by the Catholic Church. In this context Hume, ever alive to opportunities that might advance his Ulster agenda and concerned about a lack of direction in the South's approach to the North, proposed a forum of Ireland's constitutional parties to address the issue. In particular, he wanted political parties in the Irish Republic to seriously consider how they would achieve Irish unity by consent, and how they would protect in a new Ireland the identity and interests of Ulster Protestants.

Duly established, the New Ireland Forum comprised representatives of four of the major constitutional parties in Ireland – SDLP, Fianna Fail, Fine Gael and Labour – and deliberated for a year from 30 May 1983. It received written submissions from 317 individuals and groups and heard oral evidence from 31 of these. It also commissioned a number of research papers. Supported by government funding and a full-time staff it was the most important nationalist contribution to the debate on the Ulster problem since the Second World War (Whyte, 1991). No UUP or DUP members took part, though Protestant Church representatives did. Probably the most important of the Forum's conclusions, though dissented from by Fianna Fail, was that the traditional consensus among nationalists that the Ulster problem was primarily the fault of the British, was no longer credible. Dick Spring, the Labour Party leader, argued that both nationalism and unionism had failed, while both FitzGerald and Hume focused on the problem of national identity. Hume, in fact, expressed what would become the dominant nationalist approach to the Ulster problem when he acknowledged that the British identity of Ulster Protestants was not a form of false consciousness, but a valid tradition and allegiance that could not be ignored, and that the core of the problem was their belief that their 'ethos' could not survive in an Irish political structure.

Given the historic divisions within Irish nationalism, it was unlikely that the Report of the Forum would demonstrate a homogeneity of recommendations and conclusions. It was, in fact, characterised by ambiguities and inconsistencies in places. Awareness of the concern to finalise the Report before the European elections of June 1984 allowed Haughey considerable leverage to insist that its main conclusions demonstrate a preference among all parties for a unitary state. Nevertheless, two other options were considered, a federal/confederal state and joint authority over Northern Ireland by London and Dublin. Also, it was made clear that the participants remained open to other options (Kenny, 1986; Whyte, 1991). Thus, seen as a whole, while the sentiment for Irish unity was expressed, the realities of the Ulster problem were largely addressed. It was a problem of identity the solution to which could only be arrived at by consent and which might include a continued British presence.

The Forum Report, dismissed by unionists still confident of Thatcher's backing and less than willing to produce an initiative of their own, became the basis of the negotiations that would result in the Anglo-Irish Agreement (AIA) of 1985.

Indeed, its very radicalism may well have appealed to Thatcher's own radical instincts, especially given the failure of the NIO's preferred policy of devolution plus power sharing (Bew *et al.*, 2002). But there were more substantial reasons for action, especially increased American interest in the North.

The early 1980s had seen the rejuvenation of the republican network, and this had prompted the Friends of Ireland (FOI) group of leading Irish-Americans to further action in support of constitutional nationalism. Members of the group visited the North, met the Minister of State for Northern Ireland, Lord Gowrie, at the NIO and expressed concern at lack of political progress. In Congress the FOI tabled resolutions calling for a ban on the use of plastic bullets in Northern Ireland and the outlawing of the UDA (Wilson, 1995). These initiatives signalled a wider attack on direct rule, which had hardly been an overwhelming success. Britain had failed to pursue a fair and firm policy, particularly in the security field, and had also failed to secure an effective voice for northern Catholics in the government of Northern Ireland, or to significantly improve that community's position of relative unemployment and social deprivation (Boyle and Hadden, 1985; Whyte, 1991). Britain was thus exposed on a wide front and the FOI maintained pressure on the Ulster question. Encouraged by Hume and FitzGerald the group sponsored support in Congress for a united Ireland and for the Forum Report as the means by which the peaceful reunification of Ireland could be secured. As part of this project Prior's Northern Ireland Assembly was criticised as 'unworkable', and the PIRA's campaign of violence condemned as incapable of delivering a solution. But most significantly, the FOI was successful in persuading President Reagan to raise Anglo-Irish relations in his meetings with Margaret Thatcher (Wilson, 1995).

This was deemed necessary given Thatcher's cool response to the Forum Report at the Anglo-Irish summit of mid-November 1984. Despite prior indications that the British would give the Report a 'magnanimous' response, they were, in fact, quite unwilling to embrace its options. At a joint press conference following the summit, on 19 November, Thatcher delivered a public humiliation to FitzGerald by abruptly dismissing any consideration of the three major Forum proposals, a united Ireland, confederation and joint authority. Thatcher's response is perhaps understandable, given that the PIRA had bombed the Grand Hotel in Brighton the previous month, during the Conservative Party conference, killing five people and injuring more than 30. Thatcher herself narrowly escaped serious injury. Nevertheless, anxious that her stance would work to the advantage of militant republicanism Hume and FitzGerald pressed the FOI to intervene with Reagan. Accordingly, the President made known to Thatcher his concern about Ulster at a meeting at Camp David on 22 December 1984, and that he would wish to discuss the matter further when she returned to the USA in February 1985.

Thatcher was thus moved to make some proposals to the Irish government before the February meeting. Yet, the process of arriving at them was not easy. With the Brighton bomb in mind it was important not to be seen to be conceding to the pressure of violence, while the sovereignty issue was also an important consideration. On the other hand, her Cabinet colleagues impressed on her that the very vehemence with which she dismissed the Forum options had damaged constitutional nationalism and encouraged the PIRA, and that this state of affairs needed to be remedied. Thus, important as the American factor was, it was not the only one impelling action. Delivered on 21 January 1985, the British plan centred on a deal which gave the Irish Republic an institutionalised role in the government of Northern Ireland but without formally infringing the North's constitutional position within the United Kingdom. It was a plan, which, while it rejected the major Forum options, was nevertheless framed within the context of Anglo-Irish responsibilities for the Ulster problem on which those options had been based. Certainly the British proposals ruled out the kind of integrationist settlement James Molyneaux, the leader of the UUP would have preferred, and to which nationalists were strongly opposed. For his part, Garret FitzGerald, having accepted that reconciliation between the two communities in the North must precede territorial unity, regarded the British plan as advancing the constitutional nationalist agenda in a way that would stall the progress of militant republicanism, while not alienating northern Protestants beyond redress. The plan may not have been joint authority but it was significant progress nevertheless. And despite Thatcher's reluctance to move, the plan also carried substantial gains for Britain.

Her initial hopes that the Irish government might respond by repealing articles 2 and 3 of the Irish constitution were soon disappointed, but there was an obvious British interest in weaning nationalists away from PSF. There was also the prospect of securing improved co-operation with Dublin, and of retaining American support for Britain's role in Northern Ireland while deflecting international criticism. These considerations over-rode her real fears of what the unionist response would be. The only significant opposition to the deal from within the constitutional nationalist camp came from Charles Haughey, leader of Fianna Fail, who saw it as a sell-out to British interests (Bew *et al.*, 2002). But when, in October 1985, his attempt to gain the support of the FOI in opposing it was firmly rebuffed, no hurdle to the enactment of the Agreement remained (Wilson, 1995).

4

AGREEMENT AND PROCESS

The Agreement Formalised

Signed by Margaret Thatcher and Garret FitzGerald at
Hillsborough Castle, county Down, on 15 November 1985,
the AIA was an international treaty between the United
Kingdom and the Irish Republic. It was a multi-dimensional
response to the Ulster problem premised on the understanding that the involvement of both states was an essential basis
for any solution. At its heart was the Inter-Governmental
Conference, established to enable London and Dublin to
harmonise their approaches to the North, and in this context
the agreement committed both governments to promote the
establishment of devolved government in the North based
on agreement between the constitutional parties. Until such
a government emerged, however, the Irish government
would represent the interests of the Catholic community at
the Inter-Governmental Conference, Dublin's role in the government of the North being symbolised by a permanent
Secretariat of Irish civil servants at Maryfield, outside Belfast.

In sum, the AIA implied a British commitment to reform
Northern Ireland, especially the administration of justice,

and to guarantee equality of treatment, in terms of rights and identity, for the two communities; while both governments were pledged to political, legal and security co-operation with specific reference to the North, and to cross-border co-operation on security, economic, social and cultural matters (FitzGerald, 1991; O'Leary and McGarry, 1993). Moreover, the Agreement was framed so as to avoid the weaknesses of past initiatives. Thus, unlike the Sunningdale experiment of 1974 there were no local institutions of the AIA vulnerable to destabilisation – the Maryfield secretariat was both immune to local community pressure and easily defended by the security forces. Accordingly, the AIA nullified the unionist practice since 1912, of making unworkable any arrangements for Ulster to which they were opposed. What made the AIA so difficult to oppose effectively, was that it was not a final settlement to the Ulster problem, but a 'process' by which a settlement might emerge (Whyte, 1991).

But the Agreement was not just defined with the errors of the past in mind, it also drew positively on the ideas produced by a wide-ranging debate on the Ulster problem that took place in the early 1980s. An unofficial inquiry set up by the British Irish Association in May 1984, consisting of several academics, a journalist, politicians and headed by Lord Kilbrandon, produced a report whose findings would be expressed both in the AIA itself and in the proposals that followed from it. *Northern Ireland: Report of an Independent Inquiry*, recommended the abolition of the Flags and Emblems Act and the Diplock Courts, together with a form of devolution for Northern Ireland on a shared-responsibility basis, and the introduction of courts with judges drawn from the Irish Republic sitting with those from the United Kingdom. But its central principle was a trade-off between increased security co-operations from the Irish Republic in return for a say in the government of Northern Ireland in matters affecting the Catholic minority; though the committee was divided over the extent of southern influence. To allay unionist fears of 'betrayal' any arrangement between Dublin and London would be formalised in an international treaty and registered with the United Nations.

This idea was also supported by another important contribution to the debate. Kevin Boyle and Tom Haddens' *Ireland: a Positive Proposal* added to the Kilbrandon case by stressing that the formalisation of an agreement between London and Dublin in an international treaty was necessary as a means of re-defining the British-Irish relationship in general and their relationship over a disputed territory in particular. Further, the conclusion of Kilbrandon and Boyle and Hadden, that any settlement should have a London–Dublin framework, was supported by a Social Democratic Party–Liberal Alliance study in July 1985 (Cochrane, 1997).

But as much as the form of the AIA was shaped by the findings of recent studies, it also drew on long-standing approaches to dealing with the North; for example, the British practice of seeking the maximum possible agreement between parties in the North together with harmonious relations with Dublin and the USA. For the Irish government, and perhaps more explicitly, the AIA embodied its position on Northern Ireland since the early 1960s, when Sean Lemass effectively abandoned anti-partitionism in favour of the role of guardian of the Catholic minority and its interests, while at the same time expanding co-operation with Britain so as to contain the conflict (O'Leary and McGarry, 1993).

Nevertheless, while a sophisticated approach to the Ulster problem, the AIA, having left the specific form of a final settlement to be determined by a combination of events and political negotiations, inevitably created, especially for unionists, a degree of uncertainty about the North's constitutional future. In particular, they detected a fundamental contradiction between clause 1 of the Agreement, which guaranteed Northern Ireland's constitutional position so long as a majority in the North supported it, and clause 2, which emphasised determined efforts between Britain and the Irish Republic to agree policy on the government of the region. Certainly varied and incompatible interpretations of the Agreement's meaning would abound, not helped by British statements to the effect that the AIA safeguarded the union with Britain, as against the Irish government view that this was not the case (Whyte, 1991).

As might have been expected, the reaction of public opinion in both Britain and the Irish Republic to the AIA was highly favourable. In the British case, parliamentary opinion mirrored that of the public, though in the Dail, the Agreement was accepted in the face of opposition from the largest party, Fianna Fail. In Northern Ireland, the SDLP, whose leader had largely provided the inspiration for the Agreement, gave it a vigorous endorsement. More cautious support came from the Alliance Party. The republican movement, however, was strongly opposed to it, arguing that it 'copperfastened' partition and stabilised British interests in the North by insulating Westminster from international criticism (Adams, 1995; Murray, 1998). The strongest opposition, however, came from the unionist community, which saw the Agreement as a major advance on the road to a united Ireland.

Unionists Respond

It says much about the political trauma experienced by unionists on the signing of the AIA that, almost immediately, Ian Paisley and James Molyneaux rushed to London to confer with Margaret Thatcher on a hurriedly constructed replacement involving power sharing. It was an initiative that their own followers angrily repudiated on their return to the province. The virulence of the popular unionist reaction to the Agreement would take its framers by surprise. It is true that the unionist leaders were not officially consulted about its making, chiefly out of fear that they would play a destructive role. But the assumption was made, certainly by Garret FitzGerald, that they were being kept informed unofficially, and that the Agreement would not come as a shock.

But while the unionist leaders did have their contacts with the British government, the extent of what was being planned was not known. Indeed, the British government, against the advice of Fitzgerald, was adamant that unionists not be given detailed accounts of what was taking place. Accordingly, when the Agreement emerged it contrasted sharply with assurances given to Molyneaux by Enoch Powell, among others, that nothing of any great significance was afoot (FitzGerald, 1991; Loughlin, 1995; Cochrane, 1997). To unionists its import was clear. A process by which Northern Ireland would be gradually eased into a united Ireland was now in place.

Unionists fears were exacerbated by John Hume's interpretation of the AIA, to the effect that Britain was now 'neutral' on the Union and could be a persuader for a solution acceptable to nationalists; a view given colour in 1989 by the then Secretary of State for Northern Ireland, Peter Brooke, who stressed that Britain had no selfish, strategic or material interest in Northern Ireland. Attempts by his predecessor in December 1985, Tom King, to reassure unionists by stressing that, as the majority in Northern Ireland, their will on the Union must prevail, backfired when he was criticised by politicians in the Irish Republic and was forced to apologise in the House of Commons (Aughey, 1994). The opposition of unionist leaders was mirrored among the Protestant community generally, with opinion polls showing only around 8 per cent support and with opposition ranging from 75 to 80 per cent.

The unionist community responded to the AIA with a campaign of opposition that had both parliamentary and extraparliamentary dimensions. The unionist MPs collectively resigned their seats with the purpose of forcing by-elections and thus demonstrating the extent of popular unionist opposition to the Agreement. The by-elections were held in January 1986 and produced 418,230 anti-AIA votes, representing 43.9 per cent of the total electorate (Cox, 1996). But the exercise was less than wholly successful. A target of 500,000 votes was not reached, while the Newry and Armagh seat was lost to Seamus Mallon, deputy leader of the SDLP.

As an attempt to impress the Westminster parliament it singularly failed, as did an attempt to contest by-elections in Britain. The unionist candidate at the Fulham by-election of April 1986 polled fewer votes than Screaming Lord Sutch of the Monster Raving Loony Party. Also, a projected campaign of mass demonstrations fizzled out when only 100 people turned out for the first such meeting in Liverpool. Likewise, a Friends of the Union group, established within the Tory Party in May 1986 to co-ordinate the campaign, had little effect on either Tory elite or popular opinion. Unionist frustration at their political ineffectiveness in opposing the AIA was reflected in boycotts of the NIO and Westminster; the breaking of the constitutional link between the UUP and the Tory Party; and in using the facilities of the Northern Ireland Assembly for anti-AIA protests. Mass protests, of course, were more effective in Northern Ireland than in Britain, and to these were added a one-day general strike attended by considerable intimidation, and a civil disobedience campaign, involving the non-payment of rent and rates and the refusal of unionist councillors to set local government rates.

More seriously, in the spring of 1986 loyalist paramilitaries began a campaign of violence against RUC members living in Protestant areas, because of their supposed 'collaboration' in implementing the AIA. This was accompanied by the intimidation of Catholics living in religiously mixed areas and the re-activation of a sectarian murder campaign that had been in abeyance since 1977. The framers of the AIA argued that it would contribute to the demise of paramilitary violence. The loyalist paramilitaries were determined to show that in this respect, at least, it would fail. Nevertheless, the various forms of unionist opposition failed to make much headway in the face of British determination to face it down, a resolve reflected in the closing down of the Northern Ireland Assembly. By early 1987, unionist opposition was gradually dissipating (O'Leary and McGarry, 1993); a result not only of political ineffectiveness, but also of deep divisions within the unionist family itself about the *extent* to which the AIA threatened Northern Ireland and the kind of actions that were justified in opposing it (Cochrane, 1997).

To unionist political ineffectiveness in opposing the AIA can be added self-defeating postures. Thus, the decision of the unionist leaders not to negotiate a replacement for the AIA until it was first abandoned, a decision predicated on the expected success of their opposition campaign, left them painted into a corner when that campaign failed. And political failure was soon reflected in a splintering of the unionist bloc. A group broke away from the UUP to form the Campaign for Equal Citizenship (CEC). Aiming at complete integration with Britain it directed its activities specifically towards persuading the main British parties to organise in Northern Ireland, arguing that their failure to do so prevented citizens of the North from having any impact on the making of governments which influenced their daily lives. The campaign had some success when, against the leadership's wishes, Tory constituency organisations were established in the North, though they failed to make much headway against the main unionist parties (Aughey, 1994).

Leading members of these parties responded to the political crisis occasioned by the AIA by forming a Task Force, with the purpose of charting a constructive way forward. It produced a report sympathetic to power sharing, but this was an option the party leaders, then engaged in 'talks about talks' with the NIO, were disinclined to adopt. In fact, both the UUP and DUP were increasingly riven with tensions over how to proceed, with opinion in the former divided between a pro-devolutionist wing inclined to accept regional government on the basis of a responsibility-sharing model and a larger integrationist body represented by the party leader, James Molyneaux. Opinion in the DUP was divided over whether to maintain its alliance with the UUP or to embrace more militant methods of opposition to the AIA (O'Leary and McGarry, 1993).

In pursuit of the latter, Peter Robinson and other DUP members hoped to mobilise grass-roots opinion through the

Ulster Clubs, an organisation with paramilitary links (John McMichael, leader of the UDA, was given a place on its steering committee). The loyalist paramilitaries, however, mirrored constitutional unionism in failing to establish an effective response to the AIA. Politically, the UDA did respond imaginatively with the document, *Common Sense*, which proposed a power-sharing government for the North based on a proportionality of votes at each level of government, with equality of citizenship guaranteed through a Bill of Rights. But the document drew a more favourable response from the SDLP and Cardinal Tomas O'Fiaich than it did from the unionist leaders, who sidelined it by pointing out that acting on its recommendations involved political negotiations that were not possible until the AIA was abandoned, a position the UDA was also committed to. But more importantly, it was not explained how the document was to be sold to the loyalist rank and file:

> loyalists could only be won over to 'proportionality' if the IRA stopped killing Protestants, and the only way to ensure that was to kill a lot of IRA men. Provided that such killing was followed quickly by political innovation then Catholics would accept it and there would be no surge of IRA recruitment. In McMichael's mind there was no conflict between the political and military sides of the UDA (Bruce, 1992: 238–9).

In fact, there was no groundswell of popular unionist opinion in favour of the plan, while northern Catholics had long seen through the fiction – then still accepted by the justice system in Northern Ireland – that the loyalist murder gang, the Ulster Freedom Fighters (UFF), was a different organisation from the UDA. Accordingly, they would not have been amenable to any peace proposals coming from that quarter. In this context the position of the UVF was more realistic; namely that the task of finding a political solution was a job for the mainstream unionist politicians. But this was a formidable task. As in the past, so in the aftermath of the AIA, the unionist family proved united only in destructive intent. Constructing an alternative to the AIA that all unionists could endorse, and which would also appeal to nationalists, was monumentally difficult for a leadership whose preferred idea of reform had hardly moved beyond Brian Faulkner's proposals in 1971: the old Stormont with committees that nationalists could chair. The fragmentation of the unionist family that occurred at that time had left its several sections more concerned to secure support through out-doing each other in hard-line stances than in thinking constructively about how their fundamental interests could be secured (Arthur and Jeffery, 1996).

Nationalist Gains

As the prime mover in the process that produced the Agreement it was perhaps not surprising that John Hume argued that everything that 'has happened in the past few years stems from the Anglo-Irish Agreement' (Hume, 1996: 46). Hume's assessment was upbeat and positive, but it deflected attention away from a critical assessment of just how advantageous for the minority the AIA was, and it is unlikely that his view was widely shared by Catholics. An opinion poll in April 1988 reported that only 16 per cent of Catholics believed the Agreement had benefited them. 'Benefit', however, has to be assessed psychologically as well as materially, and with respect to the former, the fact of unionist hostility to the Agreement was itself a source of satisfaction. In terms of reducing nationalist support for PSF, a major objective of the AIA, a small but significant reduction did occur. But it now seems that PSF may have already reached the limit of its then achievable support in the mid-1980s, and would not have grown significantly in any case. Otherwise, concrete gains are difficult to identify.

It is true that, for Northern Ireland generally, the AIA did stimulate financial benefit through grant-aid provided through the European Structural Fund, while the Flags and Emblems Act, long a device for preventing the display of the Irish Tricolour, was repealed. But a number of specific initiatives, such as abolition of the 'supergrass' system – whereby a member of a terrorist organisation gave evidence that convicted several of its members – fair employment measures and changes in regard to the policing of Orange parades, were in train for other reasons, or out of necessity (Cochrane, 1997).

Anglo-Irish Difficulties

As a framework which existed to facilitate the emergence of a solution to the Ulster problem, its most significant aspect was the institutionalisation of Anglo-Irish co-operation. This included regular sessions of the IGC covering all aspects of Northern Ireland politics; regular meetings and communications between the NIO ministers and their counterparts in the Irish Republic; the working of the secretariat at Maryfield; and attempts to harmonise the statements and policies of London and Dublin following negotiations. Nevertheless, these activities had to cope with a variety of tensions, produced by Irish changes of government when Fianna Fail replaced Fine Gael, and by different interpretations placed on aspects of the Agreement as the two governments addressed their respective constituencies. But most seriously, problems arose over the objectives and priorities of public policy for Northern Ireland.

In this respect, Britain's major concern was improved security, on cross-border relations and extradition in particular, with reform in the North a major concern to the SDLP and the Irish government. The latter proceeded only slowly so as not to antagonise unionists; and when, following the acquisition of substantial arms shipments from Libya in 1986–87 PIRA activity increased significantly, the British emphasis on security and crisis management was enhanced with any commitment to reform of the administration of justice in the North being further delayed. The tensions produced by the different and changing priorities of Westminster and Dublin were to find expression in a number of highly controversial issues.

When, for instance, Britain reneged on its promise to reform the court system in Northern Ireland – to change the single judge Diplock Courts to mixed courts with judges drawn from the Irish Republic – in 1987, the Irish government amended the Extradition Act of 1986 to ensure that a crime had actually been committed before extradition could take place. This amendment was apparently vindicated in 1988 when, despite serious misgivings about the evidence on which they had been convicted, the British Court of Appeal rejected an appeal against their sentence by the Birmingham Six. In fact the Six were only one of a number of groups of prisoners – the Guildford Four, the Maguires, the Winchester Three – whom had been convicted by English courts of PIRA-related offences in controversial circumstances and whose cases became *causes celebres* in Ireland. Irish opinion was further enraged in 1988 by the British failure to prosecute RUC officers involved in 'shoot to kill' controversies in the early 1980s; by the British Army's killing of an innocent Catholic, Aidan McAnespie; by the early release of a British soldier convicted of manslaughter, the only one until then convicted in the Northern Irish courts; and by the controversial killing of three unarmed PIRA members in Gibralter by the SAS.

On the British side, the Thatcher government was outraged by the refusal of the Irish Attorney-General to extradite Fr Patrick Ryan, a priest suspected of terrorist involvement, on the grounds that, following an attack on him in the House of Commons by Thatcher, he could not get a fair trial. The difficulties experienced in Anglo-Irish relations during the period 1985–88 alerted both sides to the need to co-ordinate their activities better. The jointly published 'Review of the Inter-Governmental Conference' in 1989 indicated that they were sensitive to the charge that the IGC lacked strategic co-ordination and had become a form of crisis management (McKittrick, 1989; O'Leary and McGarry, 1993).

At the same time, however, there was never any possibility that these incidents would undo the AIA. As an initiative which established a 'process' for dealing with the Ulster problem its success or failure was not tied to the fortunes of specific proposals. Despite its deficiencies in the period 1985–88 both Dublin and London had gained considerably by it. For Britain especially, the way in which the AIA enhanced its international reputation was important at a time when a highly effective campaign by pro-republican activists such as Fr Sean McManus and the Irish National Caucus had persuaded several American firms with branches in Northern Ireland, together with a number of state legislatures, to adopt the 'McBride principles' – a commitment to implement measures to ensure fair employment for Catholics. Nevertheless, Irish- American success in this area would force the British government to strengthen fair employment legislation in the North (Guelke, 1994).

Republican Reaction

Claiming that the AIA 'copperfastened' partition republicans yet responded in a dualistic fashion, reflecting the movement's need to attract votes while at the same time retaining its militant support base. Thus, despite the 'copperfastening' claim, Gerry Adams, in late 1985, could argue that the AIA's introduction showed that the British could be moved by republican pressure. In fact, this was reflective of the traditional republican attitude to Britain: conscious of its ability to damage their movement yet anxious, at the same time, to interpret British initiatives in terms of PIRA effectiveness. However, it now seems that the PSF leadership's public position at this time was a less than comprehensive indicator of the depth and nature of its political engagement.

Apparently, Adams had, with the inspiration and support of Fr Alex Reid of Clonard monastery in west Belfast, been secretly attempting to forge his own peace process since 1983, seeking in the first instance to mobilise senior Catholic clerical support, an effort that found support from Cardinal Tomas O'Fiaich, Primate of all Ireland, among others, and through them, support among the Catholic hierarchy in the USA which would be influential in smoothing Adams's path with US political opinion and in winning over important figures in the Irish-American business community. By 1986, Adams and O'Fiaich were hinting publicly at ideas that could easily be dovetailed with those of John Hume, and would later be central features of the nationalist dimension to the peace process – a pan-nationalist alliance, an all-party conference to hammer out a settlement, and a declaration of political 'neutrality' from the British. Privately, Adams was also in contact with the Secretary of State for Northern Ireland, Tom King, at this time seeking to elucidate the British role in Northern Ireland. This contact was of crucial importance, for the British response – the precise authorship of which was unknown – accorded, apparently, with his own ideas. It stated that Britain had no selfish interest for remaining in Northern Ireland and would respect any solution to the conflict that accorded with the principle of consent; that it was prepared to accord PSF a role in negotiations in the context of a PIRA ceasefire and, moreover, offered to convene the kind of all-party conference nationalists desired; and that Britain would implement any settlement in legislation (Moloney, 2002).

If the British response was in accord with Adams's own views, then his personal understanding of the politically acceptable at this time was considerably in advance of the republican movement generally; and his initiatives, accordingly, highly personal. It would be going too far to read his acceptance of the Agreement of Easter 1998 as implying positions fully formed from the mid-1980s, especially in regard to unionism, but it would nonetheless seem that a politically realistic approach to the Ulster conflict was already informing his thinking, and significantly in advance of the Hume–Adams discussions of the late 1980s from which his 'conversion' to this approach has usually been dated. Moreover, the logic of PSF's political activities would gradually provide a supportive context for his endeavours (Moloney, 2002).

The PSF decision, in November 1986, to abandon abstention from the Dail – provoking O'Bradaigh and O'Connell to depart and form Republican Sinn Feinn – was a logical consequence of the process of deepening its political engagement in conjunction with an ongoing armed struggle. Certainly at this time there was no serious consideration being given to the idea that the military struggle would be ended. The PIRA had just acquired large quantities of high quality arms and many members were convinced that military success was now within its grasp, while the dropping of abstensionism was only achieved at the cost of accepting a number of hardliners in leadership positions on the Army Council.

There was, however, an inverse relationship between the ferocity of PIRA activity and electoral support for PSF. And it was clear that many nationalists would never support the latter while the former was still active. It was also evident by 1987 that the AIA, which the southern government was employing to ease the impact of the British security apparatus on nationalist areas, was serving to diminish the alienation that was in the past highly conducive to PIRA support. By the time of the Westminster general election of 1987 it was evident that the republican vote had settled down at around 35 per cent, and that to advance politically pressure to restrain the PIRA was needed together with a radical political departure (Moloney, 2002).

As it happened, developments occurred which facilitated the Adams project. For example, in May 1987 eight essential PIRA personnel were killed by the SAS in an ambush at Loughgall, county Armagh, an ambush which had the effect of removing the heart of the highly active east Tyrone brigade. But much more importantly, at the beginning of November a large consignment of sophisticated weaponry from Libya destined for the PIRA was seized aboard the *Eksund*, off the French coast. This consignment was intended to provide the PIRA with the military supplies to enable it to undertake a massive surprise attack on the British security apparatus; a surprise attack based on the Vietcong Tet offensive of 1968 – an offensive which cost the Vietcong dearly, but which was also credited with breaking the will of the USA to stay in Vietnam. The failure of the *Eksund* shipment, the last and largest of a series of hitherto successful expeditions, meant that an offensive on the scale intended could not take place, something that, arguably, saved the infant peace process (Moloney, 2002).

The armed struggle continued at a reduced level, but was attended by some appalling blunders. For instance, the PIRA bomb which killed 11 people and injured 63 at the Remembrance Day service at Enniskillen on 8 November – itself a consequence of the PIRA's cellular structure and the freedom of initiative that now lay with local commanders – only provoked an intensified Garda security operation and did great political damage to the republican movement in general. Further, the amendment in 1987 to the Irish Extradition Act, while it made the extradition process more stringent, also made it very difficult for PIRA activists in the South to escape extradition to the United Kingdom on the grounds that their acts were 'political'. Moreover, the successes of the security forces, not least the killing of three PIRA operatives during the failed attempt to bomb Gibralter in March 1988, which marked the beginning of the reduced 'Tet offensive' – it consisted of a wave of violence until September – had a depressing effect on operatives and induced demoralisation and hunts for informers. In sum, the revived military campaign did not produce the achievements the militants had hoped for. At most, it merely reiterated the depressing reality that while the Provisionals were capable of perpetrating individually effective strikes against the security forces they were incapable of winning the war. Moreover, their activities offered a rationalisation for an intensified loyalist murder campaign, which in Tyrone accounted for 60 nationalist lives, 20 of whom were PIRA members, in the five years from the disaster at Loughall. But while their military weaknesses in the late 1980s may have been depressing for republicans, depression informed by the strong suspicions of traitors in their midst, these reverses – not to mention the loyalist killings which struck at the core of the PIRA's *raison d'être* in the North and which it was inhibited from responding to in like fashion – nevertheless, served to make the political course Adams favoured more attractive (O'Brien, 1993; Smith, 1995; Moloney, 2002). In a wider context, republican reverses, together with an apparent lessening of support for right-wing unionism, stimulated Peter Brooke's hopes for advancing the political process.

The Brooke Initiative

Appointed Secretary of State for Northern Ireland on 24 July 1989, Brooke was a politician unassociated with either the implementation or selling of the AIA. He seemed well placed to make a new beginning. At the outset, however, he was regarded as something of a political lightweight, an impression given colour by initial injudicious statements about the nature of the Ulster problem (Cox, 1996). In this respect he undoubtedly suffered, to some extent, from the widely held perception in Northern Ireland that the post of Secretary of State is filled by politicians of low calibre.

Brooke's approach to the problem, however, was realistic. He, like Tom King, had already been contacted by Adams, and his observation in November 1989, that the PIRA could not be militarily defeated and that if, and when, republican violence ended he would not rule out speaking to PSF – that the government's response to the ending of violence would be 'imaginative' – was clearly informed by those contacts and drew positive responses from both the SDLP and PSF, though not from unionists. More immediately, in January 1990 he initiated talks between the constitutional parties. These were especially welcome to the SDLP as they were premised on Hume's conception of the multi-dimensional nature of the problem, comprising relationships between the two communities in the North; between North and South; and between Britain and Ireland. But Brooke's optimism proved to be misplaced. There was too big a gap between the SDLP and unionist positions for progress to be made. The break came with a dispute about when Dublin should become involved in the talks, with the unionists insisting that this could only occur after substantial agreement was made on internal governmental structures for Northern Ireland, and the SDLP equally insistent on prioritising talks on 'sharing the island of Ireland'. Yet, despite their disagreements, no party was prepared to accept the opprobrium of being held responsible for the failure of the talks process and more substantial negotiations would soon follow (Cox, 1996).

The necessity for talks was given point by an upsurge in paramilitary violence which illustrated the failure of the AIA on the security front. From a low point of 54 for 1985, fatalities due to the conflict rose to 95 for 1991 (O'Brien, 1993). Depressingly, 1991 opened with the PIRA killing of eight Protestant workers at Teebane Cross, county Tyrone, in January, while loyalist paramilitaries retaliated with the killing of five Catholics at Graham's betting shop on the Lower Ormeau Road, Belfast, early in February. On 9 February the PIRA bombed 10 Downing Street. Accordingly, despite SDLP reluctance to negotiate an alternative to the AIA, and unionist insistence on talking only with the object of replacing it, and even then not when it was in operation, the security situation brought both sides to agree on a formula for talks in late March. Their three-fold dimension, unionist–nationalist, North–South, and Anglo-Irish, was now defined as Strands One, Two and Three, and with all parties accepting that a settlement could only be arrived at if there was agreement on all three strands, leading to the oft- repeated phrase, 'nothing is agreed until everything is agreed' (Bew and Gillespie, 1993).

Getting the talks under way was something of an achievement in itself, involving difficulties over where the location for the different strands should take place, especially Strand Two, and who should act as chairman, an issue eventually resolved with the appointment of Sir Ninian Stephens, a prominent Australian lawyer and politician. Again, the difficulty of how the talks were to proceed given the unionist condition of not engaging in negotiations while the AIA was in place, was resolved by the device of holding them in a gap between meetings of the IGC, an 11-week period from the end of April to mid-July (Guelke, 1995). The hopes for a political settlement were raised when an umbrella group of loyalist paramilitary organisations, the Combined Loyalist Military Command (CLMC) declared a unilateral ceasefire for the duration of the talks.

Despite the hopes raised, however, no settlement emerged. On the unionist side, the UUP and DUP agreed on opposition to Dublin involvement in Northern Ireland affairs, but disagreed otherwise, with the former preferring integration with Britain and the latter, devolved government. Not surprisingly, the talks had difficulty getting beyond procedural questions and broke up on 3 July following a British refusal to extend the talks period. The failure to make progress was widely blamed on the unionists, not just by political commentators but also by the leaders of the mainstream Protestant churches (Bruce, 1994). Moreover, in their insistence on continuing the meetings of the IGC, London and Dublin were signalling the importance they placed on the AIA and the improvement in their relationship it had produced; and, accordingly, how difficult it would be to replace (Cox, 1996).

Nevertheless, escalating paramilitary violence, especially a loyalist determination to match and exceed the PIRA in the toll of killings, something that would finally lead to the banning of the UDA in August 1992, acted as a recurrent coercive factor driving the political parties back to the negotiation table. Thus, on the tenuous evidence produced by the result of Westminster general election of April 1992, when Gerry Adams lost the west Belfast seat to Dr Joe Hendron of the SDLP and the DUP vote fell significantly, the time was deemed appropriate for another attempt at fruitful discussions (Guelke, 1995; Bew *et al.*, 2002).

Initiated by a new Secretary of State, Sir Patrick Mayhew, on 30 April 1992, this round did produce significant progress on Strand One, with the two unionist parties, Alliance and the British government agreeing on a governmental structure for Northern Ireland consisting of a number of leaderless committees drawn from a Northern Ireland assembly, plus three 'commissioners' emerging through popular election. The latter element had been introduced to meet SDLP concerns. John Hume would not accept an executive elected from the assembly, arguing for a six-man executive of whom three would be elected along the lines of the European elections in Northern Ireland to represent the three main parties, and with the remaining three to be appointed by Dublin, London and the European Community. The other parties, while accepting in principle the idea of commissioners, rejected the proposal to appoint them, especially any from outside the United Kingdom. There was deadlock then on this issue, but it was at least possible to resolve it, unlike the problems that emerged on Strand Two, with the SDLP and the Dublin government wanting to maintain the influence that Dublin had on the administration of Northern Ireland through the AIA, and with the unionist parties seeking to remove the accord and to reduce North–South links to the 'cordial relations between separate states' envisioned by the agreement of 1925 which resolved the boundary question (Bruce, 1994).

Unionists, in fact, approached this round of talks in a more assured frame of mind than in the past, illustrated by their innovative action in going to Dublin in autumn 1992 to discuss North–South relations, and in their involvement in

Strand Two of the talks despite the fact that a prior condition, that Strand One be first agreed, had not been fulfilled. That assurance derived in large part from the Westminster parliamentary arithmetic following the general election, which produced a Tory majority of 21, large enough to hold office but not enough to guarantee victory in all Commons' votes, especially on the European issue, a subject on which the Tory Party was increasingly fractured. In this context, the Ulster unionist contingent at Westminster would find opportunities to exercise leverage on government policy for Northern Ireland in return for their support. Relatedly, the safeguarding of the Union in a wider British sense – supposedly under threat from Labour's devolution plans for Scotland – emerged as a central Tory theme during the election, one which they considered vital to their victory and which undoubtedly worked in the Ulster unionist interest. Certainly the NIO team appointed after the election was decidedly pro-unionist.

The unionist negotiations with the Dublin government failed to produce significant results, especially in regard to articles 2 and 3 of the Irish constitution, and with Strand Two in deadlock the whole talks process once again came to a halt. Yet their collapse was not accompanied by the usual recriminations. The participants issued a statement stressing a positive outcome in terms of a clearer understanding of each other's positions, with the possibility of future progress (Cox, 1996; Bew *et al.*, 2002). But the persistent failure of talks between the constitutional parties to make substantive progress had already moved Hume to seek a way forward by a more unorthodox route.

Hume and Adams Confer

What would become known as the Hume–Adams initiative began with a series of talks held in the course of 1988. Hume had been persuaded by Fr Reid to meet Adams, the latter keen to involve the SDLP in his own initiative, as was the Irish Taoiseach, Charles Haughey, then pursuing his own secret contacts with Adams, but fearing the consequences of public association with the PSF leader and therefore keen to use Hume as a go-between. Adams, impressed with Haughey's 'anti-British' stance during the Falklands War and after, had apparently contacted the Irish leader at the same time, or shortly after, his approach to the British, and presented a set of proposals that included elements destined, in somewhat varied form, to become central features of the 1998 Agreement. Crucially, they included a re-definition of the principle of self-determination to incorporate the need for unionist consent by specifying the Irish people as consisting of two traditions, the consent of both being necessary to a settlement of the Ulster problem. It was a radical departure from republican orthodoxy, as was another proposal which re-defined British withdrawal to mean a declaration of constitutional disinterest and a promise not to dictate or influence the outcome of all-party talks – a declaration intended to nullify section 75 of the Government of Ireland Act which gave Britain power to veto a settlement of the Ulster problem, even one agreed by Northern Ireland's political representatives. In fact, the British response to Adams's approaches had included such an assurance; however the PSF leader was concerned to have private assurance translated into public policy and needed Haughey's assistance to do so.

Adams brought the same set of proposals to his meetings with Hume. Hume, however, was kept in ignorance of the Adams–Haughey contacts to date, and for long afterwards was convinced, as were most commentators, that the peace process began with his meetings with Adams. The meetings, which also came to include delegations from PSF and the SDLP, ran over 1988; however, the prospect of substantive peace talks was still remote. The Army Council of the PIRA was apparently ignorant of the far-reaching nature of Adams's proposed compromises; the destructive armed struggle was ongoing and constituted a public contradiction of Adams's private initiatives; and Margaret Thatcher was an unlikely partner for negotiations with the republican movement. However, the Hume–Adams talks were significant as a conditioning process that demonstrated to party activists the ability of former bitter enemies to engage in meaningful dialogue, dialogue which introduced into their political discourse many of the key concepts and language of the peace process, while also giving what had hitherto been secret contacts a public identity – the Hume–Adams process – and, moreover, through Hume's involvement, respectability for Adams. Further, when the public talks ended, secret contacts between Adams and Hume continued (Moloney, 2002).

If the progress of the peace process was slow, it nevertheless did exist. In February 1989, Charles Haughey told the Fianna Fail Ard Fheis that an end to PIRA violence would open the way to a broad nationalist campaign to persuade unionists of the merits of a partnership of equals with their nationalist fellow-countrymen, and the British government that the future of Ireland should be left to all the Irish people to decide for themselves. In November 1990, Peter Brooke sought to encourage the development of republican non-violence with the statement that Britain had 'no selfish, strategic or economic interest' in Northern Ireland – a statement made on Hume's prompting with the intention of validating an argument he had made to Adams, but also informed by Brooke's own prior contacts with Adams. The statement would become one of the central building-blocks leading to the PIRA ceasefire. But more importantly, just three weeks after Brooke's 'neutrality' statement an internal Tory Party crisis forced the resignation of the republican hate figure, Margaret Thatcher, and her replacement by John Major, who had no personal and negative Irish baggage. Also, changes in the bureaucracy at the NIO brought the arrival of senior officials with a supportive approach to the peace process (Moloney, 2002), while world events were also working to provide a congenial environment for progress.

PSF had argued that, in the face of the Soviet threat, a vital strategic interest of Britain in Ireland had been the need to counteract the weakness in Western defences occasioned by Irish neutrality. But with the unravelling of the Soviet bloc at the end of the 1980s that argument lost credibility. In October 1991, Hume and Adams produced a document which, after many changes, would emerge as the Joint Declaration of 1993. The purpose of the paper, entitled 'A Strategy for Peace and Justice in Ireland', was to find common ground in the ideological positions of all parties. Framed within the context of the AIA, its key features included self-determination; a statement of British neutrality on Ulster and Ireland generally; a special emphasis on agreement between the North's divided communities; and the establishment of institutions of government, North and South, which would respect the diversity of the Irish people but allow them to expand common ground in order to build the necessary trust for an agreed future. In this context the Dublin government would establish a permanent Irish Convention in order to plan and implement the steps and policies required to break down community divisions.

Although it did not demand it, it was clear that these developments presupposed the existence of a PIRA cease-fire. Also, in accordance with Adams's ideas, it framed the British position in a very different way from that in which PIRA had traditionally conceived it: Britain was now a part-ner with Dublin in the search for an agreement. The most crucial aspect of the document, however, was its attempt to address the republican demand for self-determination, which, it declared, could not be achieved without the people of Northern Ireland:

> the principles of self-determination would be recognised and acknowledged, but nationalists would be conceding that unionists had rights. Partition would still be in place, for the moment at least, but it would continue, not because Britain wanted it, but because Irish nationalists were, in the

exercise of self-determination, granting unionists the right to choose it. The border would therefore exist by nationalist choice rather than British imposition (Mallie and McKitterick, 1996: 120).

Hume took the document to the Haughey government, which duly informed John Major. But it was only when Albert Reynolds, who succeeded Charles Haughey – forced to resign over a scandal involving telephone tapping – as the leader of the Fianna Fail government in January 1992, that progress on the initiative quickened.

A Dublin Boost

Reynolds, fully briefed by his predecessor on the state of play, was more adventurous than Haughey. More willing to take risks, he would be largely responsible for effecting the PIRA ceasefire of August 1994. He made the initiative his primary concern and got Major, whom he already knew and was friendly with, to pursue it jointly with himself. Moreover, during the British general election of April 1992, PSF provided peace hints with a document entitled 'Towards a Lasting Peace'. Although the continuing violence of the PIRA – especially the massive bomb at the Baltic Exchange in the City of London on 10 April which caused damage estimated at £700,000,000, over £1,000,000 more than all the compensation paid out in Northern Ireland since 1969 – determined that it would receive little immediate attention, it was of major significance in marking out the political distance PSF had travelled since 1987.

The document was framed in the light of recent developments which had been seen to undermine the traditional republican position on reunification. It accepted that there was now no significant constituency for traditional republicanism in the Irish Republic. Adams effectively encapsulated the organisation's new position when he said that republicans might have to accept 'interim phases and interim arrangements' while still being committed to the aspiration of a united Ireland. Tellingly, armed struggle was now described as an option of last resort. But Adams was prepared to move further in the direction of a peaceful strategy. A new PSF paper in June 1992 moved away from the April document, which sought to commit Britain to Irish unity within an agreed period, and now gave the principle of consent much greater prominence. The British were asked to commit themselves, not to Irish unity, but to self-determination, while the consent principle was accorded fundamental significance. These proposals registered a radical shift away from traditional republican notions of an Irish settlement, and when ideas consistent with them were aired at the annual Provisional address at the grave of Wolfe Tone at Bodenstown in the same month confusion was sowed among the assembled republican faithful, ignorant of the true nature of Adams's political agenda. What was important, however, was that the London and Dublin governments took note of the new departure. Taken as a whole and with some minor changes, the document, known as 'Hume–Adams', would be sent to London a year later as the basis for a PIRA cessation. In the meantime, its existence remained secret. Publicly, attention became focused on the Mayhew follow-on to the Brooke initiative (Coogan, 1995; Mallie and McKittrick, 1996; Moloney, 2002).

In the light of his contacts with Adams, however, it seems likely that Hume regarded the talks as little more than a preliminary to the real negotiations that would take place following an end to paramilitary violence. Mayhew repeated Brooke's guarantee of an 'imaginative' British response in that event and signalled it by removing the ban on Irish street names.

The Ulster problem, however, seemed as intractable as ever in the spring of 1993. The violence continued with the PIRA bombing campaign showing no sign of letting up, either in the North or England, where a bomb at Warrington in March killed two small boys and injured 56 people. Loyalist paramilitaries continued their grisly murder campaign against the Catholic population in general, and nationalist and republican politicians in particular. Moreover, the Major government was seen to move closer to the Ulster unionists, whose votes would be needed in a forthcoming Commons vote on the social chapter of the Maastricht Treaty.

At the same time, however, given the future of both Ireland and Britain in Europe, the EU was being sold to the republicans by the British as a context within which both parts of Ireland would gradually come 'to be as one'. They were also assured of Britain's acceptance that there could be no solution to the Ulster problem without republican participation. In this context, the Opsahl Commission, established to assess the Ulster problem on the basis of popular, rather than elite or party political opinion, published a report in early June which recommended a form of power-sharing government for Northern Ireland, informal government contacts with PSF, and that if the party rejected violence, it should be allowed into talks.

The privacy surrounding the Hume–Adams talks ended in April 1993, when evidence of their meeting was confirmed by a joint statement in which the objectives of the meetings were spelt out. The expected condemnation from unionists was duly forthcoming, but there were also signs of unease from within the SDLP and concern in Dublin that publicity would enlarge the difficulty of bringing Britain on board. Yet, a significant sign of progress also emerged when the Army Council of the PIRA, on the basis of the June 1992 document, expressed approval of the Hume–Adams initiative, though accompanied with the traditional demand for a British withdrawal. This was not obtainable, and Reynolds, deciding that the process had went as far as it could, decided to present the 1992 document, as it stood, to Major.

Coming in the midst of the PIRA bombing campaign, having trouble with his own right-wing, and increasingly dependent on unionist support as his parliamentary majority diminished, Major was in no position to offer active support.

Indeed, when Hume and Adams went public in late September – against the advice of Dublin – saying they had made significant progress on the path to peace, he pressed for the whole initiative to be abandoned. This appeared quite likely when, a month later, a mishandled PIRA bomb attack on the Shankill Road resulted in the death of the bomber, Thomas Begley, and nine others. Gerry Adam's decision to attend the Begley funeral and carry his coffin made perfect sense in terms of maintaining his credibility with the republican movement; however, it angered Major and intensified his opposition to the Hume–Adams initiative. The inevitable loyalist retaliation for the Shankill bombing – itself provoked by the loyalist murder campaign – in which six Catholics were killed in Belfast and a further eight during an attack on a Hallow'een party at a bar in the village of Greysteel, county Londonderry, brought the total killed to 23, all in the space of a week (Bew and Gillespie, 1993, 1996; Coogan, 1995; Mallie and McKittrick, 1996).

Retrieving the Initiative

Seeing that radical political surgery was necessary if the gains made during the Hume–Adams talks were not to be lost, Reynolds used a European Community summit meeting in Brussels at the end of October to persuade John Major that they, as the two government leaders, should take the initiative in pursuing the peace process. Accordingly, a joint communique was issued after the summit, in which secret negotiations with terrorist organisations were rejected, together with a statement that any proposals had to come from London and Dublin. Thus, politically contaminated by his association with Adams and, implicitly, with republican terrorism, Hume's achievement could only be saved if its author was abandoned.

But while this was Reynolds's reading of the situation, it was soon obvious that it was not Major's. Major had come

away convinced that he and Reynolds had agreed to abandon
the avenue Hume had taken to achieve peace in favour of
inter-party talks. And deadlock between the two governments might thereby have ensued had not a public reaction
in Ireland against media attacks on John Hume for his association with Adams not emboldened Reynolds to raise the
political stakes with London. At his party's annual conference, on 7–8 November 1993, Reynolds was forced to publicly recommit himself to the Hume–Adams process. With
the force of Irish public opinion behind him he even
declared that, if necessary, he would walk away from John
Major and put forward his own proposals.

At this point, however, the scope of the initiative began to
widen. Originally intended to wean the republican movement away from violence, this remained its primary objective,
but the idea then took hold that it should be aimed at loyalist paramilitaries and unionists as well. Both London and
Dublin were worried that its original focus, if persisted with,
would spark a wave of unionist anxiety. Accordingly, steps
were taken through the Church of Ireland Archbishop of
Armagh, Dr Robin Eames and Revd Roy Magee, a
Presbyterian minister, to assess unionist concerns so that they
could be addressed in any future declaration. The result was
a list of six points, which included the rights to free political
thought, to pursue constitutional reform by peaceful means
and to equality of opportunity, that would find expression in
the Joint Declaration promulgated by Reynolds and Major in
December 1993. They were included on the understanding
that they addressed unionist concerns when, in fact, they
were offered by loyalists to reassure Catholics, which was not
quite the same thing. Major, however, remained sceptical of
the whole enterprise, neither endorsing or rejecting it, and
when a Dublin leak about a 'framework document' on
Northern Ireland revealed the southern government's
demand for a major say in the North's affairs he evidently
decided to abandon the whole process in favour of renewed
inter-party talks.

Shaped chiefly with unionist concerns in mind and apparently produced by Mayhew, whose attitude to the Hume–Adams initiative was at best lukewarm, a British 'alternative' document in early December dealt with the question of self-determination in a statement to the effect that each part of Ireland should be able to determine freely and without coercion whether or not a united Ireland should be established. At the same time Reynolds's acceptance of unionist concerns about articles 2 and 3 of the Irish constitution was stated. But there was never any chance that Dublin would accept this arbitrary attempt to side-line the strenuous efforts nationalists had made to bring about a PIRA ceasefire. Dublin had hardly time to respond when news of the British government's own secret contacts with PSF emerged to create an embarrassing controversy. Major was on record as having stated that the idea of negotiating with Gerry Adams made his stomach turn, and had assured unionists that no contacts had taken place. The controversy intensified when British documents, intended to demonstrate the limited nature of those contacts, were compared to more convincing PSF copies of their correspondence with the British, and shown to have been substantially falsified. On 1 December Sir Patrick Mayhew admitted to 22 inaccuracies in the British version of the documents.

But dismay and a sense of betrayal extended beyond the unionist community to include members of the RUC and the NIO, whom had also, in good faith, been denying the existence of British-PSF contacts. It was in Dublin, however, that indignation was greatest. Major had not infrequently lectured Reynolds on the inadvisability of talking to terrorists. Now Reynolds' fury at British 'double dealing', expressed directly to Major during an ill-tempered Anglo-Irish summit on 3 December, was such that the British alternative document was immediately buried. Major was persuaded to revive the joint initiative with Reynolds, with 15 December set as the date of publication (Bew and Gillespie, 1993, 1996; Mallie and McKitterick, 1996).

The Joint Declaration

The centrepiece of the Declaration, drawn from the 1992 document, was a statement to the effect that Britain agreed that it was for the two parts of Ireland, if they so wished, to establish a united Ireland through agreement, freely and concurrently given. The attempt was made thus to address both the nationalist aspiration to unity and the unionist anxiety about being coerced to accept it. As to the latter the most significant addition to earlier drafts was the inclusion of the six points supplied by the loyalists together with a substantial section intended to reassure unionists of their rights and the commitment of both governments to the principle of consent. Nevertheless, it was not a document shaped primarily with unionist sensibilities in mind. Its thrust was the conciliation of republicanism, though very much in the sense of Adams's revisionist ideas. Unionism was guaranteed the constitutional status quo on the basis of majority will, but with the clear indication that the document's framers did not regard them as authentically British (Cox, 1996; Moloney, 2002).

The Joint Declaration was widely welcomed in Britain and Ireland, with even the unionists, after an uncertain start, putting up no significant protest against it. The popular republican reaction, however, was distinctly hostile. The document made no concession to the demand for a British withdrawal, while at the same time 'consent' was now raised to a principle of the utmost importance. And the document's revisionist nature was immediately apparent. As one Belfast republican put it: "if we accept this we accept that everything we stood for in the last 25 years is for nothing" (Moloney, 2002: 413). Yet, a decision to reject the Declaration would have been costly. It would not only have undermined Adams's partnership with Hume, but would also have been likely to provoke a severe security reaction, North and South. Irish opinion, given the recent slaughter, was yearning for peace. But at the same time, acceptance of the document, given its limited nature from the republican perspective, could only have resulted in internal division.

Consequently, the republican leadership decided to make no immediate public decision, but, at Adams's urging, to buy time by calling for 'clarification' of its contents, something John Major immediately refused, thereby initiating a stalemate that would last for months. The only attempt to assuage republican feelings came from Reynolds. A 20-year ban on television and radio interviews with PSF was lifted while a Forum for Peace and Reconciliation was established in Dublin as evidence of his concern to bring republicans to the negotiating table, and these measures undoubtedly made an outright rejection of the Joint Declaration undesirable (Coogan, 1995; Bew and Gillespie, 1996; Mallie and McKittrick, 1996; Moloney, 2002).

The tortuous process by which the Joint Document emerged served to illustrate some of the most fundamental characteristics of the Ulster problem, especially in regard to the British role. As in previous phases of the problem, they had failed to develop a positive conception of what that role should be, with the result that it largely came to be determined by whichever of the indigenous actors – PSF, SDLP, Dublin, the unionists/loyalists – could exert the most pressure at any given time. This state of affairs would not change.

Towards the Cessation

Ostensibly, the Joint Declaration heralded a new departure in the handling of the Ulster problem. In reality, pre-existing mindsets continued to determine political developments. The SDLP and Dublin remained anxious to press forward in the hope of bringing the PIRA campaign to an end. London, antagonistic to the republican movement, determined to oppose it at every opportunity, but with limited success. Thus, the determined efforts made by Major to prevent Gerry Adams from getting a visa to enter the USA in January

1994 resulted in humiliation when those efforts, publicly reported, failed.

That they did so indicated how well Hume, Reynolds and Adams's own contacts had mobilised Irish-American opinion, and also the increasing receptivity of the Clinton administration to their efforts. That receptivity went back at least to the presidential campaign of 1992, when two influential Irish-Americans, Niall O'Dowd and Bruce Morrison, brought together a group of wealthy members of that community to support Clinton. Now they were able to persuade him that, against the background of the Joint Declaration, allowing Adams a visa would give him a glimpse of the political opportunities open to republicans if they gave up violence, and would accordingly be a significant contribution to the peace process.

British failure on this occasion presaged similar disappointments as the year wore on, seeming to illustrate just how devalued the 'special relationship' between the USA and Britain had become. It was all the more galling to British sensibilities that Adams proved highly adept at courting the American media and political community. In fact, Adams's task in the USA was much easier than that of holding the republican military and political wings together on the same course. A series of PIRA attacks on Heathrow airport in April 1994, designed, apparently, more to create publicity and to sustain morale among the republican rank-and-file than to inflict damage, nevertheless caused great injury to the political gains Adams had made in America. In May, Major threw the political onus back to the republicans by providing a statement of 'amplification' in reply to their call for 'clarification'.

The statement addressed several PSF areas of concern but without any hint of the British withdrawal it had set its hopes on. Nor was this a real likelihood. It would only have undermined the pledge given to the unionists. But the time that had elapsed between the demand for 'clarification' and the eventual 'amplification' worked to Adams's advantage.

The republican movement got used to the idea of cessation, making it easier for him to put his case.

A novel aspect of the British document was a hint that, in return for an amendment of articles 2 and 3 of the Irish constitution, the Government of Ireland Act of 1920 could be amended, a hint regarded by nationalists as evidence of British concern to address the issue of self-determination. At any rate, the 'amplification' document served to break the political log-jam at a time when the loyalist murder campaign had developed a ferocious intensity, outdoing republicans both in numbers killed and in the depravity of the acts committed. The most appalling was the random murder of six Catholics watching a televised football match in the hamlet of Loughinisland, county Down, on 18 June 1994. However, hopes that a republican conference in late July to review the peace process would produce a breakthrough were dashed when the Joint Declaration was roundly condemned. The reality was rather different from the appearance, condemnation of the Joint Declaration being something the leadership had to endure as the price of keeping the republican movement united behind it. But the political consequence of such criticism was to induce serious misgivings among the parties to the peace process. In particular, tensions between Dublin and London were revived, with Sir Patrick Mayhew making plain his concern to promote inter-party talks, believing that unionists would respond generously to an amendment of articles 2 and 3 of the Irish constitution.

His efforts were frustrated by the determination of Reynolds and Hume to pursue a PIRA ceasefire. A definite signal that those efforts were not fruitless came in mid-August 1994 when Danny Morrison stated publicly that the republican movement had moved away from demanding a British withdrawal and were thinking in 'different time scales', considering whether a totally unarmed strategy (TUAS) might bring about 'a just settlement, however defined'. This was a neat encapsulation of the way the Adams faction had worked to shape the development of republican thinking since the late 1980s. But it was also indicative of Adams's political methodology that TUAS was simultaneously presented to the politically unreconstructed republican rank-and-file as meaning Tactical Use of Armed Struggle.

By the end of the month the movement was convinced that the road to a democratic 32-county socialist republic could now best be pursued by creating a broad consensus with the SDLP and constitutional nationalism in the South, in a context in which the Irish-American lobby in the USA was exerting a powerful influence on the Clinton presidency, and with support expected also from the European Community (Cox, 1996; Mallie and McKittrick, 1996; Moloney, 2002).

The Paramilitary Ceasefires

It was confidence in the alliance with Dublin and the SDLP that enabled the republican movement to declare 'a complete cessation of violence' on 31 August 1994 despite the fact that no specific concessions had been made by the British government. The basis for it was a 14-point proposal in which the Dublin government promised to respond to a ceasefire by removing all restrictions on the functioning of PSF as a political party; work with it and the SDLP to pursue a pan-nationalist settlement of the Ulster problem; move quickly towards the release of PIRA prisoners; work to persuade the British government to scrap all restrictive measures against PSF, re-open border roads and deal speedily with PIRA prisoners in British jails; and make sustained efforts to persuade the Clinton administration to remove restrictions on republicans – especially to allow a member of the Army Council entry to the USA to reassure supporters there before a ceasefire was announced – and engage with nationalists in pursuing a peace settlement. Militarily, the PIRA would cease all warlike activities, North and South, as would the Irish and British forces – the latter well aware of the impending ceasefire through various intermediaries.

Agreement on these terms allowed the PIRA to declare an open-ended ceasefire on 31 August 1994. It was the culmination of a long process stretching back to the mid-1980s and incrementally shaped by diverse factors, including botched PIRA operations; the activity of informers and the undermining of the 'Tet offensive'; British military sophistication; the need to 'dovetail' the war according to the needs of the increasingly important political agenda, designed by the Adams strategy to steer the republican movement in a direction few were fully aware of; the effects of the grisly loyalist murder campaign; and also, it should be noted, the example of Derry, where a de facto ceasefire, carefully constructed between the local PIRA and British forces through the mediation of peace groups, had been in place well before 1994: all were factors taking the Provisionals to a position which the leadership had repeatedly claimed was wholly unacceptable – ceasefire without British withdrawal (Moloney, 2002). It was, accordingly, essential to reassure the republican grass-roots about the new departure.

This was done by keeping the precise terms of the ceasefire secret, describing the ceasefire as a 'suspension', or by the Irish term, *sos*, meaning 'pause', and by claiming that a great victory had been won and celebrating it. In fact, it was a victory of hope over reality. The fundamental reality of the Ulster problem for republicanism had been spelt out in the Joint Declaration, with its insistence that Irish unity could only come about with the consent of a majority in Northern Ireland. PSF's final position on the Declaration, indicated in the statement announcing the ceasefire, was to note its significance but to reject it as the basis of a settlement, something which could only come about through 'inclusive negotiations'. Quite how negotiations would bridge the vast gap between republican and unionist perspectives was not inquired into too closely. For the present, Adams, the President of PSF, had an increasingly favourable media coverage at home and abroad, while the Irish government and the SDLP created the impression of political movement through a publicity event in Dublin at which Hume, Adams and Reynolds declared themselves totally committed to peaceful means to resolve the Ulster problem.

For unionists the announcement of the PIRA ceasefire was a source of some unease, activating suspicions about a possible secret deal between the British government and republicans. But as these fears proved unfounded loyalist paramilitaries came to reciprocate with their own ceasefire on 10 October, an outcome to which David Ervine, the most personable of loyalist fringe politicians, made an instrumental contribution. This provided the occasion for the emergence of a new political party associated with UVF, the Progressive Unionist Party (PUP), fronted by articulate spokesmen such as Ervine and Billy Hutchinson. They would work closely with Garry McMichael of the UDA-linked Ulster Democratic Party (UDP). Surprisingly, both these parties would be more conciliatory in approach and more open to negotiation with republicans than either the UUP or DUP (Sinnerton, 2002). These parties were reluctant to accept that the PIRA ceasefire was genuine, while Ian Paisley refused to negotiate with republicans under any circumstances.

The most important reaction, however, was that of the Major government. It had not expected a complete cessation of PIRA activities, but there was to be no 'flexible and imaginative' response such as Peter Brooke had promised in 1990, and which had been so influential in initiating the peace process. Instead, the suspicions of the republican movement remained, and were expressed in a set of further tests of its genuineness. The first was a public insistence that the cessation be declared not just 'complete' but 'permanent', something that was seen by republicans as an attempt to humiliate them and was met by a refusal to comply. Gradually, as the peace held, a 'working assumption' was made that it was permanent, but then another test of republican credibility emerged. The British made plain that there would be no quick engagement in talks. Major envisaged a period of up to two years before these would take place, a prospect that contradicted assurances given by Hume and Reynolds to Adams and which would put the ceasefire at risk. The danger in the British position was summed up by a Dublin government source in September 1994: 'It can't be permanent until they say it is; the longer the British take to say its permanent the more they undermine the chances of it truly becoming so' (quoted Mallie and McKittrick, 1996: 340).

At the same time, however, while the stance the Major government was taking was inconsistent with the promise made by Peter Brooke in 1990, and was not even hinted at in the Joint Declaration, it was, nevertheless, clearly prefigured in public statements made by Major and Mayhew in the autumn of 1993. These specified plainly that before PSF could be involved in substantive negotiations there would have to be a total PIRA ceasefire, followed by a sufficient period of time to assess its effectiveness, and also by the surrender of arms to demonstrate the PIRA's good faith. It was also made plain at this time that Britain would not be a persuader for a united Ireland (Bew and Gillespie, 1996).

The British response to the PIRA ceasefire was determined by a number of factors. Personally Major's only acquaintance with republicans was through their violence. The Ulster politicians he knew were unionists whose support at Westminster he was increasingly dependent on to remain in office. He was, therefore, inclined to heed their advice on how to deal with republicans. The intelligence services, moreover, were a poor guide to the republican mentality in general and to current developments within the movement in particular, while Sir Patrick Mayhew had shown no great insight into the Ulster problem and had been highly doubtful about the Hume–Adams initiative from the start. At the same time, republican activities gave some colour to British suspicions. Punishment beatings, a means by which the PIRA enforced its authority in the urban ghettoes, continued to be inflicted, while during an 'unauthorised' PIRA robbery in Newry, county Down, a postal worker was shot dead.

But the most serious threat to the peace process came from an unexpected quarter. Soon after the Newry robbery, Albert Reynolds's government collapsed over a controversy about his handling of the case of a pedophile priest wanted in the North. Reynolds's administration was replaced by a Fine Gael-led coalition with Labour and the small leftist party, Democratic Left. The accession of the new government was a disappointment to the republican movement. Fine Gael's history had been one of antagonism to militant republicanism, while its leader, John Bruton, was more concerned about addressing unionist sensibilities as a basis for political accommodation than that of republicans. Once in office he committed himself to the peace process, but he lacked the enthusiasm for the enterprise that had fired Reynolds and moved distinctly closer to the British attitude to the Provisionals (Mallie and McKittrick, 1996; Moloney, 2002).

In January 1995, some signs of political movement emerged. PSF representatives met government officials at Stormont, while in the South government ministers held the first formal talks with republicans. On 22 February the Framework Documents were published. These were two documents agreed between the London and Dublin governments dealing, respectively, with how a form of government acceptable to the two communities in the North could be established, and how relations within the island of Ireland and between Britain and Ireland could be established to the mutual advantage of all. The documents were not blueprints for implementation but, in the context of an ongoing political process, guidelines to resolving difficulties that had emerged in previous negotiations. In the main, they presented a scenario for the future premised on the basis of Northern Ireland's continued membership of the United Kingdom and stressing unionist consent, but with the stipulation that the involvement of nationalists should be formally expressed through an increased Dublin input, most visibly through new cross-border institutions (Bew and Gillespie, 1996; Mallie and McKittrick, 1996).

As with most Anglo-Irish initiatives since 1985, the expected favourable reaction of British and Irish nationalist opinion was matched by unionist opposition based on the belief that its ultimate purpose was to deliver Northern Ireland into an Irish republic. Alternatively, they stressed the importance of an internal settlement as providing the most realistic way forward (Cochrane, 1997). The republican leadership, exploiting its new respectability and media attention, and having embraced the politics of 'process', ignored the documents' unpalatable aspects and read their 'real' significance as indicative of a historical tide that was declaring partition to have failed. Colour was given to the republican view in April when, after much prompting from Hume and Dublin, the British government agreed that meetings could take place between PSF and ministers (Bew and Gillespie, 1996).

Yet, the Framework Documents were not to signal a rapid transition to all-party talks. A new condition for republican engagement in talks had emerged in the 'decommissioning' issue. Speaking in Washington on 7 March, Sir Patrick Mayhew outlined a three-point plan defining the specific terms on which PSF would be allowed into political negotiations. Popularly known as 'Washington 3', it stipulated: (i) the demonstration of a willingness to disarm progressively: (ii) agreement on the method of decommissioning weapons: (iii) a beginning to the process of decommissioning as a 'confidence building measure' (Bew and Gillespie, 1996). The rest of 1995 would be taken up with this issue. Decommissioning came as an unpleasant surprise to the SDLP and Dublin. It had not been formally proposed previously as a condition for negotiations, though in substance it was publicly bruited by Mayhew in late 1993. There was no precedent for it in recent Irish or international history and any attempt to have proceeded on that basis would have killed the peace process at birth. Gerry Adams did not reject decommissioning but saw the issue being settled in the process of building a comprehensive settlement, and British insistence on it as a condition for entry to talks soon came to be seen by republicans as an attempt to humiliate and defeat the PIRA, something the British had failed to achieve on the battlefield.

Republican suspicions were enhanced by the fact that prior decommissioning, if accepted, would not prevent a return to violence if a peace settlement broke down. Much PIRA materiel was in the form of home-made explosives, which could easily be manufactured, something the security forces were well aware of. Accordingly, and given the loyalist rejection of it, they had advised ministers against insisting on decommissioning as a precondition for talks. That Major persisted with it is largely explicable in terms of intelligence sources on the republican movement – not always nuanced and insightful – his problems with the nationalistic right-wing of the Tory Party, and his parliamentary dependence on the unionist MPs. In this context, their views on how the peace process should be dealt with would have been influential.

Accordingly, while a PSF delegation headed by Martin McGuinness met the NIO minister, Michael Ancram on 10 May, and the PSF President, Gerry Adams, met with Sir Patrick Mayhew in Washington on 24 May, no progress was made. Republican frustrations increased, moreover, with British reluctance to make concessions on the prisons issue. Unlike Dublin, which began early releases soon after the ceasefires began, London did nothing until September 1995 when it increased remissions from one-third to one-half. The latter had been in force until 1989 and its restoration meant that only 40 prisoners would benefit from the new rules. Relatedly, the Home Office proved reluctant to transfer Irish prisoners from British to Irish jails (Bew and Gillespie, 1996; Mallie and McKittrick, 1996; Moloney, 2002)

On the ground the ceasefire continued but in an increasingly fraught atmosphere, with tensions occasioned by Orangemen insisting on marching through Catholic areas in July; disturbances in Belfast and Derry in mid-August; and the controversial release, after only two years, of Private Lee Clegg, a paratrooper jailed for life for the murder of a girl travelling in a stolen car. In sum:

> Sectarian tensions were heightened in 1995 because both
> nationalists and unionists were looking at events for sub-
> liminal messages about potential political trends on a wider
> level. Thus, increased re-routing [of Orange parades]
> would be taken by some to indicate a greater Dublin influ-
> ence in Northern Ireland's internal affairs, while less may
> be regarded by others as evidence of British government
> insincerity over the peace process (Cochrane,1997: 337).

The centrality of the marching issue as an interpretative
framework for assessing the constitutional issue for unionists
was quite brilliantly expressed by Ian Paisley at Drumcree in
July 1995: 'If we don't win this battle all is lost, it is a matter
of life or death. It is a matter of Ulster or the Irish Republic,
it is a matter of freedom or slavery' (Paisley quoted in Bew
and Gillespie, 1996: 108).

By August 1995, the ceasefire had been in place for a year
with little to show for it from the republican perspective. Nor
were the prospects for progress enhanced in September, when
James Molyneaux, increasingly compromised by the misplaced faith he had invested in British politicians going back
to Margaret Thatcher in 1985, was succeeded as party leader
of the UUP by David Trimble. Trimble had enhanced his
credibility with the unionist population through a leading
role in the 'Siege of Drumcree' in July. He was credited, along
with Ian Paisley, with the 'victory' that enabled Orangemen to
march through the Catholic Garvaghy Road area of
Portadown on their way home from an annual religious service at Drumcree Anglican Church (Cochrane, 1997).

Trimble, however, while continuing Molyneaux's hard line
on the ceasefire in general, made the intriguing suggestion
in early October that he would be prepared to talk to PSF in
an assembly even if no arms were handed in. This was taken
as a cue by the Major government to consider an election to
such a body, and the idea took specific form as a result of the

setting up of a commission to report on the decommissioning issue. Dick Spring had originally proposed such a body in June, but it was only decided upon hurriedly at an Anglo-Irish summit in late November as a way out of the political deadlock, in advance of President Clinton's impending visit to the North. Headed by former US senator, George Mitchell, together with Harri Holkei, former Prime Minister of Finland, and a Canadian general, John de Chastelain, it was due to report in January 1996 (Bew and Gillespie, 1996; Mallie and McKittrick, 1996).

The Mitchell Report

The setting up of the Commission did not indicate a sea-change in the fortunes of the peace process. London still remained committed to decommissioning. When the Mitchell Commission reported on 22 January 1996 its major conclusion that *prior* decommissioning was unobtainable and that decommissioning should proceed in parallel with political negotiations – each of the participants having accepted a list of six anti-violence statements – it was effectively rejected by John Major. Instead Major declared that progress could only be made either through prior decommissioning or the holding of an election in Northern Ireland to provide each party with a popular mandate as a basis for meeting in a discussion Forum. It was a statement which delighted unionists and infuriated the nationalist-republican camp, which saw it as evidence of lack of commitment to the peace process and the extent to which the unionists were dictating the government's stance. Major's action also diverted attention away from the problems that the six 'Mitchell principles' on non-violence could cause for republicans. It is noteworthy that Gerry Adams did not commit himself unequivocally to the Mitchell Report; he welcomed it generally as a basis for 'moving forward'.

Whatever the appearances, however, it is important to see Major's stance in the light of the fundamental problems involved in getting Ulster unionists and republicans to the same negotiating table, quite apart from the much more problematical task of reaching an agreement that both sides – whose stated objectives were incompatible – could accept. There were, thus, some very awkward realities that the politics of 'process', with its ambiguities, could not disguise forever. Accordingly, Major's opting for elections to a Forum for Northern Ireland in which, as Trimble had already indicated, he would be prepared to talk to PSF, may have seemed a useful acclimatising and time-buying exercise that could make the possibility of meaningful negotiations between these bitter enemies more likely. That such a procedure also facilitated Tory interests in the House of Commons was merely a happy coincidence. At any rate, Major persisted with the election option, rejecting as premature a proposal by Dick Spring that they might adopt the procedures employed in the Bosnian negotiations, whereby intermediaries shuffled between bitterly opposed adversaries who did not actually have to meet personally. It was at this stage, with relations between Dublin and London on the peace process difficult and distrustful, that the whole exercise effectively came to an end with the massive PIRA bomb at Canary Wharf in London's dockland area on 9 February 1996, killing two people and causing massive destruction costing around £100,000,000.

The reason given by the PIRA for the bomb was the undermining of the analysis outlined in the unarmed strategy. Not only had the 'imaginative' response to a republican cessation of violence promised by Peter Brooke not been delivered on, but on the Irish side, John Bruton not only lacked the credibility with the republican movement that Albert Reynolds had established, but was too sympathetic to unionist and British concerns while maintaining pressure on republicans. Moreover, it appeared that the British thought that the longer the ceasefire lasted the more difficult it would be for the PIRA to reactivate their campaign. The Canary Wharf bomb demonstrated how erroneous such thinking was (Mallie and McKittrick, 1996).

For a Prime Minister determined not to allow republicans into negotiations until they were deprived of any political leverage the possession of arms might give them, the London bombing proved highly effective in moving Major to set a firm date for the opening of all-party talks, and to suggest that the republicans could become involved if the PIRA called another ceasefire. The bomb, however, together with a successful attack on Thiepval barracks in Lisburn, the British army's headquarters in Northern Ireland, also, paradoxically, appears to have assisted Gerry Adams's efforts to retain the republican movement's support for his problematic peace strategy. Deeply critical of the way the strategy was working out and its apparently deleterious impact on PIRA effectiveness, these high-impact bombings put the organisation in better heart than would otherwise have been the case when an extraordinary PIRA convention met to review the peace process in early October. The upshot was that despite suffering setbacks and a verbal mauling the Adams faction emerged with its ability to shape the republican movement's political direction intact (Moloney, 2002).

Drumcree '96

The procedure for initiating all-party talks – acquiring a democratic mandate through elections to a discussion forum – was proposed by Trimble and argued against by Hume, on the basis that it was unnecessary and was likely to strengthen extremist parties. And so it proved. Both PSF and, to a lesser extent, the DUP increased their vote compared with the general election of 1992. Nevertheless, both elections and an assembly were important to unionists for reasons that did not apply to nationalists; the first to ensure that any negotiations undertaken were not vulnerable to the charge of lacking a mandate from the unionist people, the second as a means of establishing a physical symbol of the integrity of Northern Ireland that would elevate the 'internal' dimension to the talks process, insulating it from the Dublin interference that had caused unionists such anxiety during the Brooke– Mayhew initiative. No less importantly, such a body, with its inevitable unionist majority, was seen by unionists as a means of controlling the talks process. Both elections and the Forum proposal were accepted by the SDLP. But the price of acceptance was the de-coupling of the Forum from the negotiating process. It would still function as a symbol of Northern Ireland, but deprived of any substantive political role (Cochrane, 1997). And as its proceedings became engulfed in endless acrimonious debate it became symbolic of Northern Ireland in a way the unionists had not quite intended. Moreover, from the start the talks process faltered.

Barred from the negotiations after the collapse of the PIRA ceasefire, PSF, whose performance in the elections to the Forum registered the party's best ever performance, 17 seats and 15.5 per cent of the votes, boycotted the institution. The talks process, moreover, soon got bogged down in procedural wrangles. When, on 31 July, the Chairman, George Mitchell, called a break until September, the issues on the agenda – the topics for discussion and the order in which they would be dealt with – had still not been settled. And the political environment worsened significantly in July as a result of the controversy over marching rights in Portadown. Given the experience of July 1995 – a compromise between Orangemen and residents allowing a limited number of marchers to proceed through the area without bands was celebrated afterwards as an Orange triumph – a controversy here was inevitable.

The RUC acceded at first to the Catholic residents' demand that the march should not be allowed through the area – another more direct and convenient route was available. But a crisis developed from Sunday 7 July when the Orangemen refused to disperse. It continued until 11 July, during which time civil disorder on a scale unseen since the UWC strike of 1974 engulfed Northern Ireland. In this period, encouraged by the unionist leadership, Orangemen paralysed the North through the erection of roadblocks, unhindered by the security forces. At the same time, a wave of attacks on the homes of policemen and Catholics, churches and businesses occurred. The crisis worsened dramatically on 11 July when unionist leaders threatened to call on Orangemen across the North to attempt to march in nationalist areas, virtually a threat to initiate civil war.

Faced with this scenario the RUC abruptly reversed its policy and proceeded to force the Orange procession down the Garvaghy Road, vigorously beating the protesting residents out of the way. Widely seen in Ireland, Britain and abroad as a capitulation to loyalist thuggery, the consequences of Drumcree '96 were profound. On the ground it provoked disorder in nationalist areas, the response to which was seen to exhibit anti-Catholic bias. The nationalist violence, much more geographically confined than the loyalist protests, occasioned the discharge of 5500 plastic bullets causing 40 casualties, in contrast to the 400 used during the Drumcree stand-off, which inflicted no injuries. In the biggest episode of demographic re-alignment in 25 years 600 families suffered 'ethnic cleansing', while up to £50,000,000 worth of damage to property was inflicted. A boycott of Protestant shops began in certain areas, which put some out of business. Loyalists began an abusive picket of a Catholic Church in the Harryville area of Ballymena, county Antrim that would last 20 months, in protest against a ban on Orange marches in the nearby village of Dunloy. In general, a 'melt down' of inter-community relations occurred, while the already ailing peace process was virtually killed off (Dixon, 2001).

The premise underlying the demand for paramilitary de-commissioning was that the forces of the state could be relied upon to protect the communities whose fears for their safety had led to the growth and tolerance of paramilitary groups in the first place. The Drumcree crisis posed the question of where power within Northern Ireland ultimately lay, and demonstrated that it lay with Ulster loyalism, a conclusion confirmed shortly afterwards by Sir Patrick Mayhew when he candidly admitted that he could not guarantee that such a crisis would not occur again. Gerry Adams's defence of the republican stance on decommissioning was considerably more persuasive among northern Catholics after Drumcree than it was before. But the consequences of Drumcree went further.

The effective consensus of the Hume–Adams position, in the short term at least, was that parity of esteem for the nationalist tradition in Northern Ireland would go hand-in-hand with effective cross-border institutions. Drumcree appeared to demonstrate both the unionist refusal to accept that scenario and that they could mobilise enough force on the ground to give effect to their refusal. Thus, when the inter-party talks reconvened in September 1996, an initiative which never showed much hope of delivering a settlement seemed all the more irrelevant. As the year proceeded to an end the PIRA was gradually intensifying its campaign, though in such a way as to suggest it lacked the ability and confidence to effect any significant political gains.

In late November it presented new terms for a ceasefire, demanding early entry of PSF to talks on the government of Northern Ireland; substantive negotiations to take place within an 'indicative' time frame of six months; no de-commissioning of weapons until a settlement was reached; and 'confidence building' measures such as the early release of prisoners. However, no political movement followed and none was really expected until the new Labour government, elected on 1 May 1997, formulated its Ulster policy in detail. The election registered a breakthrough for PSF when Gerry Adams recaptured west Belfast from the SDLP and Martin McGuinness won Mid-Ulster from the DUP's Revd William McCrea, with the party's overall vote rising to an all-time high of 127,000, thereby enhancing the appeal of a peace strategy. Indeed, Adams provided a quite remarkable indication of his own commitment to peace when, in February 1997, he wrote a letter of condolence to the mother of Stephen Restorick, the last soldier to be killed during the troubles by the PIRA, an organisation whose Army Council he was, apparently, a leading member of (Moloney, 2002).

Another Start

The outlook of Tony Blair's government to the Ulster problem did not differ in essentials from that of its predecessor. Blair made clear that the kind of constitutional settlement to be expected from Labour would not differ significantly from that which John Major would have conceded. Nevertheless, the change of government did influence the quest for a solution.

Shortly after the election Tony Blair came to Belfast with the express purpose of reassuring unionists about the future, declaring himself a believer in the union and ruling out any possibility of a united Ireland until well into the next century. But reassurance for the unionists went together with an all-party political initiative; and he was especially concerned not to let the decommissioning issue stall it. Blair was in a very different, and stronger, position than John Major, constrained as he was by a dependency on unionist support in the Commons and leading a party deeply divided on Europe. With a massive parliamentary majority of 179 and imbued with a radical reformist impulse, Blair was determined to make progress on Ulster no less than on other issues. The new Secretary of State for Northern Ireland, Dr Marjorie 'Mo' Mowlam, more approachable than her rather aloof predecessor – though her arrival was greeted more enthusiastically by nationalists than unionists – struck a position of equidistance between the Ulster parties, demonstrating a concern to bring PSF into the negotiating process on an equal footing with other participants.

In this task she was assisted by the result of the general election held in the Irish Republic in June, which saw Fianna Fail returned to power. Bertie Ahern, the new Taoiseach, reassured republicans by stating that he saw his role as the leader of the whole Irish nationalist family. Just as the defeat of

Fianna Fail by the pro-unionist Fine Gael was one of the factors that undermined the August 1994 ceasefire, so its return to office would be an important factor in the ceasefire's restoration. Moreover, these developments were taking place at the same time as the PIRA's revived military campaign was failing, due to a combination of operational bungling and greater security force effectiveness, and with its ability to recover debilitated by a lack of funds. Accordingly, at the same time as the peace process was reviving, the armed alternative was progressively weakening (Moloney, 2002).

Following an exchange of contacts between PSF and the Labour government – especially a letter of 9 July to the effect that decommissioning would not be allowed to stall political progress and that PSF could remain at the talks even if no PIRA arms were actually handed over, provided the Mitchell principles on non-violence were observed – and indications that the London and Dublin governments would ignore UUP advice to toughen their position on the arms issue, the scene was being set for a restoration of the PIRA's ceasefire. Crucial to this being effected, however, was a 1700-word document communicated by the Dublin government to the PIRA Army Council promising, in the event of a restored ceasefire, a series of measures to include the early release of PIRA prisoners, decommissioning in 'co-operation' with the PIRA, a thoroughgoing reform agenda for Northern Ireland, constitutional negotiations to include the Government of Ireland Act, and the participation of PSF as a full partner in all aspects of the peace process. Of these terms one of the most crucial was the approach to decommissioning, which took into account a decision of the PIRA convention of October 1996 specifying that a decision to disarm could only be made by a PIRA convention, not by the leadership. Ahern's approach sought to allow PSF to establish enough political progress to make the case for it persuasive (Moloney, 2002).

With a new British government keen to pursue the peace process, a rising PSF vote, and with both the Irish government and the Clinton administration having persuaded the British to set a date both for the beginning and end of negotiations – mid-September and May 1998 – the PIRA Army Council, on which the Adams camp had a majority, unexpectedly and without consultation with other Provisional bodies, declared an unequivocal restoration of its ceasefire, to take effect from mid-day on 20 July 1997. However, the terms of the ceasefire, as explained to the PIRA rank-and-file, apparently stressed its limitations, especially its 'tactical' nature and how it would facilitate a return to armed struggle. This was consistent with an already established Adams practice of telling the PIRA grass-roots that what PSF said in public was only for the purpose of political advantage, and should not always be taken at face value. Nevertheless, the issue of PSF participation in peace talks under the terms of the Mitchell principles was so problematic for the PIRA – with the very real threat of a split in the organisation – that adroit manipulation by the Adams camp of another PIRA convention which considered the issue in mid-October, in the Gweedore area of county Donegal, was needed to secure approval (Moloney, 2002).

PSF, meanwhile, had already renewed its contacts with government ministers and taken occupation of offices at Stormont in preparation for the political talks. In this context, it publicly indicated more clearly than in the past that while it would be working for the ultimate objective of a united Ireland, it had its sights set on more immediate reforms to transform the position of the nationalist community in the North.

The government's determination to include PSF in negotiations created severe strains within the unionist family. Whether any major unionist representative would be there to negotiate with them was problematic. The unionist-dominated Forum voted to reject the government's plan for talks, while Robert McCartney's United Kingdom Unionist Party (UKUP) and the DUP refused to have any talks with PSF at all, and departed to embark on an anti-talks campaign across the North.

David Trimble and the UUP, however, while rejecting the government plan, were aware, given the unionist experience with the AIA that they could not afford to simply walk away from the process. Thus, Trimble indicated that he might be prepared to negotiate through the agency of the British government, even if his party was not at the talks table, and distanced itself from the intransigent stance of the DUP on the talks issue by making clear that it was prepared to debate with PSF through the media, while a concern not to be seen as extremist was reflected in a decision to discuss its position with several groups in the North. It was of great symbolic importance that the Catholic Church was included. In fact, Trimble went further. When the talks process resumed in September he led his team, albeit with great belligerence, into negotiations that included PSF. For their part the PSF leadership bruited its entry to talks as the beginning of a project to 'smash' the Union, while its integration into negotiations proceeded with Adams and McGuinness meeting Tony Blair for the first time at Stormont, and the second time at 10 Downing Street in December. The talks process, of course, did not take place in a socio-political vacuum.

Drumcree '97

The intention of the Orange Order to march down the Catholic Garvaghy Road area of Portadown on the way home from their religious service at Drumcree on 6 July, and the eventual decision of the RUC to force the march through the area on the day, initiated, as it had the previous year, serious social disorder in nationalist areas. Nationalist anger in 1997, however, was much more intense and threatened graver consequences.

A number of relevant developments had occurred since July 1996 that affected the parading issue. In Portadown May 1997 had seen both the sectarian killing of a local Catholic man, Robert Hamill – kicked mortally unconscious by a loyalist mob while, allegedly, RUC men sat observing the incident in a police land rover and refusing appeals to intervene – and

the election to Craigavon Borough Council of Brendan
Mac Connaith, spokesman for the Garvaghy Road Residents Coalition, by the highest number of nationalist first-
preference votes ever recorded in the town, and thus
discrediting local Orange claims that the residents group was
unrepresentative of local nationalist opinion. At the beginning of June an RUC man was kicked to death shortly after
leaving a public house in Ballymoney where he had been
jostled by a crowd angry at the role of the police in preventing a loyalist parade in Dunloy. In mid-June the PIRA shot
dead two community policemen in Lurgan, five miles from
Portadown (Ryder and Kearney, 2001).

On the parades issue generally, the disorder initiated by the
Drumcree issue in the previous two years led to the establishment of a review of the parades problem in August 1996.
Chaired by Peter North of Oxford University and two local
clergymen, it was concerned primarily with both the problems
of the differing perceptions of parades held by the two communities, and how the role of the RUC in determining the
outcome of parading issues had led to the increasing politici-
sation of the force. The chief outcome of the review was the
recommendation for a Parades Commission with a five-fold
remit: 'education in community understanding; promotion of
mediation and local accommodation; imposition of conditions on specific parades if mediation failed; reviewing Codes
of Conduct that were to be introduced; and arranging
for contentious parades to be monitored' (Cunningham,
2001: 112). Dependent on Ulster Unionist support in the
Commons, the Major government responded cautiously to
the review body's report when it was published in January
1997, and it was not until October 1997, after the accession of
Labour to office in May, that it would be effectively acted
upon. Thus, while the parameters of how contentious parades
should be dealt with were clearly laid out, and the Orange
Order's recommendation – the 'classification' of parades,
whereby some parades would have a higher status than others
and be exempt from, or subject to, less regulation – was

rejected (Cunningham, 2001; Ryder and Kearney, 2001), no effective procedures for dealing with Drumcree in July '97 were in place and the likelihood of a repeat of the previous year's mayhem all too likely.

On taking up the post of Secretary of State for Northern Ireland Dr Mowlam entered enthusiastically into negotiations with both the Orange Order and the Garvaghy Road Residents Coalition, though with foreboding that it may already be too late to retrieve the situation and angry that the Major government facilitated this by failing to effectively act on the recommendations of the North commission. Moreover, her relations with the Orange Order quickly deteriorated, as the staid unionists found Mowlam's casual informality and sometimes vulgar manner of speech offensive. Her relations with the Garvaghy residents, who found her informality refreshing, were initially much better. But this seems to have facilitated the latter gaining the impression that the march would not proceed through their area without their agreement.

It was clearly how she wished to proceed; however, as the options for a resolution of the Drumcree issue disappeared in June the ultimate decision on the parade would lie with Ronnie Flanagan, the Chief Constable of the RUC, and his decision to allow a 'controlled' march on the Garvaghy Road was not taken until the early hours of the 6 July and was based on a simple security calculation. Inevitably, the decision to force the march through was perceived as an act of betrayal by the residents, and nationalist anger intensified two days later when a confidential government document was leaked, which indicated that on 20 June, two weeks before the march, Dr Mowlam and the security chiefs were agreed that the 'least worst solution' at Drumcree was for an Orange march of limited numbers to proceed along the Garvaghy Road. Dr Mowlam's claim that the document was only a 'discussion' paper, and not a secret plan to be implemented after she had gone through the motions of consultation, was not convincing.

As a decision for the RUC, Drumcree was viewed narrowly as a public order issue, shorn of its wider political ramifications. The decision to allow the march was made on the basis, as in 1996, that not to allow it would occasion far greater violence from loyalists. As such, it was a decision devoid of any consideration as to the justice of the march or equity of treatment between marchers and residents. Moreover, following the march Dr Mowlam gave every impression of allowing other contentious marches through nationalist areas – in Derry, Newry, Belfast and Armagh – to proceed on exactly the same basis. The inevitable disorder ensued over four days: 60 RUC officers and 56 civilians were injured and 117 arrests made; 2500 plastic batons were fired in response to 402 highjackings, the throwing of 1506 petrol bombs and 815 other attacks. The ambulance service responded to 500 emergency calls.

But the marches controversy of 1997 was not simply a repeat of 1996. For in the wake of the crisis then Catholic residents groups, with strong PSF involvement, had grown up across the North, and the significance of that development was now made apparent. Following Drumcree '97 the activities of these groups were co-ordinated for the purpose of mass protests at the site of contentious Orange marches in the days leading up to the annual Twelfth of July celebrations. In a context of rising sectarian attacks and paramilitary violence Northern Ireland looked set for civil disorder exceeding that of 1996. Then, unexpectedly, the deepening crisis was defused by decisions of the Orange Lodges in contentious areas not to proceed along their traditional routes; decisions taken after consultation with the Ronnie Flanagan, the Chief Constable of the RUC, and in which he painted a black picture of republican inspired disorder – for which Orangeism would get the blame – across Northern Ireland if they did so (Ryder and Kearney, 2001). The statements of explanation emanating from the Lodges all reflected this concern.

A reasonable interpretation of the events from the Drumcree march to the Twelfth would be that, in a context where decisions respecting parades were being made on the basis of which side posed the greater threat, the mobilisation of residents associations presented marchers and police with a threat that could not be ignored. In 1997, the result was the diffusion of the parades crisis with much less violence and disorder than anyone expected; and, indeed, took place in a context where, to facilitate PSF's political agenda, PIRA active service units were ordered not to engage the loyalist rioters and protesters.

Indeed, the most positive development of this period, the re-instatement of the PIRA ceasefire on 20 July, provided the basis for an attempt to have an agreed march by Apprentice Boys in Derry on 9 August. It was only partially successful. A pageant commemorating the siege of Derry went off peacefully, but the subsequent march by Apprentice Boys descended into violence when drunken bandsmen broke ranks and attacked nationalist by-standers.

Contentious parades were a reminder that any peace settlement for Northern Ireland had to resolve issues on the streets no less than in the conference chamber, a point made in another way when the 'Continuity IRA' exploded a massive car bomb in Markethill, county Armagh, in September.

5

AGREEMENT AND RESOLUTION?

Scene Setting

The new year opened with depressingly familiar developments. The killing of the LVF leader, Billy Wright, in the
Maze prison on 27 December 1997 provoked an inevitable
round of retaliatory killings by the organisation in early
January. But at the same time, the ability of sectarian violence
to de-stabilise the search for peace – a recurrent development
since 1968 – was substantially weakened. The determination
of the Blair government to drive the peace process forward
was reinforced by the determination of the new Tory leader,
William Hague, to maintain the bi-partisan approach to
Northern Ireland, while the re-admission of PSF to the talks
process in September 1997 and its signing up to the Mitchell
principles; the appointment of the Canadian general, John
de Chastelain, to oversee the weapons issue; the endorsement of David Trimble's leadership by the UUC, which gave
him the freedom to make decisions in the talks process; and,
not least, the fact that the major loyalist paramilitary organisations continued to maintain their ceasefires (McKittrick
and McVea, 2000; Cunningham, 2001) – all were powerful
factors conducive to political progress. But no less important

was the departure from the talks process of the DUP and the UKUP. Their departure left the process in the hands of parties willing to reach a compromise settlement.

The Path to Good Friday

The beginning of substantive negotiations on 23 September brought together the representatives of the British and Irish governments and eight political parties, PSF and UUP entering the process – in which unionists and republicans would meet for the first time in 75 years (Dixon, 2001) – with a belligerence that belied the inevitable compromises that a negotiated settlement would entail.

On 12 January, the British and Irish governments produced a joint document entitled 'Propositions on Heads of Agreement'. It consisted of a single document, but established the framework for the settlement arrived at on Good Friday 1998. The document was an initiative intended to break an impasse in the talks due largely to the lack of an agreed agenda for discussion, especially on a devolved assembly. It originated with Blair, and while it reflected the three-stranded 'totality of relationships' between Britain and Ireland that had been a central theme of John Hume's political agenda, it had yet a distinctly unionist flavour, reflected in a recommendation that an agreement should include a Council of the Isles – favoured by David Trimble as a counter-weight to the 'unity' focus of the North–South bodies – and with references to a 'constitutional understanding', commitment to the 'principle of consent' and changes in articles 2 and 3 of the Irish constitution, together with the subordination of North–South institutions to the northern Assembly – a clear gain for unionists against strong republican opposition – and the Dail respectively, instead of the institutions having free-standing, autonomous status as nationalists and republican desired. A new British-Irish Ministerial Council would also be established.

181

With an agenda for discussion agreed by mid-January the central issue of the negotiations was clearly established – how to reach a compromise between the SDLP and UUP positions. The debate was clarified on 29 March in a Downing Street document which balanced nationalist concerns about 'cross-community' decision-making on key issues with a 'unionist' executive proposal positing a Liaison Committee whose composition would be determined proportionately, or by bringing together the Assembly secretaries of departmental committees. Substantial differences remained about the form of an Executive; nevertheless, by 1 April agreement between the SDLP and the UUP was reached on a number of issues, that is, the d'Hondt proportionate system for the allocation of posts, and Assembly committees with secretaries and chairmen and with the power of policy formation. Also, it was agreed that the Assembly would have a legislative role and that representatives to the North–South Council would be there to fulfil the wishes of the assembly (Hennessy, 2000).

A spur to further progress came on 25 March when George Mitchell set 8 April as the deadline for the conclusion of an agreement; and, when it came, that agreement was based on nationalist/Irish government concessions to unionists on Strand Two (North–South) and consequent unionist concessions on Strand One (Northern Ireland government). One was dependent on the other. It was vital to the UUP claim to have secured the Union that the North–South Council should not be free-standing with executive functions; and that objective was secured when nationalists – apparently under pressure from Tony Blair – accepted that an overall settlement was impossible without the concession that the Assembly should have the authority to determine decision-making on North–South issues, though nationalists were assured that the North–South Council would not be an empty shell: six areas of co-operation were identified (Mitchell, 1999; Hennessy, 2000). It was the case that unionists conceded, in the interests of 'balanced' constitutional change, the abolition of the Government of Ireland Act, but this was acceptable following assurances from Downing Street that the act had no bearing on Northern Ireland's constitutional position as part of the United Kingdom. Moreover, while Trimble recognised that concessions would have to be made on Strand One, Reg Empey, a key member of his negotiating team, had already been having doubts about the 'co-ordination and decision-making' effectiveness of the unionist committee proposals and was prepared to move in the direction of power sharing anyway. Power sharing did not affect the constitutional issue, and was not the issue that brought down the Sunningdale Agreement of 1974. With the constitutional question settled to unionist satisfaction the final matters to be settled were prisoner releases and the decommissioning of paramilitary weapons (Hennessy, 2000).

Of apparently lesser significance at the time to constitutional matters, these issues received less minute and sustained attention, and would – especially decommissioning – return in the future to hamper the implementation and working of the Agreement arrived at on Good Friday 1998. It was, for instance, a mistake to many that no functional linkage was made between these two questions. On Trimble's reading decommissioning was implicit in the commitment PSF made to the democratic and peace political means embodied in the Mitchell principles. Moreover, he received assurances in a letter from Tony Blair – whose active engagement during the final stages of the negotiations sidelined the distrusted Dr Mowlam, and was crucial to the making of the Agreement – to the effect that provisions of the settlement dealing with parties ineligible to hold office due to paramilitary associations would be reviewed as to their effectiveness, and that the government's view was that decommissioning should begin immediately. Having gained the support of his mercurial Deputy Leader, John Taylor, Trimble threw his weight behind the settlement (Mitchell, 1999; Hennessy, 2000; Cunningham, 2001).

It was effectively made between the UUP, the SDLP and the two governments. The inclusion of PSF was crucial to the settlement's feasibility, but its maximalist demand for Irish unity – essential to its credibility with the grass-roots of a republican movement whose adjustment to the realities of the politically possible was a difficult process – left it sidelined from effective bargaining. At the same time, this was a politically astute stance. The essentials of the Agreement had already been settled to Adams's relative satisfaction, and with the SDLP as the apparent sole negotiators on behalf of the nationalist community, it could be made to carry the responsibility for any features of the Agreement that might prove distasteful to the republican community. PSF's mere participation in the talks process allowed it to gain the kudos from so doing – presenting the Agreement as a major advance on the road to Irish unity – while also leaving greater freedom to adopt a critical attitude to its implementation, and thus appearing to be a more reliable defender of minority interests. Unlike the relationship between paramilitarism and constitutional politics in the unionist community, there is no psychological or ethical barrier to the practitioners of the former, in the right political circumstances, expanding decisively onto the territory of the latter. Accordingly, with the military option effectively abandoned PSF, despite continuous political abuse from the UUP and temporary suspension from the negotiations due to republican violence, maintained its support for the peace process.

The participation of the political representatives of the major loyalist paramilitary groups, the PUP and UDP, in the peace process was also essential to the making of the agreement finally arrived at; and their experience was similar in some respects to that of PSF, especially with regard to temporary suspension and in the limited nature of their contribution to the negotiations – the most significant aspect of which was probably a meeting between Gary McMichael and Bertie Ahern in which McMichael stressed the necessity of meeting unionist demands on Strand Two.

The Agreement

If the Agreement concluded on Good Friday 1998 is best seen as the realisation of John Hume's ambition to achieve a settlement that addressed the 'totality of relationships within these islands', it also demonstrated how complex and multi-faceted those relationships were.

The first section dealt with the crucial constitutional dimension, emphasising the interlocking and interdependent nature of the new institutions; and that the principles of consent and the formulation of self-determination were as set out in the Downing Street declaration of 1993, declaring impartiality of treatment for everyone by whichever government had jurisdiction over Northern Ireland. However, alive to the fact that in Northern Ireland constitutional status and national identity were, for many, not complementary, the Agreement eliminated any connection between the two, declaring

> the birthright of all the people of Northern Ireland to identify themselves and be accepted as Irish or British, or both, as they may so choose ... their right to hold both British and Irish citizenship is accepted by both Governments and would not be affected by any future change in the status of Northern Ireland (*The Agreement*, 1998: 2).

The document then specified the three-stranded nature of the Agreement. The internal government of Northern Ireland would be the province of an Assembly of 108 members and would exercise legislative and executive functions over matters formerly within the competence of the Northern Ireland departments, and elected by Single Transferable Vote from the existing Westminster constituencies. Also, Members of the Legislative Assembly (MLAs) would be required to declare whether they were unionist, nationalist or 'other' for the purpose of cross-community voting. Specified key decisions, or others which could be so determined through a petition of at least 30 MLAs, would necessitate one of two procedures to be valid, either parallel consent – in which a majority of both nationalists and unionists present and voting had to support a proposal, or a weighted majority, where 60 per cent of MLAs, including 40 per cent of both nationalists and unionists had to be in support. 'Non-key' decisions would be taken by a simple majority vote.

Committees would be drawn from the Assembly both to scrutinise the Executive and aid it in policy formation, with the Chairs and Deputy Chairs allocated in proportion to party strength. The Executive would consist of the First Minister and Deputy First Minister, jointly elected on a cross-community basis together with up to 10 ministers appointed under the d'Hondt system and reflecting party strength in the Assembly, thereby guaranteeing executive positions for those parties with sufficient popular support. Additionally, this section of the Agreement specified the roles of the Secretary of State and the Westminster parliament, and outlined a consultative 'Civic Forum' to be established comprising representatives of business, trade unions, the voluntary sector and others with relevant expertise for a body whose purpose was to promote a civic culture in an ethnically divided society.

Strand Two of the Agreement dealt with the North–South Ministerial Council, which would bring together those with executive responsibilities in the North and the Irish Republic for 'consultation, co-operation and action' on six areas concerning the island of Ireland: transport, agriculture, education, health, environment and tourism. These areas would be dealt with by six implementation bodies, for Ireland waterways, food safety, trade and business development, special EU programmes, language, agricultural and marine matters. Council decisions would be based on agreement by both sides, with each side accountable to their respective parliament. Participation in the Council would be an essential responsibility of those holding Executive posts, a stipulation designed to reassure nationalists who might be concerned that unionists would use every opportunity to emphasise

Strand One – the 'internal' dimension – of the settlement. In fact, the interdependence of both strands was stipulated to the effect that one could not function without the other, though it was also specified any further development of the North–South arrangements would require the assent of the Northern Ireland Assembly.

Strand Three specified a British-Irish Council and Inter-governmental Conference, to be composed of representatives of devolved institutions within the United Kingdom, together with representatives from the Irish Republic, the Isle of Man and the Channel Islands (*The Agreement*, 1998; Cunningham, 2001; Dixon, 2001). The purpose of the British-Irish Council, like the North–South body, would be to discuss matters of mutual concern to its members. However, since participation would be voluntary and its role advisory, it would lack comparable institutional significance; and is best seen as a support for the British identity of unionists.

More significant in this section of the Agreement was the outlining of a new British-Irish Agreement that would subsume the structures established under the AIA and provide bi-lateral cooperation at all levels on all matters of mutual interest within the competence of both governments. These would include non-devolved matters, especially rights, justice, prison and policing in Northern Ireland, strenuous efforts being made by both sides to reach an agreement (*The Agreement*, 1998; Cunningham, 2001).

In particular, it was pointed out that the European Convention on Human Rights was to be incorporated into British law, and would find expression in Northern Ireland in 'a statutory obligation on public bodies to carry out all their functions with due regard to the need to promote equality of opportunity in relation to religion and political opinion; gender; race; disability; age; marital status; dependants; and sexual orientation' (*The Agreement*, 1998: 16). In this context, a Bill of Rights for Northern Ireland was stipulated, together with the establishment of Human Rights and Equality Commissions, and the promise of measures to promote economic, social and cultural rights and progress. In the politically sensitive area of cultural identity the Agreement declared:

> All participants recognised the importance of respect, understanding and tolerance in relation to linguistic diversity, including in Northern Ireland, the Irish language, Ulster-Scots and the languages of the various ethnic communities, all of which are part of the cultural wealth of the island of Ireland (*The Agreement*, 1998: 19).

At the same time, however, special emphasis was placed on the promotion of the Irish language in Northern Ireland.

The remaining section of the Agreement dealt respectively with decommissioning and prisoners, and said little apart from specifying the commitment of the participants to the Agreement to use any influence they had to achieve the decommissioning of all paramilitary weapons within two years, while a complete and unequivocal cessation of activity was stipulated as an essential condition of the early release of paramilitary prisoners, whom it was foreseen would all be released within two years (*The Agreement*, 1998; Dixon, 2001). Parallel with decommissioning the British government would commit itself to making progress towards the objective of as early a return as possible to 'normal' security arrangements in Northern Ireland, consistent with the level of paramilitary threat; in other words, 'demilitarisation' through reductions of crown forces and the dismantling of security installations. For its part, the Irish government would undertake a review of its own security acts covering the period from 1939 to 1985. Lastly, provisions for radical reform of the RUC and the justice system in Northern Ireland were stipulated (*The Agreement*, 1998).

Sunningdale Two?

The obvious historical reference point in assessing the Agreement is the Sunningdale Agreement of 1974. Seamus

Mallon sarcastically described it as 'Sunningdale for slow learners'. But how close are the similarities? Certainly the essential features are the same – power sharing government with an Irish dimension. There are also, however, significant differences. For example, the linkage between Strands One and Two and the explicit subordination of the North–South Council to the northern Assembly did not exist in 1974, while the innocuous nature of the implementation bodies forestall both rejectionist unionist accusations that the North is being trundled into a united Ireland, and republican boasts to the same effect. Furthermore, significant differences exist in terms of procedures, especially in respect of the d'Hondt proportionality in the Executive, reflecting the relative assembly strength of parties – a departure from the governing Grand Coalition of parties in 1974, and complex voting procedures in the Assembly ensuring virtual veto rights in each of the two communities (McDonald, 2001; Wolff, 2001; Bew *et al.*, 2002). Again, what PSF calls the 'equality agenda' – human rights legislation and safeguards, commissions on policing and the justice system, the British commitment to demilitarisation – is another departure from Sunningdale, and can be seen, to some extent, as compensation for the weak nature of the North–South dimension to the Agreement. Certainly, of all the major parties to the Agreement PSF found that its stated agenda – Irish unity – was addressed least. Not only was unity not delivered on, but nor did republicans succeed in convincing Tony Blair of the idea that he should act as a persuader for a united Ireland (McIntyre, 2001).

Probably the most significant difference between Sunningdale and the Agreement, however, is that whereas the former was a settlement framed in terms of the interests of the centre parties, with no involvement by paramilitary representatives, the Agreement of Good Friday 1998 is conceived comprehensively with a concern to address the needs of all parties to the Ulster problem, and thus holds the promise of a complete end to violence. In this context also, it offers to the people of Northern Ireland, to a greater extent, the opportunity to determine their own constitutional future (Ruane and Todd, 1999; Arthur, 2000).

Furthermore, the making of the Agreement of 1998 benefited from an international input unavailable in 1974. Canadian, Finnish and African expertise was drawn on, but the influence of the USA, in the personal commitment of President Clinton, and especially George Mitchell, was crucial (Arthur, 2000). Additionally, the wider constitutional context is different. Devolution in Scotland and Wales makes Northern Ireland 'British' in a way that was not possible formerly, especially in the way that it facilitated the creation of the Council of the Isles; though the specificity of the arrangements in Northern Ireland are different from those that apply in Scotland and Wales.

But it was some aspects of the Agreement that distinguish it from Sunningdale that laid the seeds of the difficulties that would hamper its progress; for example, republican involvement and the decommissioning issue, and the failure to make a functional relational relationship between the two (Bew *et al.*, 2002), though the RUC did not consider decommissioning as a central issue and thought an undue stress on it could produce dangerous splits in the republican movement (Dixon, 2001). More generally, it has been suggested that despite the failure to effect Irish unity, the Agreement delivered an effectively bi-national polity (Patterson, 2001), with symbolic and cultural changes that did much to persuade many in the unionist community that the Agreement was a one-way process of advantage for the nationalist/republican community.

The People's Verdict

The period from the promulgation of the Agreement on Good Friday, 10 April 1998 to the referendum on 22 May which registered the popular verdict on it – North and

South – was short. Nevertheless, positions on the Agreement were struck then which both determined the nature and extent of its endorsement and shaped outlooks for the future.

The Agreement sought to mark a radical departure from the traditional zero-sum character of Ulster politics, where the perception existed that one side could only gain at the expense of the other. Instead a 'level playing field' would be established as the basis on which the politics of Northern Ireland and Anglo-Irish relations would be conducted in future. Instead of zero-sum, Ulster politics would be 'win–win'. Through the Agreement's complex arrangement of checks, balances and safeguards both nationalism and unionism would be validated, and a multi-ethnic civic polity created. However, it was never likely that the debate on the Agreement would rise above the inter-party, intra-party and ethnic divisions of Northern Ireland.

For those parties such as the DUP and the UKUP, which left the talks process on the entry of PSF, the argument of sell-out and betrayal of Ulster was employed from the outset, and was hardly surprising. The UUP, however, whose leadership might have been expected to enthusiastically support the settlement, was riven with doubts and misgivings, and it was soon clear Jeffrey Donaldson represented a significant body of rejectionist opinion within it. Accordingly, David Trimble, whose own personal evolution from right-wing to conciliationist unionism was far from complete, was driven to sell the Agreement in terms of narrow ethno-party advantage, and would come under repeated criticism for failing to enthusiastically promote its overall societal benefits (McKittrick and McVea, 2000). Undoubtedly this task was not made any easier by a republican movement which, since 1994, had brazenly made a virtue of military failure by adopting the line that politics rather than paramilitarism was a surer road to Irish re-unification; and now fastened on the North–South Council and implementation bodies as a significant step on the road to Irish unity, together with the 'equality agenda', especially security, justice and language reform, as real gains that would strengthen the position of the nationalist community in Northern Ireland and thus aid the unity project. Nevertheless, like Trimble, the Adams camp could not take republican endorsement of the Agreement as given. Its control of the PIRA leadership meant that that organisation's reaction was, somewhat surprisingly, unproblematic. Rather it was PSF, ostensibly a party of open debate, which would prove more difficult, especially over the issue of a revived Stormont assembly which most republicans had traditionally regarded with visceral hatred. Indeed, when the Heads of Agreement document of January specified an Assembly Adams felt compelled to repeatedly echo grass-roots condemnation of it.

A consultative Ard Fheis in April provided clear indications of widespread dissatisfaction, and when it was reconvened on 10 May for the purpose of making a definitive judgement on the Agreement a successful strategy was needed to effect acceptance. In fact, realising the position Adams was in, the British and Irish governments had arranged for the wholesale temporary release of PIRA prisoners for the occasion, with the result that a highly emotive event took place in which the permanent freedom of the prisoners was clearly seen to be functionally related to approval of the Agreement. Accordingly, it was endorsed by an overwhelming majority of 331 out of 350 delegates, 94.6 per cent (Moloney, 2002).

With the UUP and the republican movement assessing the Agreement in chiefly party political terms, the only major party actually promoting it as a comprehensive solution to the North's ethno-political problems and the development of a new civic polity was the SDLP, which saw it fundamentally as the embodiment of John Hume's vision of the political future for Northern Ireland, the benefits of which were self-evident. Accordingly, the party's approach to the referendum campaign tended to be somewhat complacent (Dixon, 2001). In the event, enthusiastic support for the Agreement as a means of ending the North's sectarian divisions came chiefly from the Prime Minister, Tony Blair;

the Tory opposition, concerned about the continued existence of paramilitary violence, paramilitary-related parties
in government, and the decommissioning issue, offered only
qualified support.

The government moved quickly, both to provide legislative
effect to the provisions of the Agreement and to rally support
for it in the run-up to the referendum. Tony Blair visited
Northern Ireland three times during the campaign, largely to
support David Trimble, aware of the particular difficulties he
had in selling the Agreement to the unionist community and
offering a sweetener in the form of increased public expenditure (Cunningham, 2001). Certainly support was needed.
Anti-Agreement unionists were united behind the powerful
negativism of Ian Paisley's DUP, supported by six of the
10 UUP Westminster MPS, the Orange Order, and Jeffrey
Donaldson exploiting the lack of a clear linkage between
republicans in government and decommissioning, as well as
prisoner releases and the 'threat' to the RUC suggested by
policing reform (Bew *et al.*, 2002).

Thus, while the pro-Agreement parties, especially PSF and
the UUP, used the campaign to address their varying and
incompatible political agendas, rejectionist unionists had a
clear single message that proved highly effective in diverting
attention away from Trimble's success on constitutional safeguards for their community. They were aided undoubtedly
by the triumphant welcome given to recently released PIRA
members convicted of bombing and kidnapping in London
in the 1970s at the Ard Fheis organised by PSF to debate the
Agreement in May. Intended to demonstrate support for the
settlement from one of republicanism's vital constituencies,
it nevertheless played powerfully to the emotive negativity
of rejectionist sentiment (Dixon, 2001; McDonald, 2001;
Bew *et al.*, 2002; Patterson, 2002).

The weakness of the rejectionist case, however, was the failure to produce a realistic alternative to the Agreement that
addressed the unionist position. For the unionist community
in general the shadow of the AIA still hung over the whole

political process. The necessity of demolishing its effectiveness by bringing political power back to the unionist community, combined with a pro-Agreement campaign that had powerful media and political support from home and abroad, enabled Trimble to mobilise a considerable swathe of unionist opinion that was not usually politically engaged to endorse the Agreement at the referendum on 22 May.

At 81 per cent the referendum saw the highest turnout ever in Northern Ireland: 160,000 more people voted than had turned out for the previous Westminster general election, though in the Irish Republic only 56 per cent of the electorate did so. In Northern Ireland 71 per cent of the electorate endorsed the Agreement. The figure was impressive, but it disguised a serious weakness. For while the nationalist/republican community gave it overwhelming support, only a bare majority of the unionist community approved it. According to an exit poll conducted by the Irish television company, RTE, 51 per cent of Protestants voted yes compared to 99 per cent of Catholics (Dixon, 2001).

The failure of the unionist community to more fully support the Agreement demonstrated the depth of unionist fears and suspicions about constitutional reform, based on a combination of anti-nationalism and anti-Catholicism. Certainly the most powerful politio-religious organisation in the community, the explicitly anti-Catholic Orange Order, whose leader, Robert Saulters, publicly suggested that Tony Blair was unfit for office because he had married a Roman Catholic (Ryder and Kearney, 2001), had been a consistent opponent of power-sharing and was unlikely to agree to a system that included nationalists and Catholics in government. Further, the declaration by the PIRA on 30 April that it had no plans to decommission its weapons also played powerfully in the anti-Agreement interest.

At the same time, pro-Agreement unionist leaders failed to offer inspired leadership, with Trimble, Taylor and Ken Maginnis, either going on foreign holidays, or focusing on other issues, while party managers made the mistake of preparing for elections to the Assembly in June rather than the referendum. Thus, while five weeks before polling day 90 per cent of Catholics in Northern Ireland supported the Agreement, only 62 per cent of Protestants did so. In mid-May Catholic support was still holding up at 87 per cent, but Protestant support had fallen to 36 per cent, with the issues of greatest concern to 'no' voters being, respectively, release of paramilitary prisoners followed by 'the beginning of a move towards a united Ireland' (Hennessy, 2000; McDonald, 2001). Despite the fact that the Northern Ireland Act of 1998, which gave validity to the provisions of the Agreement, specified the primacy of domestic law over international agreements and that Westminster retained sovereign power over Northern Ireland (Hennessy, 2000), the rejectionist exploitation of unionist fears had substantially nullified what constitutional reassurance the act afforded.

Moreover, despite assurances from Tony Blair during the referendum campaign on paramilitary decommissioning designed to bolster pro-Agreement support, these assurances were not followed up by legislation making a functional connection between decommissioning and the release of paramilitary prisoners; nor was such a relationship established between decommissioning and republicans in government. Accordingly the result of the elections to the Assembly in June recorded the worst ever UUP result in non-European elections. The DUP came within 3 per cent of the UUP vote, with the anti-Agreement unionists winning 27 seats, just three short of the number needed to deadlock the Assembly: 'The high turn-out for the referendum campaign, which was thought to have brought out "Yes" voting unionists, was not repeated for the Assembly elections' (Dixon, 2001: 274).

The first meeting of the Assembly saw David Trimble elected to a shadow Executive as First Minister designate in readiness for the devolution of power, with Seamus Mallon as Deputy First Minister designate, developments which reflected party strength in the Assembly:

UUP	28
SDLP	24
DUP	20
PSF	18
Alliance	6
UKUP	5
PUP	2
NIWC	2
Others	3

The results of the referendum and the election, however, failed to provide the kind of popular endorsement for the Agreement needed to make a convincing new beginning in Northern Ireland politics; and developments on the streets would soon demonstrate the continued virulence of community divisions.

Drumcree '98

It was inevitable that the annual crisis over the Orange march at Drumcree would have a special significance in 1998. Having been defeated in the referendum on the Agreement, it was only too likely that rejectionist unionists would shift the terrain of debate on the issue, and the public and national awareness that annually attended the Drumcree controversy made it a tempting site. As Jeffrey Donaldson was to remark:

> The nature of the protest changed after the Agreement and referendum. Drumcree became not just symbolic of a stand for Protestant civil rights but a stand, also, against the ideals underpinning the Agreement, including the partici-pation of Sinn Fein-IRA in government. It was regarded by many Orangemen as the last stand (Donaldson quoted in Ryder and Kearney, 2001: 257).

Accordingly, for rejectionists, the Drumcree issue became again what it was for Paisley in 1995 – a synecdoche for the Ulster crisis in general – the part which subsumed the whole. And when the usual ritual of attempted negotiations between residents and marchers failed to reach a compromise there was the inevitable descent into civil disorder. But the disorder was more intense and vicious now, because unlike previous years the legally established Parades Commission had issued a ban on the Portadown Orangemen marching on the Garvaghy Road and the government had pledged to uphold it. For the Orangemen, however, the ban was not the product of an objective assessment of the Drumcree issue but an expression of the Agreement agenda to betray Ulster. Certainly that a relationship between Drumcree and the Agreement existed – though not the one imagined by the Orange Order – was accepted by all sides is clear; for the anti-Agreement unionists and loyalist paramilitaries such as the LVF disorder generated by the Drumcree issue might engulf Northern Ireland and the settlement with it. The scene-setting had already taken place with the burning of 10 Catholic churches on 2 July and 400 attacks on the security forces over the following four days. David Trimble, the Orange hero of Drumcree '95 was now recast as a Lundy and was himself highly anxious that a prolonged impasse at Drumcree could fulfill the ambitions of the rejectionists (McDonald, 2001).

With the Drumcree crisis now invested with wider political dimensions, the passions it generated were reflected in an escalating level of disorder. One 24-hour period, for example, in which Orange roadblocks were constructed across the province, assisted by loyalist paramilitary involvement, resulted in '384 outbreaks of disorder, 115 attacks on the security forces, 19 injuries to police, with petrol bombs thrown on 96 occasions, 403 petrol bombs seized, 57 homes and businesses damaged, 27 vehicles hijacked and another 89 damaged' (McKittrick and McVea, 2000: 223). In Portadown passions among the Garvaghy Residents were as high as among the Orangemen. When Seamus Mallon,

Deputy First Minister designate, gave voice, in the company of David Trimble, to an SDLP view that the situation required resolution by 'accommodation' between both sides, his arrival on the Garvaghy Road met with a hostile reception from residents erroneously suspecting a 'dirty deal' in the offing (Ryder and Kearney, 2001).

The civil disorder and violence unleashed by Drumcree continued until the early hours of 12 July, when, against a background of loyalist death threats to Catholics living in the Carnany Park housing estate at Ballymoney, county Antrim, a UVF petrol bomb attack on the Quinn household resulted in the incineration of three young brothers, Richard, Mark and Jason. The shock across the community at the attack brought the Drumcree protest to a shuddering halt. The association between the two, and the Orange Order, was immediate, while the latter's response, which included the suggestion that the attack was nothing to do with the Orange protest but had its source in drug dealing, was an irresponsible and wholly unjustified slur on the stricken family (McDonald, 2001; Ryder and Kearney, 2001). Despite protests of Orange non-involvement, the Order would have known, from the experience of previous years, that to extend the Drumcree protest from Portadown to include the six counties as a whole was only too likely to result in heightened sectarian violence and to create an environment where the Carnany atrocity was likely. That the moral stain of the killings was attached to the Order was wholly understandable. Also, in a wider political context, the context in which the existence of the Agreement was threatened by the fallout from Drumcree, the atrocity undoubtedly served to remove its immediacy. The Agreement's prospects, moreover, benefited from the consequences of a more serious atrocity a month later when the 'Real IRA' exploded a massive bomb in Omagh killing 29 with hundreds wounded, an appalling atrocity which did much to discredit physical force republicanism and enhance the attractions of the peace process.

In fact, before the Omagh Bomb the LVF declared a cease-fire, and after it the INLA followed suit. At the same time, that unreconstructed mentalities would persist to complicate the Agreement's progress was indicated by demands from extremist elements in the Orange Order that Trimble and a colleague, Denis Rogan, who had attended the funeral mass in Buncrana of children killed in Omagh, be expelled from the Order for so doing; a striking example of insensitivity – if not outright bigotry – and an indicator of the value placed on Catholic lives by many in the organisation (McKittrick and McVea, 2000; McDonald, 2001; Ryder and Kearney, 2001).

The Way Forward

Northern Ireland came out of a long hot summer with more reason to be optimistic than might have been expected. Nevertheless, the results of the referendum and the Assembly elections had clarified the obstacles in the path of implementing the Agreement. In particular, the divisions in the unionist community left David Trimble's room for political manoeuvre severely restricted, especially on the related issues of decommissioning and republicans in government. Undoubtedly republican movement on decommissioning would have significantly strengthened his position.

At the same time, decommissioning had to be handled delicately by the republican leadership. Armed force, as republicans saw it, was a legitimate response to state oppression while the possession of arms was evidence that the PIRA had not been militarily defeated. Decommissioning, accordingly, carried the inevitable import of defeat. Concerned above all to maintain unity within a movement that was being effectively sold partition as a route to reunification, and including elements that remained suspicious of the whole project, it was simply not possible for Gerry Adams to facilitate Trimble on decommissioning without a substantial *quid pro quo*. Accordingly, the terms he set for progress on this issue were the implementation of all aspects of the Agreement, especially policing reform. Until then the PIRA would continue to remain inactive: unionists needed to appreciate the historical significance of the ceasefire. From the unionist perspective, however, an intact paramilitary organisation with representatives in government represented the politics of threat and was simply unacceptable (Bew *et al.*, 2002). As the political process resumed after the summer break it was already clear that the dynamic of Agreement politics in the future would lie in the tense and mistrustful PSF–UUP relationship, a relationship that would sideline significantly the SDLP, left urging 'commonsense' on its recalcitrant partners.

The autumn of 1998 saw a number of developments, informed by the need to make progress on the implementation of the Agreement. PSF declared violence to be a thing of the past and nominated Martin McGuinness to speak to the arms decommissioning body. Tony Blair and President Clinton travelled to Omagh to meet the relatives of the dead, but also called at Stormont to offer encouragement to the new Assembly members. Additional positive noises came from David Trimble, who adapted the slogan 'a Protestant parliament for a Protestant people' in pledging himself to creating a 'pluralist parliament for a pluralist people', and from Bertie Ahern, who suggested the establishment of a timetable for the handover of paramilitary weapons.

The continuing gap between pro-Agreement aspirations and Northern Ireland's sectarian realities, however, was also evident, not least in loyalist resentment in Portadown at the outcome of the Drumcree crisis – a permanent Orange presence was established on Drumcree hill, manned by Harold Gracey, the District Master of Portadown Lodge – and in a continuous stream of sectarian attacks on local Catholics, in the combating of which a Catholic-born RUC officer, Frank O'Reilly, was killed by a bomb blast. Against this background the clarification of positions on the decommissioning issue took place, with Trimble emphasising to the UUP annual conference in October that it was an essential condition for PSF membership of the Stormont Executive, while John

Hume replied pointing out that the Agreement made no explicit connection between the two, but that it was the will of the people that decommissioning should take place (McKittrick and McVea, 2000).

The Trimble and Hume statements on decommissioning were significant. They clarified the central site of controversy over the issue – the difference between the spirit and the letter of the Agreement. But as the year drew to a close the political mood was largely upbeat. Hume and Trimble were jointly awarded the Nobel prize in December, though with some reason Trimble stated that the award might be somewhat premature. His position was a difficult one, though offset by the failure of the rejectionists to produce a viable constitutional alternative (McKittrick and McVea, 2000; Aughey, 2001; McDonald, 2001).

The dialectic of incremental progress and loyalist violence – especially the killing of the high-profile solicitor for the Garvaghy Road residents, Rosemary Nelson – continued in early 1999, together with rumblings of discontent in the UUP and rejectionist predictions of sell-out. But it was clear that the latter could make little headway unless or until a major crisis on the Agreement arose among the parties to it. At this stage, signals of possible crisis could be detected, but were overshadowed by evidence of political progress and the ongoing implementation of the Agreement, such as a reported doubling of Catholic applications to the RUC since the ceasefires of 1994; UUP plans for a review of the party's links with the Orange Order; a police announcement of the closure of seven border army bases; the confirmation by the Assembly in February of the new government departments and cross-border bodies; the establishment of the Northern Ireland Human Rights Commission in March, together with the signing by the British and Irish governments of treaties establishing the new North–South, British-Irish and inter-governmental arrangements. An investigation into the loyalist killing of Pat Finucane – another prominent nationalist solicitor – in 1989 was instituted, conducted by John Stevens,

Deputy Commissioner of the Metropolitan Police. However, it was also clear that with the passage of 11 months since the signing of the Agreement, the decommissioning problem remained a formidable obstacle to the formation of an Executive. When pressed by Trimble on the issue PSF leaders pointed to the dangers decommissioning posed of a split in the PIRA, and how difficult it would be to effect in a context of ongoing dissident loyalist attacks on Catholic homes and businesses. For his part, aware of the extent to which republican violence was diminishing unionist faith in the Agreement, Trimble argued that to accept PSF in government without decommissioning would be to risk losing the leadership of his party. Inevitably, a deadline of 10 March set for the devolving of power to Northern Ireland passed without effect (McDonald, 2001).

In an attempt to break the impasse the two governments convened new talks between the parties at Hillsborough; however, the issue at stake now between the UUP and PSF left very little room for compromise between them. Satisfying the terms of either side involved such potentially dangerous consequences for the party making the first move that no real progress was likely. Accordingly, another sequenced attempt by the two governments also failed. The difficulty of the decommissioning issue for the PSF leadership was graphically illustrated at Easter when the PIRA declared bluntly that it would not be coerced into surrender under the guise of decommissioning, while Trimble's difficulties were evidenced both in a lack of UUP enthusiasm for a reform of its relationship with the Orange Order and in the UUP performance in the European elections in June, when the party got its lowest ever share of the vote, 17.6 per cent, narrowly avoiding fourth place behind PSF. Responding to these difficulties, Trimble called for the sacking of the 'pro-nationalist' Dr Mowlam. In fact, loyalist violence was much more significant than that emanating from republicans, and had occasioned the killing in Portadown of a Protestant woman married to a Catholic earlier in June.

But Unionists were much less concerned about violence from this source, excusing their emphasis on republican activities as due to the fact that the political representatives of the PIRA were candidates for government while those of loyalist paramilitaries were not.

The summer months saw further unsuccessful attempts by Blair and Ahern to establish a Stormont Executive, with Trimble baulking at the prospect of 'government before guns' (Cunningham, 2001). The one positive development that occurred at this time was the passing of the annual crisis at Drumcree with minimal violence and disorder. Clearly chastened by the events of 1998 the Order opted to settle for a formal protest to the security forces on being prevented from marching on the Garvaghy Road and then to disperse quietly, thus claiming the moral high ground. However, it soon became clear that the Orange policy on Drumcree was based on a misunderstanding, a belief on the part of the Orangemen that Tony Blair had guaranteed them a march on the Garaghy Road at some date in 1999, when Blair had merely expressed the desirability of a march when the circumstances were right (Ryder and Kearney, 2001). The upshot was an intensification of Orange and rejectionist unionist beliefs about treachery and betrayal associated with the Agreement. With all existing domestic options apparently exhausted, and Mowlam infuriating unionists further by declaring in August that the PIRA ceasefire was still intact – despite ongoing punishment beatings, the killing of a west Belfast man and arrests in the USA over alleged PIRA transatlantic gunrunning – Blair and Ahern turned again to George Mitchell.

Mitchell Recalled

Mitchell returned to Northern Ireland to conduct a review of the implementation process in a context where relations between the parties were fraught and soon made worse on the unionist side by the publication of a report into policing by former Governor of Hong Kong, Chris Patten, and which recommended far-reaching reform, including changing the name of the RUC to the Police Service of Northern Ireland (PSNI). Convening the first meetings between the parties at Castle Buildings, Mitchell was struck by the bitterness between them, and the impossibility of progress in these circumstances. Accordingly, he decided on a change of location and moved several of the meetings to London, to Winfield House, the residence of the American ambassador to the United Kingdom, situated in 11 acres of grounds in Regents Park. Moreover, Mitchell clearly took a long view of the route to progress. Setting conditions under which discussions on political matters would take place – for example, none during meal times and a limit of two negotiators from each party – he sought to create circumstances that would allow the bitter antagonisms between the politicians to abate. After ten weeks this strategy did show results. Personal relations were much improved and the unionists were showing sign of softening their line on the 'guns and government' issue (Cunningham, 2001; Trimble, 2001; Mallie and McKittrick, 2002).

At the same time, however, it would be naïve to think that social engineering alone could have removed the most serious obstacle hampering progress on the implementation of the Agreement since April 1998. In fact, a significant political change, intended to address unionist concerns, took place in early October – the replacement of the 'pro-nationalist' Mo Mowlam with Peter Mandelson as Secretary of State for Northern Ireland. In the long unionist memory it was significant that Mandelson was the grandson of the pro-unionist war-time Home Secretary, Herbert Morrison, and indications were already forthcoming that the grandson was of the same ilk. Accordingly, believing that the unionist interest would be safeguarded to a greater extent than had been the case since the signing of the Agreement, and influenced by the former Official republican, Eoghan Harris's views on the advantages of abandoning a hard line on decommissioning, Trimble began to prepare his party for this eventuality at a party conference in Enniskillen on 9 October. George Mitchell could conclude his review of the implementation process in mid-November with the opinion that the basis now existed for the formation of an Executive to take place accompanied by a start to decommissioning through an agreed series of moves between the parties and the two governments.

The specific compromise made by Trimble was acceptance of statements from the PIRA and PSF re-stating the republican commitment to the peace process and confirming that the PIRA would appoint a go-between – Interlocutor – to meet General John de Chastelain's disarmament commission. But his gain, arguably, was even more significant – a republican commitment to a process that had an end-point in disarmament, something republicans had always ridiculed, and with blame for the failure of the Agreement if they failed to do so laid firmly at their door. Moreover, unionist anger at the proposed reform of the RUC was assuaged by the declaration that the force was to be awarded the George Cross, while a new terrorism bill was also announced to replace the Emergency Provisions Act (NI) and the Prevention of Terrorism Act. It was to operate across the whole United Kingdom and apply to domestic and international terrorism, its remit pointing up Northern Ireland's constitutional position (Cunningham, 2001; McDonald, 2001; Mallie and McKittrick, 2002).

Thereafter, progress was quite rapid. On 22 November, Mandelson informed the Commons that Interlocutors would take up their roles on the day that devolution took effect, but that if there was evidence of default on either devolution or decommissioning then the institutions would be suspended. This stipulation was essential. The remaining task to be accomplished before the plan could be implemented was securing the support of the governing body of the UUP, the UUC, and a meeting to effect this was set for 27 November. Certainly UUC support for Trimble could not be taken for granted. It included a large representation of Orangemen whose organisation had publicly declared its opposition to the Agreement while the rejectionists in general were well represented. The meeting had to be carefully prepared for, and to secure UUC approval – especially that of his influential deputy, John Taylor – Trimble promised that he and his ministerial team would resign in February 2000 if the republican movement did not deliver on their promises. It was enough to secure the endorsement of nearly 60 per cent of the delegates, 480 in favour to 239 against (Cunningham, 2001; McDonald, 2001).

Devolution was established on 2 December, with Trimble as First Minister and Seamus Mallon as Deputy First Minister, together with 10 other ministers, including two from the DUP, taking office but not joining cabinet meetings with PSF. The parallel Strand Two and Three institutions were also established; articles 2 and 3 of the Irish constitution, which laid claim to Northern Ireland, were changed and the PIRA appointed an Interlocutor to the de Chastelain commission. But almost immediately problems emerged as the PIRA failed to deliver sufficiently on decommissioning. Accordingly, bound by his assurances to Trimble and, not least, assurances also given to John Taylor – instrumental in persuading the party to support Trimble's devolution initiative – Mandelson moved to suspend the governing institutions, which took effect on 11 February.

The first attempt at devolution was thus short-lived, but it was still significant. What experience there was of it alarmed and infuriated many unionists as Martin McGuinness took up the position of Minister of Education. Thus, while nationalists and republicans found the experience congenial and positive, and were angered by its early demise, the effect within the unionist community was to add passion to the rejectionist argument and misgivings among many of the Agreement's supporters. But more importantly, the procedure which made possible David Trimble's accession to office – debate and prior sanction by the UUC – would offer ample opportunity for attack by his critics in the future, especially so as council rules allowed for a mere 60 members to call a meeting of all 860 delegates to debate party policy at any time. For nationalists and republicans, moreover, not only was the decision to collapse the governing institutions objectionable, but they were angered further in January 2000 by the attitude to the Patten Report of Peter Mandelson.

Mandelson and Policing

Designed to address the related problem areas of police relations with the community, accountability and the transparency of police objectives, Patten recommended, first, a new police authority with a wider range of responsibilities and, departing from the practice of appointment by the Secretary of State, composition drawn from Assembly members of parties represented in the Executive, with remaining members drawn from business, trade unions, the legal profession and the voluntary sector. In the event of devolution members could be appointed by the First and Deputy First Ministers, while to increase its authority the power of the Secretary of State to offer 'guidance' to the police would be abolished and the 'independence' of action currently accorded the Chief Constable restricted to 'operational' responsibility.

Second, Patten advocated the replacement of 'elitist' Community and Police Liaison Committees by District Policing Partnership Boards (DPPBs), composed of committees of district councils and with advisory, explanatory and consultative functions, in addition to facilitating public discussion about annual policing plans. To this end all general principles about policing were to be in the public domain, unless it was in the public interest to withhold them. Further, the role of the new Police Ombudsman, created under the Police (Northern Ireland) Act of 1998, would be proactive rather than limited in function to specific complaints received.

The remaining principal recommendations of the report covered the structure of the force, size, composition, culture, ethos, symbols and human rights. Simplification and rationalization of the command structure to facilitate police–community inter-linkages was recommended. The Special Branch, widely criticised by the nationalist community as a 'force within a force', was recommended for reform and integration into normal policing structures. Reduction in the size of the force was recommended with peace-time conditions in mind, from 13,000, including 1300 part-time reservists, to 7500.

The composition of the force was a vital concern given its overwhelmingly Protestant character (91.7 per cent in 1998). To effect a radical compositional shift to make it acceptable to Catholics a target of 50 : 50 recruitment over 10 years was recommended, while to enhance the feasibility of this objective Patten suggested four significant changes: (i) re-naming the force the PSNI: (ii) a new badge and symbols unconnected with either the British or Irish states: (iii) abandonment of the practice of flying the Union flag from police buildings, with a police service flag flown when one was required: (iv) a new police oath emphasising the upholding of human rights, together with a new code of ethics developed which integrated the European Convention on Human Rights into policing practice (Cunningham, 2001).

The policing issue was a central one in the Ulster problem. Regarded historically by nationalists and republicans as the oppressive arm of the unionist state and largely responsible for the conflict Northern Ireland had experienced since 1969, the abolition of the RUC had been a central demand for many years. For unionists, however, it was a force that had struggled manfully at appalling cost to maintain civilised order against cowardly enemies. Moreover, as a fundamental state institution, it also represented an embodiment of Northern Ireland's Britishness. Accordingly, the radical reforms recommended by Patten seemed to unionists as both a slur on the RUC's policing record and an attack on the Britishness of the region. The cultural and symbolic changes recommended by Patten, together with the abolition of the Special Branch, would be at the heart of the unionist critique of Patten's report.

It was inevitable that Peter Mandelson, in determining his approach to the report's proposals, would be influenced by their sensitivities. He could be seen, as his occasional anti-republican comments suggested (O'Connor, 2002), as offering a counterpart for unionists to the role played by the Irish government in relation to the nationalist and republican communities in the North; and in response to unionist criticisms, bolstered by Conservative support, Mandelson made a number of significant departures from Patten. He declared, for example, that the new police oath would only be taken by new recruits and not existing officers; that the new title would not take effect until the autumn of 2001; that DPPBs would initially have a purely consultative role, while measures would be taken to exclude anyone convicted of a terrorist offence from serving on a DPPB as an independent member. Moreover, a number of structural changes, such as the phasing out of the full-time police reserve and amalgamating Special Branch with the Criminal Investigation Department, would be dependent on the Chief Constable's assessment of the level of terrorist threat (Cunningham, 2001).

The policing bill giving effect to the Patten recommendations was, to say the least, based on a minimalist reading, likely to reduce democratic accountability and transparency of operation, while the fact that at its second reading in June a clause was included specifying an RUC George Cross Foundation to keep the RUC name alive – to demonstrate that the force was not actually being disbanded, and a concession deemed necessary to gaining UUC support for Trimble's policy on 'guns and government' – was evidence of the extent to which Mandelson was inclined to address unionist concerns.

At the same time, in terms of the wider peace process, Mandelson's perceived alignment with unionism served merely to alienate nationalists and republicans in the same way that Mo Mowlam had unionists. More specifically, his police bill provided republicans, unable or unwilling to deliver quickly on decommissioning, with the perfect excuse for not doing so: the need to properly and fully implement the Patten Report remains one of PSF's standard responses to complaints about republican failure to live up to their Agreement commitments. And when the SDLP agreed to operate the procedures established by Mandelson's bill, policing became a useful electoral weapon for republicans in the struggle for political hegemony in the Catholic community.

Re-activating Devolution

Despite the suspension of the governing institutions in February, bitter accusations between the SDLP and the UUP, and a PIRA withdrawal from arms talks, there was no real expectation of a collapse of the Agreement. Rather, the by-now established pattern of talks to re-activate devolution got under way, but the most dramatic and unexpected initiative came from Trimble. Contrary to expectations, he had found that his withdrawal from government did not incur the expected media condemnation in the USA; instead PIRA obduracy on decommissioning tended to be the focus of criticism. Apparently emboldened by this Trimble took the opportunity of a Saint Patrick's Day visit to Washington to suggest that the Executive could be re-established without prior PIRA decommissioning if there were firm guarantees that it would take place. It was a statement that came out of the blue to friend and foe – inside and outside the UUP – alike, and was intended to pressurise Gerry Adams, due to meet President Clinton, to move on the issue.

As he would have expected, it produced the inevitable UUC inquest and also a rejectionist backlash in the form of a leadership challenge from Revd Martin Smyth, a standard bearer for traditional Protestant unionism. The contest took place at the King's Hall on 24 March, and despite ridicule of Smyth from the Trimble camp the result was close. Trimble won by 457 to 348 or 56.7 per cent to 43.22. A contest bruited by the Trimble camp as one to resolve finally the direction of party policy merely gave heart to rejectionists delighted to have done so well with an ageing, indifferent candidate; and who looked forward to ultimate success in the future given that the archaic rules of the UUC allowed for any number of leadership challenges. Moreover, although their attempt to oust Trimble had been defeated they did succeed in passing a motion linking re-entry to talks to the maintenance of the RUC name.

Nevertheless, despite these setbacks, and with a background of hopeful signs throughout April, Trimble continued to expect a PIRA move on decommissioning. His expectations were vindicated in early May when Tony Blair unveiled a plan for the re-establishment of the Executive in conjunction with a commitment by the PIRA to put its arms completely 'beyond use' and the full implementation of the Patten Report. In due course Cyril Ramaphosa, former Secretary-General of the ANC, and Martti Ahtisaari, former President of Finland, were appointed to monitor PIRA arms dumps. For its part, the government continued the process of closing selected security bases.

Yet another UUC meeting followed on 20 May to decide whether the party should go back into government with PSF, with the decision to do so being narrowly endorsed, by 459 votes to 403, a 53–47 per cent split. On 29 May devolution was restored (McKittrick and McVea, 2000; Cunningham, 2001; McDonald, 2001). It would be the longest period of government, lasting until July 2001, when Trimble again resigned accusing the republican movement of failing to take the decommissioning process seriously. But with the restoration of the executive in May 2000 the politics of the peace process was coming to have a predictive, even theatrical quality, whereby expected actions produced predictable responses. In this context, crises in the process appeared to lose much of their destructive potential as both the UUP and the republican movement ultimately seemed prepared to act in such a way as to ensure its survival, and with the British and Irish governments firmly supporting the Agreement. At the same time, and following the Ballymoney atrocity of 1998, the Drumcree controversy lost much of its moral credibility as a site of anti-Agreement agitation, a process enhanced by the events of July 2000, when the Orange Order, infuriated by Blair's 'betrayal' in 1999, organised mass protests across the North aided and abetted by loyalist paramilitaries. The outcome, however, was merely to seriously compromise the Order by association with the widespread violence and disorder that their actions initiated (*Belfast Telegraph*, 10 July 2000). The mayhem ended with both the Garvaghy ban and the Agreement intact; and incremental change proceeded with the final release of paramilitary prisoners under the terms of the Agreement, an announcement that the Maze prison would close at the end of the year, and the last graduation of RUC recruits before the Patten proposals took effect.

Inauspicious Portents

While at one level the outlook for Northern Ireland was optimistic in the autumn of 2000, as the marching season ended and the Executive got down to work, there was, nevertheless, disturbing evidence of the effective disengagement of loyalist paramilitaries from a process in which their representatives had failed to gain the electoral endorsement necessary for the exercise of power at government level. In August a vicious feud broke out between the UVF and the UDA in the lower Shankill district of Belfast which claimed seven lives – with more to come – and involved attacks on houses and businesses, resulting in requests for re-housing by 160 families, the drafting of troops into the area and the re-incarceration of Johnny Adair who was believed to be largely responsible. On the republican side, dissident activity continued, most seriously with a rocket attack on the headquarters of MI5 in London. Unionist disillusionment with the peace process – enhanced by squabbling among the Agreement partners over the implementation of the Patten Report and PIRA foot-dragging over decommissioning – was registered markedly in September when Revd William McCrea of the DUP won what had previously been the safe UUP seat of South Antrim in a by-election; a double defeat for Trimble in that his preferred candidate was rejected by the local constituency party. In October, the killing of a Real IRA member, Joseph O'Connor, believed to be the work of the PIRA, was enough to provoke yet another rejectionist-initiated meeting of the UUC to re-consider involvement in the Executive. Only after Trimble announced a plan to exclude PSF ministers from North–South ministerial meetings unless the PIRA delivered on decommissioning did the council, on 26 October, narrowly support continuance in government. But Trimble's plan was unlikely to hasten decommissioning, and when he put his threat into effect PSF ministers tested his decision in the courts (McKittrick and McVea, 2000; McDonald, 2001). Republicans were further angered in November when the House of Lords rejected the Disqualifications Bill, a measure intended to allow members of the Irish parliament to stand for election to the House of Commons and the Northern Ireland Assembly, a measure that clearly facilitated the republican agenda by blurring the constitutional boundaries between North and South (*The Times*, 21 November 2001). And though the year drew to a close with an Agreement-boosting visit from President Clinton, the last significant development was a pessimistic report by General de Chastelain on the decommissioning process (Mallie and McKittrick, 2002).

However, serious enough as republican activities were in complicating the implementation of the Agreement, much of the blame for its difficulties lay with Trimble himself, who preferred to indulge his critics in the UUP rather than ruthlessly root them out. Excusing such weakness on the grounds of encouraging healthy debate (McDonald, 2001), it was more exactly the case that his own conversion to the compromises entailed in the Agreement was far from complete (O'Connor, 2002). Despite twice heralding it, the promised revision of the UUP's links with the Orange Order has yet to take place. Together with poor leadership and people-management skills, in a party with an archaic structure and riven with internal divisions, Trimble, accordingly, made his own contribution to the problems in the peace process. As 2001 opened there was every prospect that the depressing stop-go pattern into which Agreement politics had fallen would continue.

New Year, New Broom

If Peter Mandelson's appointment as Secretary of State for Northern Ireland was not entirely unheralded, his departure certainly was. He resigned abruptly on an issue unconnected with Northern Ireland and was replaced by John Reid, a Glasgow Catholic and Celtic supporter. Aware of the record of both of his predecessors, Reid opted for a low-key, pragmatic approach, designed to resolve problems by gaining the trust of both sides (O'Connor, 2002).

This would be difficult in a political context where the gains from the peace process were strongly disputed. Outraged by the Patten proposals on policing, Trimble cited republican objections to the flying of the Union flag and crown emblems as evidence that they did not accept the settlement of Northern Ireland's constitutional position specified in the Agreement. Thus, the rejection of the Disqualifications Bill offered little satisfaction to unionists, appearing merely as an exception to the rule of an Agreement which seemed to be giving everything to republicans. Moreover, the response of the DUP to the Agreement – moving beyond Paisley's negativism to a policy favoured by Peter Robinson and Nigel Dodd combining formal rejection and the demand for a more pro-unionist settlement with effective management of the two executive departments it controlled – showed every sign of being attractive to the unionist electorate, and signalled UUP losses at the general election expected sometime in 2001 (*Fortnight*, January 2001).

But it was in the loyalist-controlled working-class estates that disillusionment with the Agreement was strongest. Lacking the dynamism and sense of purpose of the republican movement, together with its success in engineering an electorally effective transition from paramilitarism to politics – Gary McMichael's *appointment* by Trimble to the politically ineffectual Civic Forum illustrated only too well the UDP's electoral weakness – loyalist activities, especially those of the UDA, were increasingly characterised by drug dealing and other criminal activities together with an ongoing campaign of sectarian attacks on the Catholic community in east Ulster. It was reported that up to 75 per cent of the membership of the UDP was opposed to the Agreement, due to the belief that it 'hands everything to Sinn Fein/IRA' and that 'loyalists and unionists are being sold down the river' (*Derry Journal*, 7, 12 January 2001; *Sunday Times*, 7 January 2001).

It was not surprising that such an outlook would find paramilitary expression in sectarian attacks on Catholics: loyalist paramilitaries were responsible for 70 per cent of sectarian killings in the period 1969–99 (O'Leary and McGarry, 1995; Morrissey and Smyth, 2002). But loyalist violence, of course, was, and is, not just directed outwardly against Catholics, but internally also. The UDA–UVF feud which took a vicious turn in late 2000 had claimed 16 lives by April 2001 (Morrissey and Smyth, 2002).

Much as Reid believed that he could pursue an even-handed approach his intentions would be undermined by his hands-on Prime Minister, whose attempts to address PSF concerns in an effort to facilitate progress on decommissioning, would leave him exposed to – often sectarian – unionist criticism (O'Connor, 2002). Accordingly, Reid's ability to stamp his imprimatur on the peace process would be complicated by the interaction between political variables and traditional prejudices. As his first six months in office drew to a close he was faced with what was becoming a familiar scenario as David Trimble wrote another letter of resignation as First Minister to the UUC, due to take effect on 1 July unless the PIRA made 'significant progress' on decommissioning, to which it responded with an announcement that it had established 'regular contacts' with General de Chastelain (Mallie and McKittrick, 2002). It was hardly surprising that an opinion poll in May registered a substantial fall in the percentage of people who believed the Agreement would deliver a sustained period of peace, down from 40 per cent in 1998 to 33 per cent, while those who were 'not very' or 'not at all' confident of it doing so rose from 56 to 65 per cent. Among Catholics the survey showed that confidence in the Agreement had fallen to a lesser extent – one-third – than among Protestants – one-half. This was predictable enough; however, where the survey did mislead was in a finding on Irish unity which suggested that support for this option among Catholics had only risen from 2–3 per cent since 1998, to stand at 27 per cent (*Belfast Telegraph*, 25 May 2001). It was a poor guide to the republican performance at the Westminster general election of June 2001.

An Electoral Climateric

The election campaign was bitter, with both the UUP and the SDLP on the receiving end of verbal and, on occasion, physical abuse from supporters of the DUP and PSF, and with accusations, and some evidence, of electoral fraud. Such treatment, however, did not translate, via popular revulsion, into electoral advantage for those on the receiving end of it. Indeed, pundit expectations that the UUP and SDLP would get the credit for effective government proved wide of the mark as the DUP and PSF made gains at their expense.

The UUP won six seats, as compared to 10 in 1997, with many MPs lukewarm on the Agreement and one, Martin Smyth, MP for South Belfast, outrightly hostile. The picture was somewhat misleading. In fact, the party's popular vote registered a 5 per cent rise on the Assembly elections of 1998. Again, the party's better electoral performance in 1997 was due to the fact that the DUP did not contest as many seats then as it did in 2001. Nevertheless, when Trimble, who was returned for Upper Bann with a much reduced majority of 2000, sought to put a brave face on the result, it was only to be expected that Jeffrey Donaldson (majority 18,342 in Lagan Valley) would read the result as indicating how party policy on the Agreement was leading to the loss of its dominant role in the unionist community.

Trimble, however, was also subject to criticism from pro-Agreement sources, which pointed to his failure to pursue party reform and civic unionism before the signing of the Agreement, and which proved much more difficult given the party divisions that emerged thereafter. There was also an inconsistency in his political rhetoric: talk of the unacceptability of 'terrorists in government' provided a hostage to electoral fortune, feeding rejectionist sentiment at the same time as he was in government with PSF, while his emphasis on decommissioning as the touchstone of the latter's right to government positions was unwise given the RUC's own view of its irrelevance and merely provided more ammunition for his party critics. Finally, when Peter Mandelson suggested introducing proportional representation for Westminster elections in Northern Ireland after the loss of South Antrim in late 2000, it was Trimble, not the SDLP or Alliance, who rejected it, doubtful that it would help his party and fearful it might damage the link with Britain (*Fortnight*, July/August 2001). With Jeffrey Donaldson, a future likely leadership contender, reading the election result as pointing to the need for a closer relationship with the DUP, it was clear that Trimble's room for political manoeuvre on the question of power sharing with PSF would be severely restricted in the future.

For the SDLP the election result was no less depressing. For the first time it lost its lead in the popular vote to PSF (21–21.7 per cent), while as to seats, the latter took four to the SDLP's three. PSF took Fermanagh-South Tyrone and, depressingly, West Tyrone, which the SDLP and much media assessment suggested would go to Brid Rodgers on the basis of her excellent performance as Minister of Agriculture during the recent foot-and-mouth outbreak. In the event, she came in third after the winner Pat Doherty and the UUP's Willie Thompson. Both Gerry Adams in west Belfast and Martin McGuinness in Mid-Ulster achieved higher personal votes than John Hume in Foyle.

The lesson of the election for Hume's heir designate, Mark Durkan, was that the party had to spend as much time looking after its own interests as that of the peace process in general, reflecting private party criticism of John Hume for failing to better prepare it to meet the PSF challenge (*The Times*, 10 June 2001). Rational calculations, that a record of achievement in bringing the Agreement about and administrative effectiveness thereafter would receive the approbation of a grateful nationalist electorate, proved misplaced in the face of a vastly superior PSF constituency machine and a political practice which, like the DUP, sought to validate traditional notions of national identity and objectives in preference to uncertain political departures and sophisticated notions of 'post-nationalism' which, while attractive to political elites and academics, were incomprehensible and unattractive to the nationalist electorate. Such notions had an abstract, unreal quality, whereas the reforms that PSF emphasised – equality, human rights, policing and criminal justice, and which found expression, often emotively, in such issues as the Irish language, Orange marches, loyalist violence and plastic bullets – affected the Catholic community directly and personally on an everyday level.

Moreover, in terms of political skills, a party with a traditionally weak constituency organisation needed good leadership performances to be successful, but at this election Hume was uninspiring. Moreover, and perhaps ominously, the success of PSF – which suggested an increasing preference for an ethno-national solution to the Ulster problem in the Catholic community – was likely to be repeated in the future, given the advantages it had over the SDLP as a party – a stronger sense of purpose, youth, energy and effective constituency organisations (Breen, *Fortnight*, July/August 2001; Harvey, *Fortnight*, September 2001). A sharp revision of SDLP objectives was clearly felt to be needed. It came when Mark Durkan officially took over from Hume at the party's annual conference in November 2001 and signalled more aggressive competition with PSF for the nationalist vote, with the party's objective clearly specified as being the creation of an all-Ireland state (*Fortnight*, December 2001/January 2002). The result of the general election of June 2001, then, was to register the weakness of civic cross-community politics and the strengthening of more traditional ethno-national preferences. Consequently, the room for political accommodation in the near future continued to narrow.

Crisis and Response

In the context of the UUP's poor electoral performance, and, not least, another Drumcree crisis – with attendant attacks on Catholic persons and property though without the power to fundamentally influence the political landscape – David Trimble's resignation as First Minister on 1 July was a forgone conclusion when the PIRA failed to meet his decommissioning deadline. As ever, it fell to the British and Irish governments to pick up the pieces. But if, as Trimble clearly hoped, the method of procedure would be coercive action to compel the PIRA to live up to its commitments, then the policy pursued by Blair and Ahern was somewhat disappointing. They accepted that decommissioning was the most serious obstacle to the peace process, but following an intensive round of talks with the political parties at an English country house, Weston Park, balanced the decommissioning demand with a range of initiatives that addressed republican concerns on policing, demilitarisation, controversial killings and fugitives still on the run (*The Times*, 2 August 2001).

There were a number of reasons why the talks did not work out quite as Trimble intended. First, focusing on the one issue of decommissioning made it easy for republicans to construct a trade-off, while at the same time reinforcing the idea of republican strength as against an SDLP that was apparently weak and easily pleased. Again, the moral credibility of Trimble's accusations about PIRA breaches of their ceasefire was significantly weakened by the ongoing loyalist attacks on Catholics, the most objectionable of which was the harassment and abuse of schoolgirls at the Holy Cross school in north Belfast. Against the background of shocking scenes at Holy Cross and loyalist sectarian violence – responsible for 31 deaths between 1998 and 2001, as against nine attributed to the PIRA, none of which were directed against the 'British' presence – about which unionists seemed largely unconcerned, Trimble's attempt to identify the PIRA as the only major complicating factor in the peace process failed to convince. Nor was his case helped when it emerged during the talks that unionists had objections to the equality agenda and reform of the police.

Certainly for many working-class Catholics a rush to decommission in the face of so much loyalist violence would have seemed rash, something the republican leadership was well aware of (O'Connor, 2002). No major act of decommissioning followed the Weston Park talks, and Trimble resigned as First Minister; a development John Reid responded to by the novel device of suspending the Agreement for one day, which immediately allowed a further six weeks of negotiations, a device he would have to employ again to facilitate attempts to resolve the decommissioning crisis.

The stimulus to action on decommissioning came from the international environment, now an established element of the wider context of the Ulster problem and which the republican movement had exploited to advantage in the past (Guelke, 2000). Now, however, it was to provide embarrassment as three republican agents were apprehended in Colombia, apparently assisting Revolutionary Armed Forces of Columbia (FARC) guerillas to overthrow the established government, and which the PSF leadership struggled to explain away. But more importantly, the Islamic terrorist attacks on New York on 11 September – which occurred during the visit to Belfast of Richard Haass, the Washington administration's overseer of the peace process, and who was apparently reading the riot act to republican leaders – created an environment in which terrorism and the support for it was wholly unacceptable. It was a development that left the republican leadership, which had depended so heavily on American support for paramilitary activities in the past, vulnerable. At the same time, that leadership knew that decommissioning was needed to save the peace process, and undoubtedly these external developments enabled it to act earlier than it might have. Accordingly, it was announced in October that by arrangement with General de Chastelain a significant act of decommissioning had taken place, an event that did not occur without evident pain within the republican constituency given the leadership insistence that it would never happen. Nevertheless, enough was done for Trimble to resume office – with the new SDLP leader, Mark Durkan, as Deputy First Minister – and the process began of bringing the governing institutions back into operation. However, this did not take effect before difficulties were encountered in electing Trimble to office. A rebellion by two UUP MLAs left him short of the necessary majority, and this was only secured by persuading a reluctant Alliance Party to re-designate itself as unionist for a day. Rejectionist frustrations were expressed in an unseemly brawl which developed in the hall of the parliament building after the election (O'Connor, 2002; Mallie and McKittrick, 2002). The whole business was another reminder of just how precarious Trimble's position was becoming.

Sectarian Deterioration

The PIRA act of decommissioning was the most significant development of the autumn of 2001, but it was accompanied by a worsening of inter-community relations in inter-face areas. The Holy Cross controversy deteriorated drastically with loyalist verbal and physical attacks on Catholic parents and their children, presenting local working-class Protestantism in the worst possible light and serving to discredit the list of grievances that community claimed to have. As was often the case, these tended to be unfocused, but having the broad theme of republican gain and loyalist loss. Another expression of that mentality was the murder of the Catholic investigative journalist, Martin O'Hagan, in Lurgan, county Armagh, the first journalist to be killed in the troubles. It was an act which finally moved John Reid to declare officially what had been obvious for some time, namely that the UDA, UVF and LVF ceasefires were over. The declaration, of course, did nothing to stem loyalist violence – accompanied in November by the dissolution of the UDA's political wing, the UDP, suggesting a complete disengagement from the peace process – which found expression on a regular basis, both against Catholics and, not least, 'unreliable' elements, as the murder in December of William Stobie, the only person to stand trial for the murder of Pat Finucane in 1989, was to show.

As the year ended the *Irish News* reported that 99 people had died in sectarian or paramilitary incidents since January 1998 with only one person convicted; and that loyalists were behind over 500 bomb and 540 gun attacks, with republicans responsible for 80 bomb and 237 gun attacks. Of recent months, the SDLP claimed, 82 loyalist pipe-bomb attacks had occurred with a detection and prosecution rate of only 2 per cent (*Fortnight*, February 2002).

Certainly an observable difference in police approaches to loyalist and republican violence was detectable, with quite limited transgressions by the latter often attracting an aggressive response while much more serious loyalist activities were treated in the 'due process' manner of normal policing. This discrepancy was worrying – it drew concerned comment from Bertie Ahern – especially to the SDLP, which joined the new Policing Board and committed itself to support of reformed policing arrangements on the assumption that a new era of objective and fair policing had begun, and was now open to the charge of political naivety from PSF which, speaking more directly to the suspicions of the nationalist working class, had already interpreted the difference as due to British government and police 'cover' for sectarian violence perpetrated by the UDA (*Fortnight*, February 2002; *Derry Journal*, 31 August 2001).

It was inevitable that such violence – either for the purpose of forcing the PIRA back to war, or 'ethnic cleansing' – would serve to reinforce a growing apartheid of communal residency. Nigel Dodds, Minister of Development, would inform the Assembly at the end of January 2002 that in Belfast 344 people had been made homeless due to intimidation in recent months (*Fortnight*, March 2002). A survey of segregation in Belfast showed that 66 per cent of the city's population lived in areas at least 90 per cent Catholic or Protestant, and that 68 per cent of 18–25 year olds never have a 'meaningful' conversation with a member of the other community (*Fortnight*, February 2002). However, if support for the police was problematic for the SDLP, its commitment to all aspects of the Agreement meant that it had little real choice. In December it actively participated in the construction of an emblem for the new PSNI, one which included the symbols of the harp and the crown, but sited separately so as to avoid the contentious relationship evident on the old RUC badge, representations of which were removed from police stations around the North as the PSNI was officially inaugurated in November. November was also noteworthy for the decision by the Gaelic Athletic Association to abolish the controversial rule 21 which banned members of the Northern Ireland security services. The year ended in controversy, however, as the new Police Ombudsman, Nuala O'Loan, delivered a scathing report into police handling of the Omagh bomb inquiry, one which saw sectarian divisions crystalise as union- ists rallied round the Chief Constable, Ronnie Flanagan, and assorted nationalists defended the Catholic Ombudsman from accusations of anti-police bias (*Belfast Telegraph*, 13 December 2001; O'Connor, 2002; Mallie and McKittrick, 2002).

A Cold Place for Protestants?

By the end of the year the security situation, especially as it affected the Catholic community, was seriously deteriorating, but the Secretary of State had already prioritised the need to address Protestant alienation; a concern he gave expression to in a speech to the Institute of Irish Studies, University of Liverpool, in mid-November, in which he registered the progress that had occurred under the Agreement but warned that if Northern Ireland became a 'cold place for Protestants' it would have failed (*Belfast Telegraph*, 29 November 2001).

It was both a general appeal to the Catholic community – experiencing the sectarian sharp end of that alienation – and, more specifically, to its nationalist and republican political class, and quite what specific responses Reid expected is difficult to determine. However, Gerry Adams, who with his three fellow PSF MPs took possession of Westminster offices together with allowances of around $400,000 on 20 January, recognised another overture in the by-now well-established political choreography of the Agreement and took the oppor- tunity of a meeting of the World Economic Forum in New York in late January to make a significant conciliatory gesture to unionists by stating that republicans could not force upon them an all-Ireland state which did not have their agreement (Bew *et al.*, 2002; O'Connor, 2002).

In the main, however, Reid's attempt to shape the direction of politics in the North by focusing on Protestant alienation was complicated by the consequences of the June 2001 Westminster election. Thus, the SDLP, from which some substantial compliance with his wishes might have been expected, was now much more concerned with its own political survival. In a speech to the Oxford Union on 26 February, Mark Durkan reinforced the party's abandonment of Humeite 'post-nationalism' in a speech which committed it to the traditional nationalist objective of a united Ireland. Arguing that care needed to be taken to ensure that unity did not mean the 'entrapment' of a new minority, Durkan, nevertheless, clearly saw the future of unionism in terms of Irish reunification, from which he claimed they would benefit (*Fortnight*, May 2002).

Trimble, no less than Durkan, was fighting to recover lost ground, and likewise did so by appealing to fundamentalist sentiment, and in a way hardly conducive to the improvement of inter-community relations, attacking suggestions that the government might introduce an amnesty for fugitives still on the run as 'the last straw' for unionists; and more viscerally, denouncing the Irish Republic as 'a pathetic, sectarian, mono-ethnic, mono-cultural state'. Reassurance for unionists came in February in the form of a declaration by Richard Haass stating that the White House was not an advocate for Irish unity; and also through evidence of royal interest with the conferring of city status on Lisburn and Newry, though they were quick to detect 'a touch of politics' in the fact that one town was predominantly Protestant and the other Catholic (*Fortnight*, May 2002; O'Connor, 2002).

What made Protestant alienation difficult to address was a fundamental clash between belief and reality. Such a central theme of Agreement politics as 'parity of esteem' suggested equality of grievance and redress to a unionist political class that refused to accept that Catholics had any really legitimate grievances under the old Stormont system. The equality agenda embodied in the Agreement was a glaring affront to that perception. At the same time, given their reservations about policing reform, especially the policy of

50:50 recruitment and what it could be seen to imply about the RUC, the fact that the most recent figures showed a Catholic intake of 43 per cent was not wholly greeted with enthusiasm. Again, the costs of the Saville Inquiry into the events of Bloody Sunday – John Taylor, ennobled as Lord Kilclooney, was to give evidence declaring his belief that all those shot were terrorists – the thirtieth anniversary of which on 3 February 2002 attracted 30,000 people, were, to union-ist annoyance, consistently growing at the same time as the killing of Protestants by republicans seemed to pass without official acknowledgement.

Against the background of these developments Trimble's attempt to stem the rejectionist challenge while remaining in government with PSF received a severe setback on Saint Patrick's Day when a break-in occurred at the Castlereagh police base, involving the loss of sensitive security files and which was almost immediately attributed to the PIRA. Republican denials lost credibility as supportive evidence gradually mounted.

A Summer of Discontent

As the Agreement went into its fourth year the frustrations and distrust that had characterised relations between the parties to it since 1998 intensified. For unionists, increasing evidence of PIRA breaches of its ceasefire, especially repub-lican activities in Colombia, was inconsistent with Bertie Ahern's opinion that PIRA weapons would be put beyond use before the Assembly elections of 2003, and John Reid's view – based on a strict reading of its terms – that the PIRA ceasefire was still intact.

The British and Irish governments sought to address unionist/loyalist as well as nationalist/republican concerns about controversial killings by asking a Canadian judge, Peter Cory, to investigate the murders of Pat Finucane, Rosemary Nelson, Robert Hamill, Billy Wright, Lord Justice and Lady

Gibson (killed by a PIRA bomb in 1987), and the RUC officers, Harry Breen and Bob Buchanan in Lurgan in 1997. Blair and the Chancellor of the Exchequer, Gordon Brown, also visited the North to announce a multi-million pound spending pro-gramme (*Fortnight*, July/August 2002; *Sunday Times*, 28 April 2002). Moreover, May brought some relief to the centre par-ties when a projected advance by PSF at the general election in the Irish Republic, raising the prospect of the party hold-ing the balance of power, failed to materialise. The five seats it gained was a good result but not enough to prevent Fianna Fail from returning to power having almost achieved an overall majority. At the same time, when, during the election campaign, Bertie Ahern declared that PSF was unacceptable as a partner in government because of its links with a private army, unionists, who were expected to do just that, were greatly offended (*Fortnight*, June 2002). Indicative of the UUP mindset at this time was a survey demonstrating that less than half of UUP members thought the party had achieved its objectives through the Agreement, while 64 per cent said they would vote against the Agreement if another referen-dum were held 'today'. The failure of cross-community polit-ical values to develop was reflected in a finding which revealed that for UUP members the DUP was, by a comfort-able margin, the preferred recipient of transferred votes. Alliance members marginally preferred the SDLP over the UUP on voting transfers (Tonge and McAulay, 2002).

Against a background of intensifying UUP alienation from the peace process, Mark Durkan's attempt to appeal to union-ists by re-designing the SDLP party emblem in the shape of a politically non-contentious shamrock whose three branches represented nationalism, socialism and Orangeism/unionism (*Derry Journal*, 25 June 2002), seemed whimsical. Alex Maskey, the first PSF Lord Mayor of Belfast, got more credit for laying a wreath in commemoration of the Somme dead on 1 July – though not as part of the official commemoration (*Irish Times*, 1 July 2002). However, such gestures hardly addressed the crisis in the peace process, which deepened as civil strife in the shatter-zones of Belfast and attacks on Catholics across the North served to embitter relations between the parties; and which – apart from the annual Drumcree crisis which passed with limited violence and noticeable evidence of police determination to pursue law-breakers – provided a disturbing backdrop to political developments over the summer months. The seriousness of the crisis was acknowledged at the beginning of July when Blair, Adams and Ahern met in Dublin to consider what could be done to calm sectarian tension and stabilise the leadership of David Trimble. The meeting was a precursor to a conference of both government leaders and all the parties to the Agreement at Hillsborough on 4 July. It was requested by Trimble under pressure from critics in the UUP and concerned about civil strife.

The Hillsborough meeting, however, was largely a replay of the Weston Park meeting a year earlier, with Trimble's concern to prioritise decommissioning and PIRA breaches of its ceasefire being undermined by the fact that much the greater violence in the North was emanating from within the unionist family – as it proceeded a PSNI commander in Magherafelt condemned sectarian attacks against Catholics in the town (*Belfast Telegraph*, 4 July 2002) – and with PSF ready to counter Trimble with their own list of priorities. Accordingly what Trimble highlighted as a major crisis in the peace process seemed more accurately a crisis within unionism (*Irish Times*, 3 July 2002); and since Trimble's only policy for getting republicans to move on decommissioning was to threaten to collapse the governing institutions, instability had become an increasingly established element of the political practice of the Agreement.

Apparent British willingness to indulge 'unreasonable' unionist behaviour infuriated both Mark Durkan and Gerry Adams. But it was Adams who spoke directly to working-class Catholic concerns when he responded thus to statements at Westminster by Blair and Reid warning republicans about the consequences of 'future' republican ceasefire breaches: 'Those [Catholics] living in the inter-face areas will find it crazy that the Prime Minister is zeroing in on republicans when they are victims of a loyalist campaign (Adams quoted in *Irish Times*, 24 July 2002).' Adams's comments came just after the murder of Gerald Lawlor in north Belfast by loyalist paramilitaries on 22 July.

In fact, a clear division was emerging in the peace process, between the Prime Minister and John Reid, focusing on the difficulties of David Trimble in maintaining UUP support for the Agreement and responding with warnings to republicans about their continued membership of the Executive; and nationalists and republicans – the latter repeatedly pointing out that the PIRA had held to the terms of its ceasefire – alarmed at apparent state indifference to the ongoing campaign of violence against the Catholic community. They noted, in particular, that despite the killings and violence perpetrated by the UDA none of its leadership had been charged and arrested, and that despite Reid's admission in October 2001 that the organisation's ceasefire had collapsed, none of its ex-prisoners had been returned to jail (*Irish Times*, 25 July 2002). Concern about police failure to offer Catholics adequate protection also found expression on the Policing Board in the person of its Deputy Chairman, Denis Bradley, while John Reid's promise to address the situation by the creation of new offences was criticised by the Chairman of the Human Rights Commission, Professor Brice Dickson, who argued that new offences were not needed as the necessary legislation was already in place: it 'just needed to be properly enforced' (Dickson quoted in *Belfast Telegraph*, 25 July 2002). It was an argument that resonated strongly with the Catholic community, and would have gained point by the speed with which the PSNI responded to the killing of a Protestant civilian worker, David Caldwell, by a dissident republican blast device at an army base in Derry, quickly arresting five suspects (*Irish Times*, 2, 5 August 2002).

Evidence of how the new political era that the Agreement was supposed to inaugurate was failing to emerge increased with a marked rise in shootings and bombings and reports that the Civic Forum – whose purpose was to cultivate civic values and to give social, economic and cultural advice to the new governing institutions at Stormont – was failing badly, with poor attendance and its reports ignored by the devolved administration (*Belfast Telegraph*, 29 August 2002; *Irish Times*, 25 September 2002). The Human Rights Commission was likewise open to the criticism that it was not capable of fulfilling the mandate accorded it under the Agreement. Indeed, Mark Durkan blamed Tony Blair for devaluing human rights by failing to have two soldiers convicted of murder in the North expelled from the army (*Belfast Telegraph*, 9 September 2002).

Durkan's accusation had followed shortly after his speech at a Michael Collins commemoration in county Cork, in which he appropriated the Collins mantle for his campaign to push the SDLP in a more overtly nationalist direction, arguing that the Agreement was evidence that Collins's vision of Ireland's democratic potential 'had a resonance which was still valid', and proposing the creation of a North–South parliamentary forum – envisaged in the Agreement – bringing together parties across Ireland (*Derry Journal*, 27 August 2002; *Irish Times*, 27 August 2002); though an SDLP summer 'kite' about possible unity with Fianna Fail signally failed to soar.

As relations between the parties worsened against a background of ongoing sectarian strife that increased community polarisation, and in turn increased the potential political costs of any cross-community peace and reconciliation activities by political leaders (*Sunday Times*, 25 August 2002), Trimble's critics in the UUP succeeded in calling another meeting of the UUC – the ninth – for the purpose of attacking his involvement in government with PSF; and, though they could hardly have been aware of it at the time, thereby initiated the most serious crisis of the Agreement to date, one that would lead, in mid-October, to its suspension for the foreseeable future.

Ultimatum and Collapse

Trimble's grilling by the UUC was set for 21 September, and with past experience in mind – supportive words and deeds by the British government, close voting, with Trimble just managing to hold on to his post – the parties adopted their expected positions. But it was increasingly clear that this crisis was of a more serious nature than previous ones. Unionist rejectionists had made their case for an emergency meeting of the UUC on the basis of an accumulation of assumed republican transgressions, especially Colombia, Castlereagh, involvement in street violence, and the persistently slow progress on decommissioning; all of which, given the party's poor performance at the general election of 2001, would spell disaster if it was still in government with PSF when the Assembly elections came round in 2003.

It was a persuasive argument, made all the more so by the PSF Lord Mayor of Belfast, Alex Maskey, grievously offending unionist sensibilities in early September by giving the Tricolour equality of status in the Lord Mayor's office with the Union flag (*Belfast Telegraph*, 4 September 2002). Against this background, rejectionists could be sure of attracting rather more support than they could normally depend on. Even Trimble supporters on the UUC thought that if he did survive as leader he might well be mortally wounded (*Sunday Business Post*, 1 September 2002).

It was a measure of the seriousness of the crisis that John Reid, together with Hugh Orde, the newly appointed Chief Constable of the PSNI – who had recently overseen the Steven's inquiry into collusion between state forces and loyalist paramilitaries in the murder of Pat Finucane – announced a series of measures to address it. Significantly, a serious effort to bring paramilitaries to book was included (*Guardian*, 3 September 2002; *Sunday Times*, 8 September 2002), thereby signalling a determination to deal effectively with one of the pressing concerns of the Catholic community. But also included was a proposal to appoint a monitor to audit the paramilitary ceasefires. It was clearly intended to both address unionist concerns about alleged PIRA violence in general, and to ease David Trimble's difficulties with the UUC.

Reid's intentions were obvious to nationalists and republicans, and the monitor proposal was objected to by Mark Durkan as a measure virtually dictated by David Trimble: it was, curiously, intended to monitor ceasefires that were still in place, especially republican, when much the greater violence was emanating from loyalist groups the government itself had declared to have gone back to violence (*Irish Times*, 14 September 2002). Moreover, as a mechanism to disable rejectionist criticism of Trimble it was ineffective, being dismissed as merely another fudging device (*Irish Times*, 13 September 2002). The time had passed when such initiatives could be relied upon to pull the irons out of the fire for Trimble.

In the event, he only secured his leadership position through a compromise resolution agreed with Jeffrey Donaldson, whereby the latter's original proposal – that the party immediately leave the North–South Ministerial Council, demand that Blair expel PSF from government and, in the event of refusal, pull out of the executive though leaving the Assembly committee system to function – was abandoned in favour of three-months notice, until 18 January 2003, for the Agreement to be fully implemented, meaning decommissioning and disbandment of the PIRA, or the party would withdraw from government (*Sunday Times*, 22 September 2002).

It was a harder resolution than Donaldson's original proposal, and surprising given a mid-week letter from Trimble to UUC delegates advising against support for wreckers interested only in destroying the Agreement (*Belfast Telegraph*, 23 September 2002). By setting demands impossible to fulfill, it was widely interpreted by the SDLP, republicans, Alliance, the NIWC and the southern government as a capitulation by Trimble to the rejectionist camp, fearing the electoral effects of power sharing with PSF. That the UUC ultimatum was accompanied by objections to the equality agenda and policing reform – unionist antagonism to the latter gaining force from Conservative Party criticism of government implementation of the Patten proposals (*Irish Times*, 6 September 2002) – seemed to many nationalists that what really lay behind the unionist ultimatum was a sectarian objection to sharing power with Catholics.

The attitude of the two governments was to forgo the temptation to lay blame and to salvage and maintain those aspects of the Agreement that were not dependent on the existence of the Executive; though the USA's representative in Northern Ireland, Richard Haass, agreed with Trimble's non-unionist critics that the UUC ultimatum to collapse the governing institutions was unlikely to effect the objectives he sought (*Belfast Telegraph*, 26 September 2002; *Irish Times*, 26 September 2002). For his part, Mark Durkan, impatient with the way PSF–UUP antagonisms had marginalised his party, threatened to take the initiative by withdrawing SDLP ministers from the Executive on the 26 October, the day set by Trimble for UUP withdrawal from the North–South Ministerial Council (*Irish Times*, 1 October 2002). The governing institutions, however, were to be brought down much earlier than either Durkan or the UUC envisaged.

A new bombshell dropped on 4 October with the discovery by the PSNI of an extensive republican intelligence gathering operation based in PSF offices at Stormont. Computer files with incriminating details of security personnel were confiscated, and resulted in charges of possession of information likely to be of use to terrorists against members of the PSF administrative staff. The operation offered David Trimble the opportunity to issue a new ultimatum, giving Tony Blair seven days to expel PSF from the executive or face a UUP departure from government, while the DUP, looking with relish at this latest crisis, rushed to deepen it by withdrawing its Executive ministers.

The choices facing the two governments were, immediate elections followed by negotiations – favoured initially by Ahern but startling to the SDLP, UUP and London, fearing triumph of the extremes at the expense of the centre; expulsion of PSF from the Executive; or suspension with the resumption of direct rule. Privately, Blair agreed with David Trimble that the expulsion of PSF was the best option, but he failed to persuade Durkan to support it, leaving suspension as a least-worst option agreed with the Dublin government. The only consolation from the crisis for PSF came from the Chief Constable, who apologised to the party for the heavy-handed nature of the raid on its Stormont offices, doubtless mindful of how its nature was open to pro-unionist interpretation (*Belfast Telegraph*, 8, 10 October 2002; *Irish Times*, 9 October 2002; *Sunday Times*, 6 October 2002).

The decision to suspend was finalised after a meeting between Adams and Blair on 10 October failed to elicit any means by which unionist trust in republicans could be restored in the immediate term, and with Monday 14 October decided upon to prevent David Trimble's planned walk out on Tuesday in the event of PSF exclusion not being effected (*Guardian*, 11 October 2002). At the same time, Trimble was aware that a collapse of the governing institutions would leave the management of the peace process in the hands of the two governments, with a possible 'joint-authority' aspect – hence his preference for PSF expulsion. Failing suspension, Trimble favoured the formation of a 'shadow administration' involving himself and the Deputy First Minister, Mark Durkan, to over-see the administration of the North, but this proposal found no favour in London and Dublin (*Irish Times*, 12 October 2002). So, for the fourth time, the Executive was suspended with disappointment all round, apart from sections of loyalist paramilitarism and the DUP, delighted with the outcome and looking forward, with more enthusiasm than rationality, to the prospect of negotiations for a more Protestant and union-ist settlement (*Belfast Telegraph*, 14, 15 October 2002; *Irish Times*, 12 October 2002). That a much longer period of sus-pension was envisaged than in the past was evident from the news that two new junior ministers would be drafted into the Northern Ireland administration to help with direct rule. If PIRA disbandment is to be the price of restoring the Executive then the prospects seem remote at present: on 12 October the Guarda apprehended a PIRA group apparently in the process of planning armed robbery (*Belfast Telegraph*, 15 October 2002).

It was a concomitant of Dr Reid's statement announcing suspension that the Assembly elections set for May 2003 would still take place. Thus, local politics still retained the focus that had driven it since the Westminster election of 2001. Reid also stressed that while the governing institutions had collapsed the Agreement itself was still in place and those aspects of it not dependent on the Assembly would still function. The central task for all parties was to work towards its resurrection and ensuring the suspension period was as short as possible. It was a scenario acceptable to all the pro-Agreement parties, though each with its own particular focus: Bertie Ahern, in particular, took pains to address nationalist and republican sensitivities, stressing the need for policing reforms and demilitarisation, and declaring his willingness, on Mark Durkan's suggestion, to re-activate the Forum for Peace and Reconciliation to promote the interests of the Agreement on an all-Ireland basis (*Derry Journal*, 15 October 2002; *Guardian*, 12 October 2002; *Irish Times*, 15 October 2002).

The immediate aftermath of suspension was characterised more by recrimination than an immediate effort to energise the peace process, with David Trimble, evidently fearing the 'joint authority' implications of suspension, blaming John Reid for 'funking' the expulsion option (*Belfast Telegraph*, 16 October 2002); but an SDLP already under threat from PSF could hardly have remained in government with the UUP in such an eventuality without risk of electoral annihilation.

The political crisis translated into an increasingly nega-tive popular unionist attitude to the Agreement: a BBC opinion poll found only 32.9 per cent willing to support the Agreement if another referendum was held, with 66.1 opposed, as opposed to 55:45 for the Agreement in 1998. Predictably nationalist support for the Agreement remained solid, though even a majority of nationalists would apparently be prepared to tolerate its re-negotiation (*Belfast Telegraph*, 17 October 2002).

In an attempt to force the pace of political development Tony Blair, with the acquiesance of Bertie Ahern, made a surprise visit to Northern Ireland on 17 October to deliver a hard hitting speech on the need for PIRA disarmament and disbandment to get the governing institutions re-established; and denying the accuracy of the belief among many nationalists that unionists 'disregard, even secretly tolerate loyalist paramilitaries'. Blair, surprisingly, declared: 'I know this not to be true.' In making his pitch for PIRA disarmament and disbandment Blair took less than due cognisance of the mythic, but nonetheless important, role of the PIRA as a community defence force for vulnerable Catholic communities under loyalist attack, and the unlikelihood of PIRA disbandment so long as that threat existed (*Irish Times*, 18 October 2002). And it was here that the security forces and the NIO had signally failed to deliver on their own commitments under the Agreement.

The Blair speech, nevertheless, was a major fillip to David Trimble as he faced the annual conference of the UUP in Derry on 19 October. With his leadership position secure Trimble delivered a more moderate and positive speech than might have been expected. He was also greatly heartened by his guest speaker, leader of the Tory Party, Ian Duncan Smith, who gave forthright endorsement to the UUP leader. Yet it could hardly have escaped the UUP delegates that when Smith spoke about Northern Ireland's constitutional position he was no different from Tony Blair in stating that membership of the United Kingdom could only last as long as a democratic majority for it existed in Northern Ireland (*Derry Journal*, 22 October 2002; *Irish Times*, 21 October 2002). And for all the support of Trimble that Smith's speech contained, it was strongly encoded with the message that a secular unionism, able to attract Catholic support – he referred to his own Catholicism during the speech – was the best way to secure it (*Sunday Times*, 20 October 2002).

Despite the series of events that led to the collapse of the Agreement, all parties to it accept that it is still the template for the political future of Northern Ireland if, and when, the gun is irrevocably removed from the political arena. But if this comes to pass, it will be under new management. John Reid's tenure as Secretary of State ended unexpectedly on 24 October 2002 as part of a Cabinet reshuffle occasioned by the unexpected resignation of Estelle Morris as Secretary of State for Education the previous day. Reid was replaced by Paul Murphy, a former junior minister at the NIO, and who was deeply engaged in the negotiations that led to the Agreement. Murphy has a reputation for fair-mindedness, patience and quiet diplomacy, and, accordingly, is regarded as someone suitably qualified to guide the peace process through its latest, most serious, crisis.

Already the shape of future negotiations is taking place. The past practice of negotiating for incremental change is discredited, as the conditions deemed necessary for the restoration of the Executive include, not just decommissioning, but the winding up – 'disbandment' is avoided by the two governments because of its prescriptive connotations – of the PIRA. Accordingly, negotiations will have to deal comprehensively with all outstanding issues and grievances, and a plan along these lines was already in preparation by London and Dublin in early November. Evidently concerned to position himself more centrally for the negotiating process, Tony Blair gave an extensive interview to the *Irish Times* (8 November 2002) in which the government's determination to deal with loyalist violence was given equal, if not more, emphasis, than the responsibilities of republicans to the peace process. For its part, PSF has sought to expand the seriousness of the threat posed by loyalist paramilitaries to the

Agreement by adopting the term 'unionist paramilitaries' to describe them (*Irish Times*, 5 December 2002), thereby implicating the wider unionist community – at least morally – in their activities, and suggesting that community's responsibility for dealing with the problem.

CONCLUSION

At the heart of the Ulster problem is a conflict of national identity. It consists not only of different national identities but different *kinds* of national identity, rooted in historical evolution.

The national identity of Ulster unionism has its origins in the period of British state formation in the early seventeenth century, a formation that took shape during the conflicts of the Reformation. Ulster Protestants were, and are, a community that defines its identity in terms of British state patriotism and constitutional membership. But while that identity was relatively secure and supported by London for over 200 years, the difficulties associated with integrating Catholic Ireland into the expanded British state after 1800 gradually forced London to move away from giving unqualified support to the Protestant interest in Ireland to a position of equidistance between the island's religious communities. The major reforms of the nineteenth century – Catholic Emancipation and disestablishment – were evidence of this. In the wider British context, they can also be seen as markers along the road of Britain's progression from the Protestant nationalism in which the state was born to the civic nationalism that characterises it today.

For Ulster Protestants, however, for whom anti-Catholicism was, and is to a significant extent, one of the most important elements binding the community together in the face of the nationalist threat, the original values and ideas which legitimised their presence in Ulster continued to have importance. As with group representatives of European metropolitan centres in colonial territories, the Ulster Protestant community came to take on the characteristics of a 'frontier' community, holding on to archaic ideas of patriotism long after they had lost their relevance in the homeland (Clayton, 1995).

Obsessed with historically determined fears of the 'native' population that inhibited ideological development, and increasingly paranoid about mainland British society's alienation from their own values and beliefs, Ulster unionism became locked into an immobilist stance that left it ill-equipped to deal with change. Accordingly, as the historical resurgence of Irish nationalism progressed from the late nineteenth century, unionism increasingly came to see the external political environment as threatening and to perceive 'conspiracies' against them and their interests. This cast of mind, powerfully reinforced by the negativism of the Revd Ian Paisley, has endured to inform the unionist outlook up to, and including, the period since the civil rights campaign of the 1960s. It allows unionists to deny any responsibility for the negative consequences of rejecting change, such as, for example, the disorder and mayhem arising from the Drumcree issue.

This mentality – reflected in the growth of 'traditional' Orange marches, which increased from 1897 in 1985 to 2404 in 1996 (North Report, 1997) – has also inhibited realistic and nuanced evaluations of the unionist position and makes a satisfactory settlement of the Ulster problem for unionists difficult to achieve. One commentator has suggested that even if they won their fight to keep Ulster British, they would suppose their victory a hollow façade (Bruce, 1994).

To a significant extent psychological security about their position is denied unionists by a zero-sum attitude which translates nationalist gain as inevitably entailing unionist loss. Pervasive throughout the unionist community, it takes on a more vicious dimension in working-class loyalism. Expressed, following the Agreement of Good Friday 1998, as a general sense of loss in terms of 'sell-out' to republicans, no specific programme of demands is articulated to address loyalist grievances, but the logic of this attitude implies the reduction of the Catholic community to the subordinate status it occupied under the old Stormont regime. While many middle-class unionists share an equally sectarian attitude to Roman Catholics, if more mutedly expressed (McKay, 2000), their economic resources allow them to respond to Catholic advances, especially residential advances, by flight to areas such as north Down: lacking their resources, working-class loyalism responds with violence.

As the expression of a visceral ethno-religious hatred of Catholics, loyalist violence has been read as denoting 'a shift in the form of the Northern Ireland conflict itself – away from a contest about sovereignty and national identity towards an internal ethnic conflict between two opposing groups' (Morrissey and Smyth, 2002: 63). But it can also be read in an ultimately re-partitionist sense, as intended to produce a solidly Protestant and unionist entity in east Ulster whose British identity and sovereignty would be secure. Re-partition was considered favourably in the 1970s by the UUP MP, the late Harold McCusker, in the event of Catholic demographic superiority, more likely now than it was then.

In evaluating the unionist dimension to the Ulster problem, however, it is worth noting that they encounter difficulties in embracing constitutional change that do not apply to nationalists. Unlike the nationalist identity, which is rooted in the *culture* of the Irish Catholic people, the British identity of unionism is a product of the constitutional structures thrown up by the British nation-making experience. Thus, whereas for nationalists, constitutional forms – whether home rule, Free State or republican – have merely been the means whereby national identity has been expressed at various times, for unionists a change in constitutional forms has a much more profound impact on identity, especially as, unlike the strongly supportive relationship that exists between Dublin governments and the northern Catholic community, the London position on Northern Ireland is one of constitutional neutrality: the most London offers the Ulster unionists is membership of the United Kingdom so long as a majority exists in the North for it.

Nor, historically, have nationalists greatly assisted the development of a unionist mind-set conducive to change. Anti-partitionist rhetoric and a denial of the validity of the unionist identity persisted for the best part of a century until the New Ireland Forum of 1983 induced a re-evaluation, leading constitutional nationalists and, to a lesser extent, republicans, to the realisation that no solution to the Ulster problem could be found without unionist agreement.

Overtly, the driving force for change was supplied by John Hume. Given his political authority within constitutional nationalism and the ideological flexibility of that tradition Hume, with the support of successive Dublin governments, had relative freedom to define the terms of a settlement acceptable to nationalists, reflected in his view that a settlement had to be one defined, not in terms of simple territorial unity, but the 'totality of relationships within these islands' (Hume, 1996). But while Hume made an enormous contribution from the Sunningdale experiment onwards to the task of defining the terms of a constitutional settlement for Northern Ireland, he could do little to bring the republican movement on board. That crucial task was taken on by Gerry Adams, employing his own considerable talents in very difficult circumstances.

Hume's achievement as a constitutional politician is sometimes compared with that of Parnell in the 1880s. But given what we now know of the PSF political project a more appropriate comparison might be with Adams. For if the secret of Parnell's success lay in exploiting the 'penumbra of revolution' to move an aggressively nationalist movement in a firmly constitutional direction, that was also Adams's achievement, and in more problematic circumstances. Certainly his

242

contribution to the making of the Agreement of Easter 1998 was of central importance.

Designed to address the fundamental concerns of all sides, it provided constitutional security for unionists and an institutional expression of the all-Ireland identity of nationalists and republicans, combined with a share in the government of Northern Ireland and an agenda to redress community and individual injustices, most complaints about which emanated from within the nationalist population. However, the progress of the Agreement to date has been complicated by differing understandings of the nature of the Ulster problem and of the Agreement, a failure to attract the support of all the major parties, and political mistakes by its signatories and supporters.

Politically centralist as the Agreement document is in establishing a position of fairness between the claims of its subscribers, a major theme such as 'parity of esteem' between the two political traditions in Northern Ireland is, as we have seen, open to quite different interpretations, and that an objective assessment of grievance, inequality and redress was bound to leave unionists disappointed. Moreover, the term lends credibility to ideas and values inconsistent with the stated objectives of the Agreement: how, for example, is the validation of such a significant element of unionist identity as the inherently supremacist Orange culture to be squared with the promotion of civic political values? As the activities of Orangemen at Portadown indicated, promotion of the latter could appear as a direct affront to their sense of self.

Nor is the attempt to address the issue of nationality by de-coupling identity and territoriality reassuring to unionists. This is attractive to academic commentators, and unproblematic for nationalists and republicans secure in their sense of communal identity. But for a unionist people whose idea of nationality is so heavily dependent on notions of sovereignty and constitutionality, and lacking unqualified support from London, it does not inspire confidence. Accordingly, these aspects, in a context where the republican movement appears to be reneging on its commitments, lend colour to the jeremiads of such a powerful exploiter of Protestant and unionist insecurities as Ian Paisley.

Gaining support for the Agreement from Paisley, whose career has been built on negative oppositionalism, was clearly never likely. Nevertheless, it could be argued that more could have been done by David Trimble to diminish Paisley's influence. Having contributed greatly to the modernisation of unionism by abandoning the immobilism of 'Ulster says No', Trimble could have made a greater effort to develop a politically centrist alliance in support of the Agreement with the SDLP to enthusiastically sell its benefits at the referendum of 1998. Instead, both the UUP referendum campaign and its campaign at the Assembly elections which followed suggested a party leadership driven by the coercive influence of the AIA to accept the Agreement as a least-worst option whose merits lay chiefly in the fact that it was not the AIA, rather than a wholehearted commitment to reform (Guelke, 2002). In this respect it is worth noting that the only unionist to have produced an intellectually coherent argument for civic unionism before 1998 (Porter, 1996), was attacked from within party ranks as a traitor (Cochrane, 1997). Trimble's political practice since 1998 likewise suggested a leader torn between a rational appreciation of what it was necessary for unionists to concede in a demographically changing Northern Ireland, on the one hand; and an emotional attachment to traditional unionist ideas and practices on the other – he again attacked the Irish Republic in terms close to sectarian abuse in mid-November 2002 (*Belfast Telegraph*, 18 November 2002; *Irish Times*, 19 November 2002). Furthermore, this cast of mind led to a preoccupation with PSF and its failings, something which served both to enhance unionist anxieties about power sharing, while also functioning to marginalise the SDLP and so weaken the political centre.

It was inevitable that if the ethno-national focus of PSF became the primary concern of minority politics then the SDLP would suffer. The party's agenda had been set by

Hume, whose arguments suggested a post-nationalist solution to the Ulster problem – though his speeches and writings could still occasionally reflect the traces of an instinctive nationalist attitude to unionism (Hume, 1996) – one in which the traditional contours of the problem have been made irrelevant by new realities. It was an outlook which owed much to his European and world roles, but which naturally had little resonance with nationalist grass-roots opinion. In a context where the party was coming under increasing threat from PSF it was undoubtedly a weakness, and destined to be jettisoned as Mark Durkan saw the road to recovery necessitating a return to the traditional objective of territorial unity. But of course this can only be pursued at the cost of cultivating the political middle-ground; territorial unity implies a resolution of the constitutional issue on the basis of a sectarian head-count, and it is not entirely surprising to find SDLP exponents of the view that Catholic demographic advance will resolve the Ulster problem (*Derry Journal*, 25 October 2002).

Certainly an overview of Northern Ireland politics since 1998 demonstrates, not an expanding civic political centre, but the strengthening of the extremes, a strengthening reflected in the success of the leaderships of the DUP and PSF in carrying their constituencies with them and expanding them. For the DUP this was not a difficult task. The leadership took no political risks, simply played to the deep insecurities of the unionist community and relied on difficulties inherent in an agreement that appeared to promise very different things to unionists and republicans simultaneously. Much more impressive was the achievement of Gerry Adams and Martin McGuinness in converting the failure of armed struggle into support for a peace process that they argue will deliver Irish unity, but which can, realistically deliver, at best, reformed partitionism for the foreseeable future. It has been a triumph of propaganda abetted by lack of alternative political options and what might be called 'the grain of history'.

If a sense of unionist loss since the end of the old Stormont regime has informed their ideas about what the Agreement is likely to deliver for them, then it is no less the case that the period since the birth of the Provisionals in 1969–70 has been one of progressive gain for the Catholic community; and republicans had long been inclined to argue that armed struggle was, effectively, central to the achievement of those gains. Accordingly, it required merely a relatively minor adjustment of historical perspective – one that eliminated or ignored the claims made for armed struggle alone, or the ballot box *and* the armalite, together with the contribution of the SDLP – to frame the Agreement as the natural product of a republican agenda that had been consistently successful since 1970.

At the same time, leadership management has not been wholly successful: recent PIRA activities that have contributed so much to the latest crisis in the peace process point up no less the limits of Adams's achievement. Alleged spying activities at Stormont were bound to be uncovered and to damage the republican movement, leaving it, rather than the usually reliable unionists, to carry the can for the collapse of the governing institutions. It is hard to believe that Adams, an accomplished political operator, would have willingly approved of such a politically dangerous operation. Either he was not aware of it, or, if he was, was unable to prevent it.

It would clearly seem to be the case that, as Adams affirmed on 26 October 2002 at Monaghan, he is committed to a future without either the PIRA as well as loyalist paramilitarism, and is aware that convincing actions leading to the PIRA being stood down are necessary for the peace process to advance. But he also emphasises that this will only be effected as part of a package that removes the reasons for its continued existence, and that the unionists, and especially the British government, have commitments to deliver on no less important than those of republicans.

For the great majority of republicans the chief obstacle to Irish unity has, traditionally, not been the unionist community, but 'perfidious Albion' acting destructively to prevent a possible solution agreed by fellow Irishmen; a view that has a long historical provenance in republican mythology. And yet, one does not have to accept this view to appreciate that the intractability of the Ulster problem in general derives to a significant extent from the nature of Britain's role in the North, which, since 1969, has been complicated by the self-perception of being an objective force for good in the North, while in reality being a participant in the conflict reacting subjectively and defensively to political and military attacks on its personnel and institutions. The former effectively acted to prevent British administrations from developing a realistic understanding of their role in the problem, with the result that that role was often determined by the play of political and military forces on the ground, as developments in the period from 1970 to 1972 so clearly demonstrate.

More recently, it is noteworthy how, in the period leading up to the PIRA ceasefire of August 1994, the approach to a resolution of the Ulster problem publicly agreed with Dublin, emphasising neutrality, imaginative responsiveness and co-operation, was undermined by political pressures and misunderstandings, and personal suspicions and prejudices regarding republicanism. The Blair government learned from the mistakes of the Major administration and had the enthusiasm and commitment to drive the talks process forward, but likewise has often acted – not neutrally as it would have preferred to think – but as another player in the conflict, tending to respond to issues, depending on personal sympathies, in an often short-term manner. Thus, Mo Mowlam, the first Labour Secretary of State for Northern Ireland, made both a huge personal and political impact, generally favourable on nationalists and unfavourable on unionists, the latter affronted by her demeanour, personal indiscretions and 'pro-nationalism', and progressively working to marginalise her by dealing directly with Blair. Her successor, Peter Mandelson, the grandson of Herbert Morrison, was much more to their liking and acted the part; but only at the expense of alienating nationalists and providing republicans with a major weapon for use in the controversy over decommissioning. Consciously seeking to avoid the apparent partisanship of his predecessors, John Reid proved more politically capable, but found his task no less burdensome and complicated by personal and impromptu interventions by the Prime Minister, to whom local parties naturally accorded more significance, if not more consistency.

Thus, unionists were promised the removal of PSF from government if decommissioning was not delivered on, only for the government to respond with ambivalence and compromise on the issue. Nationalists and republicans were promised thoroughgoing reform and demilitarisation, only for the Patten proposals to be watered down and military foot-dragging on demilitarisation to prevail. But most seriously, republicans were, and are, constantly pressed to deliver on decommissioning, while a loyalist campaign of sectarian attacks on the Catholic community – the kind of activity which, however mistakenly, is communally deemed to justify the PIRA's continued existence – was allowed to persist without a security response commensurate with its magnitude. Only as the collapse of the governing institutions became apparent was there evidence that the NIO and the PSNI were prepared to seriously address this problem.

It is difficult to be wholly positive about the future. The Assembly and Executive are in abeyance, with little prospect of their re-activation in the near future. Tony Blair's speech in Belfast in mid-October 2002 promising full implementation of the Agreement in return for acts of 'completion' by the PIRA, drew a response from Gerry Adams which shared his objectives for a peaceful future but reversed his priorities. At the same time, all pro-Agreement parties accept that there is no realistic alternative to it, while the British government has declared that those aspects of it not dependent on devolution will continue to be implemented. It is, thus, reasonable to conclude that the Ulster problem is in its endgame; however, differing perspectives on its nature will continue to complicate the pace of its final resolution.

BIBLIOGRAPHY

Adams, Gerry, *Free Ireland: Towards a Lasting Peace* (Dingle, Co. Cork, 1995 edn).

Adams, Gerry, *Before the Dawn: An Autiobiography* (London, 1996).

Anon. (*The Sunday Times* Insight Team), *Ulster* (London, 1972).

Arthur, Paul, *The Peoples Democracy 1969–1973* (Belfast, 1974).

Arthur, Paul, *The Government and Politics of Northern Ireland* (London, 1994 edn).

Arthur, Paul, *Special Relationships: Britain, Ireland and the Northern Ireland Problem* (Belfast, 2000).

Arthur, Paul and Jeffery, Keith, *Northern Ireland since 1968* (Oxford, 1996 edn).

Aughey, Arthur, 'Contemporary Unionist Politics' in Barton, Brian and Roche, Patrick (eds), *The Northern Ireland Problem: Perspectives and Policies* (Aldershot, 1994).

Aughey, Arthur, 'The 1998 Agreement: Unionist Responses' in Cox, Michael, Guelke, Adrian and Stephan, Fiona (eds), *A Farewell to Arms?: From 'Long War' to Long Peace in Northern Ireland* (Manchester and New York, 2000).

Aughey, Arthur, 'Learning From "The Leopard"' in Wilford Rick (ed.), *Aspects of the Belfast Agreement* (Oxford, 2001).

Bew, Paul and Gillespie, Gordon, *Northern Ireland: A Chronology of the troubles 1968–1993* (Dublin, 1993).

Bew Paul and Gillespie, Gordon, *The Northern Ireland Peace Process 1993–1996: A Chronology* (London, 1996).

Bew, Paul and Patterson, Henry, *The British State and the Ulster Crisis* (London, 1985).

249

Bibliography

Bew, Paul, Patterson, Henry and Gibbon, Peter, *Northern Ireland 1921–2001: Political Forces and Social Classes* (London, 2002 edn).

Birrell, Derek and Murie, Alan, *Policy and Government in Northern Ireland: Lessons of Devolution* (Dublin, 1980).

Bishop, Patrick and Mallie, Eamon, *The Provisional IRA* (London, 1987).

Boyce, D.G., 'British Conservative Opinion, the Ulster Question, and the Partition of Ireland, 1912–1922', *Irish Historical Studies*, vol. XVII, no. 65 (1970).

Boyce, D.G., *The Irish Question in British Politics 1868–1986* (London, 1988).

Boyle, Kevin and Hadden, Tom, *Northern Ireland: A Positive Proposal* (London, 1994).

Breen, Suzanne, 'The Unwashed Clean Up' *Fortnight* (July/August, 2001).

Bruce, Steve, *God Save Ulster! The Religion and Politics of Paisleyism* (Oxford, 1986).

Bruce, Steve, *The Red Hand: Protestant Paramilitaries in Northern Ireland* (Oxford, 1992).

Bruce, Steve, *The Edge of the Union: The Ulster Loyalist Political Vision* (Oxford, 1994).

Buckland, Patrick, *Irish Unionism 2; Ulster Unionism and the Origins of Northern Ireland* (Dublin, 1973).

Buckland, Patrick, *A History of Northern Ireland* (Dublin, 1989).

Callaghan, James, *A House Divided: The Dilemma of Northern Ireland* (London, 1973).

Canning, Paul, *British Policy Towards Ireland 1921–1941* (Oxford, 1985).

Clarke, Liam, *Broadening the Battlefield: The H Blocks and the Rise of Sein Fein* (Dublin, 1987).

Clayton, Pamela, *Enemies and Passing Friends: Settler Ideologies in Twentieth Century Ulster* (London, 1995).

Cochrane, Feargal, 'Progressive or Regressive? The Anglo-Irish Agreement as a Dynamic in the Northern Ireland Polity', *Irish Political Studies*, vol. 18 (1993).

Cochrane, Feargal, *Unionist Politics and the Politics of Unionism Since the Anglo-Irish Agreement* (Cochrane, 1997).

Coogan, Tim P., *The Troubles: Ireland's Ordeal 1966–1995* (London, 1995).

Cox, W. Harvey, 'From Hillsborough to Downing Street – and After' in Catterall, Peter and McDougall, Sean (eds), *The Northern Ireland Question in British Politics* (Basingstoke, 1996).

Cunningham, Michael J., *British Government Policy in Northern Ireland 1969–2000* (Manchester and New York, 2001 edn).

Darby, John, 'The Historical Background' in Darby, John (ed.), *Northern Ireland: The Background to the Conflict* (Belfast, 1983).

Dixon, Paul, *Northern Ireland: The Politics of War and Peace* (Basingstoke, 2001).

Farrell, Michael, *Northern Ireland: The Orange State* (London, 1976).

Faulkner, Brian, *Memoirs of a Statesman* (London, 1978).

Fisk, Robert, *The Point of No Return: The Strike That Broke the British in Ulster* (London, 1975).

Fitzgerald, Garret, *All in a Life; an Autobiography* (Dublin, 1991).

Girvin, Brian, 'Constitutional Nationalism and Northern Ireland' in Barton, Brian and Roche, Patrick J. (eds), *The Northern Ireland Question: Perspectives and Policies* (Aldershot, 1994).

Guelke, Adrian, 'The United States and the Northern Ireland Question' in Barton, Brian and Roche, Patrick, J. (eds), *The Northern Ireland Question: Perspectives and Policies* (Aldershot, 1994).

Guelke, Adrian, 'Paramilitaries, Republicans and Loyalists' in Dunn, Seamus (ed.), *Facets of the Conflict in Northern Ireland* (Basingstoke, 1995).

Guelke, Adrian, 'Goodbye to All That' *Fortnight* (June 2000).

Guelke, Adrian, 'Trimble's Follies and the Death of the Agreement', *Fortnight* (October 2002).

Hadden, Tom and Hillyard, Paddy, *Justice in Northern Ireland: A Study in Social Confidence* (London, 1973).

Hadfield, Brigid, 'The Northern Ireland Constitution' in Hadfield, Brigid (ed.), *Northern Ireland: Politics and the Constitution* (Buckingham, 1993).

Harkness, David, *Northern Ireland Since 1920* (Dublin, 1983).

Harvey, Colin, 'Internal Debates', *Fortnight* (September 2001).

Hennessey, Thomas, *The Northern Ireland Peace Process: Ending the Troubles?* (Dublin, 2000).

Hezlet, Sir Arthur, *The 'B' Specials: A History of the Ulster Special Constabulary* (London, 1973).

Hume, John, *Personal Views: Politics, Peace and Reconciliation in Ireland* (Dublin, 1996).

Jackson, Alvin, *The Ulster Party: Irish Unionists in the House of Commons 1885–1911* (Oxford, 1989).

Kelley, Kevin, J., *The Longest War: Northern Ireland and the IRA* (London, 1990 edn).

Kennedy, Dennis, *The Widening Gulf: Northern Attitudes to the Independent Irish State 1919–1949* (Belfast, 1988).

Kenny, Anthony, *The Road to Hillsborough* (Oxford, 1986).

Laffan, Michael, *The Partition of Ireland 1911–1925* (Dublin, 1983).

Loughlin, James, *Gladstone, Home Rule and the Ulster Question 1882–1893* (Dublin, 1986).

Loughlin, James, *Ulster Unionism and British National Identity Since 1885* (London, 1995).

Lynn, Brendan, *Holding the Ground: The Nationalist Party in Northern Ireland 1945–72* (Aldershot, 1997).

Maguire, Paul, 'Why Devolution?' in Hadfield, Brigid (ed.), *Northern Ireland: Politics and the Constitution* (Buckingham, 1992).

Mallie, Eamonn and McKittrick, David, *The Fight for Peace: The Secret Story Behind the Irish Peace Process* (London, 1996).

Mallie Eamonn and McKittrick, David, *Endgame in Ireland* (London, 2001).

McAllister, Ian, 'Political Parties: Traditional and Modern' in Darby, John (ed.), *Northern Ireland: The Background to the Conflict* (Belfast, 1983).

McDonald, Henry, *Trimble* (London, 2001).

McIntyre, Anthony, 'Modern Irish Republicanism and the Belfast Agreement: Chickens Coming Home to Roost, or Turkeys Celebrating Christmas?' in Wilford, Rick (ed.), *Aspects of the Belfast Agreement* (Oxford, 2001).

McKay, Susan, *Northern Protestants: An Unsettled People* (Belfast, 2000).

McKittrick, David, *Despatches From Belfast* (Belfast, 1989).

McKittrick, David and McVea, David, *Making Sense of the Troubles* (Belfast, 2000).

McStiofain, Sean, *Memoirs of a Revolutionary* (London, 1975).

Mitchell, George, *Making Peace* (London, 1999).

Moloney, Ed, and Pollak, Andy, *Paisley* (Dublin, 1986).

Moloney, Ed, *A Secret History of the IRA* (London, 2002).

Morrissey, Mike and Smyth, Marie, *Northern Ireland After the Good Friday Agreement* (London, 2002).

Bibliography

Mulholland, Marc, *Northern Ireland at the Crossroads: Ulster Unionism in the O'Neill Years 1960–9* (Basingstoke, 2000).

Mulholland, Marc, *The Longest War: Northern Ireland's Troubled History* (Oxford, 2002).

Murray, Gerard, *John Hume and the SDLP* (Dublin, 1998).

Nelson, Sarah, *Ulster's Uncertain Defenders: Loyalists and the Northern Ireland Conflict* (Belfast, 1984).

North, Peter, Crilly, Oliver and Dunlop, John, *Report: An Independent Inquiry into Parades and Marches in Northern Ireland* (Belfast, 1997).

O'Brien, Brendan, *The Long War: The IRA and Sinn Fein, 1985 to Today* (Dublin, 1993).

O'Connor, Fionnuala, *In Search of a State: Catholics in Northern Ireland* (Belfast, 1993).

O'Connor, Fionnuala, *Breaking the Bonds: Making Peace in Northern Ireland* (Edinburgh, 2002).

O'Duffy, Brendan, 'The Price of Containment: Deaths and Debate on Northern Ireland in the House of Commons' in Catterall, Peter and McDougall, Sean (eds), *The Northern Ireland Question in British Politics* (Basingstoke, 1996).

O'Leary, Cornelius, 'Northern Ireland 1945–1972' in Lee, J.J. (ed.), *Ireland 1945–1970* (Dublin, 1979).

O'Leary, Brendan and McGarry, John, *Northern Ireland: The Politics of Antagonism* (London, 1993).

O'Leary, Brendan and McGarry, John, *Explaining Northern Ireland* (Oxford, 1995).

O'Malley, Padraig, *The Uncivil Wars: Ireland Today* (Belfast, 1983).

O'Neill, Terence, *An Autobiography* (London, 1973).

Patterson, Henry, *The Politics of Illusion: Republicanism and Socialism in Modern Ireland* (London, 1989).

Patterson, Henry, 'From Insulation to Appeasement: The Major and Blair Governments Reconsidered' in Wilford Rick (ed.), *Aspects of the Belfast Agreement* (Oxford, 2001).

Patterson, Henry, *Ireland Since 1939* (Oxford, 2002).

Phoenix, Eamon, *Northern Nationalism: Nationalist Politics, Partition and the Catholic Minority in Northern Ireland 1890–1940* (Belfast, 1994).

Pollak, A. (ed.), *A Citizens' Inquiry: The Opsahl Report on Northern Ireland* (Dublin, 1993).

Porter, Norman, *Rethinking Unionism* (Belfast, 1996).

Bibliography

Purdie, Bob, *Politics in the Streets: The Origins of the Civil Rights Movement in Northern Ireland* (Belfast, 1990).

Rafferty, Oliver P., *Catholics in Ulster 1603–1983: An Interpretive History* (London, 1994).

Rees, Merlyn, *Northern Ireland: A Personal Perspective* (London, 1985).

Rose, Peter, *How the Troubles came to Northern Ireland* (Basingstoke, 2001 edn).

Rose, Richard, *Governing Without Consensus* (London, 1971).

Ruane, Joseph and Todd, Janet, 'The Belfast Agreement: Context, Content, Consequence' in Ruane, Joseph and Todd, Janet (eds), *After the Belfast Agreement: Analysing Political Change in Northern Ireland* (Dublin, 1999).

Ryder, Chris and Kearney, Vincent, *Drumcree: The Orange Order's Last Stand* (London, 2001).

Sinnerton, Henry, *David Ervine* (Dingle, 2002).

Smith, M.L.R., *Fighting for Peace? The Military Strategy of Irish Republican Movement* (London, 1995).

Thatcher, Margaret, *The Downing Street Years* (London, 1993).

The Agreement (Belfast, 1998).

Tonge, Jonathon and McAulay, James, 'In the Party, but Off Message' *Fortnight* (June 2002).

Trimble, David, *To Raise Up a New Northern Ireland: Articles and Speeches 1998–2000* (Belfast, 2001).

Walker, Brian, *Ulster Politics 1868–1886* (Belfast, 1989).

White, Barry, *John Hume: Statesman of the Troubles* (Belfast, 1984).

Whyte, John, 'How Much Discrimination was there Under the Unionist Regime 1921–1968' in Gallagher, Tom and O'Connell, John (eds), *Contemporary Irish Studies* (Manchester, 1983).

Whyte, John, *Interpreting Northern Ireland* (Oxford, 1991).

Wilson, Andrew J., *Irish America and the Ulster Conflict 1968–1995* (Belfast, 1995).

Wilson, Tom, *Ulster: Conflict and Consent* (Oxford, 1989).

Wolff, Stefan, 'Context and Content: Sunningdale and Belfast Compared' in Wilford, Rick (ed.), *Aspects of the Belfast Agreement* (Oxford, 2001).

For more immediate comment and analysis the following publications have been consulted:

Belfast Telegraph
Derry Journal

Bibliography

Fortnight
Guardian
Irish Times
Sunday Business Post
Sunday Times
The Times.

INDEX

Index

Index

Index

Index

Index

Index

Index

Index

Index

Index